So the Image Could Speak

While every precaution has been taken in the preparation of this book, the publisher assumes no responsibility for errors or omissions, or for damages resulting from the use of the information contained herein.

So The Image Could Speak

First edition.

Copyright pending © 2024 Susan Mouw.

ISBN: **979-8-218-98420-5**

Written by Susan Mouw.

Scripture taken from the New King James Version®.

Copyright © 1982 by Thomas Nelson.

Used with permission.

All rights reserved.

So the Image Could Speak

Dedication

This book is dedicated to my husband, Barry Mouw, for his never-ending love and support through all we have been through and will go through. I couldn't imagine my life without him and pray we will be together when that last trumpet sounds.

Acknowledgements

Paul Anderson, Elder, Calvary Chapel-Aiken. I could not have completed this work without you. Your constant scrutiny, invaluable insights, and total dedication to Scripture kept me going with direction and guidance. I cannot thank you enough.

Ronda McPherson, dear friend. A true encourager! Your comments and suggestions through each step of the way have kept me going, kept me searching, kept me looking for God's will and purpose. There were times I wanted to give it up, thinking I am not worthy, but I would get some comment or feedback from you and it would remind me for Whom I am doing this. Thank you!

Table of Contents

Dedication 2
Acknowledgements 2
Table of Contents 3
Cross-Reference 5
Foreword 6
Preface 9
Chapter 1 – Revelation or Mystery? 12
Chapter 2 – The Seven Churches 18
Chapter 3 – The Door to Heaven is Opened 52
Chapter 4 – Who is Worthy? 61
Chapter 5 – Jacob's Trouble 65
Chapter 6 – Our Eyes Deceive Us 71
Chapter 7 – The Seven Seals are Opened 75
Chapter 8 – God's Mercy Revealed 89
Chapter 9 – The Trumpets Sound 95
Chapter 10 – The Angel and the Scroll 111
Chapter 11 – The Two Witnesses 118
Chapter 12 – The Woman and the Dragon 128
Chapter 13 – The AntiChrist 135
Chapter 14 – The False Prophet 148
Chapter 15 – So the Image Could Speak 154
Chapter 16 – Mark of the Beast 159
Chapter 17 – The Harvest is Ready 166
Chapter 18 – Justice and Righteousness 174
Chapter 19 – Prelude to Final Judgment 180
Chapter 20 – Final Judgment 188
Chapter 21 – Mystery Babylon 198
Chapter 22 – The Fall of Mystery Babylon 205
Chapter 23 – Who Are the Saints? 214

So the Image Could Speak

Chapter 24 – The Second Coming 228
Chapter 25 – The Millennium.. 242
Chapter 26 – Behold! All Things are New..................................... 259
Chapter 27 – The End is Near.. 275
PostScript 277
Appendix I – Who wrote Revelation? 278
Appendix II – The Letters to the Churches 290
Appendix III – 70 Weeks Timeline.. 291
Appendix IV – Revelation Order of Events.................................. 292
Appendix V – Specific Times in Revelation 293
Appendix VI – First Song of Moses 296
Appendix VII – Second Song of Moses 298
Appendix VIII – Two Battles of Gog and Magog......................... 302
Appendix IX – The Temples of Jerusalem 303

Cross-Reference

Cross-Reference

A cross reference of the chapters in Revelation and the chapters in this book.

So The Image Could Speak chapters	Pg	Chapters of the Bible
Chapter 1 – Revelation or Mystery?	12	Revelation Chapter 1
Chapter 2 – The Seven Churches	18	Revelation Chapters 2-3
Chapter 3 – The Door to Heaven is Opened	52	Revelation Chapter 4
Chapter 4 – Who is Worthy?	61	Revelation Chapter 5
Chapter 5 – Jacob's Trouble	65	Daniel Chapter 9
Chapter 6 – Our Eyes Deceive Us	71	Revelation Chapter 6 Intro
Chapter 7 – The Seven Seals are Opened	75	Revelation Chapter 6 & 8 Seals
Chapter 8 – God's Mercy Revealed	89	Revelation Chapter 7
Chapter 9 – The Trumpets Sound	95	Revelation Chapters 8, 9, & 11 Trumpets
Chapter 10 – The Angel and the Scroll	111	Revelation Chapter 10
Chapter 11 – The Two Witnesses	118	Revelation Chapter 11
Chapter 12 – The Woman and the Dragon	128	Revelation Chapter 12
Chapter 13 – The AntiChrist	135	Revelation Chapter 13 The Antichrist
Chapter 14 – The False Prophet	148	Revelation Chapter 13 The False Prophet
Chapter 15 – So the Image Could Speak	154	Revelation Chapter 13 The Image
Chapter 16 – Mark of the Beast	159	Revelation Chapter 13 Mark of the Beast
Chapter 17 – The Harvest is Ready	166	Revelation Chapter 14
Chapter 18 – Justice and Righteousness	174	Matthew 24:21-22
Chapter 19 – Prelude to Final Judgment	180	Revelation Chapter 15
Chapter 20 – Final Judgment	188	Revelation Chapter 16
Chapter 21 – Mystery Babylon	198	Revelation Chapter 17
Chapter 22 – The Fall of Mystery Babylon	205	Revelation Chapter 18
Chapter 24 - The Second Coming	228	Revelation Chapter 19
Chapter 25 - The Millennium	242	Revelation Chapter 20
Chapter 26 - Behold! All Things Are New	262	Revelation Chapters 21-22

So the Image Could Speak

Foreword

You must read this book. It is time. Yes I am talking about this book and yes I am talking about Revelation.

It is the last book at end of the Bible, right? It is the story of how things will end. That is for another time, or is it? As Christians we say 'God will come when he is ready' yet we know Jesus will come like a thief in the night.

And Image? Speaking? What does this have to do with the last book of the Bible that was written thousands of years ago? What does that mean? How can we study what seems so hard to understand? Why are so many churches not teaching this now? How can we understand?

In the beginning of Revelation, we find a blessing:

- *"Blessed is he who reads and those who hear the words of this prophecy, and keep those things which are written in it; for the time is near"* (Revelation 1:3)

But at the end of Revelation, we are warned:

- *"For I testify to everyone who hears the words of the prophecy of this book: If anyone adds to these things, God will add to him the plagues that are written in this book; and if anyone takes away from the words of the book of this prophecy, God shall take away his part from the Book of Life, from the Holy city, and from the things which are written in this book."* (Revelation 22:18-19)

<u>How can we understand this?</u>

Revelation is a book in the Bible that has always fascinated me, captivated my imagination as well as stirred something deep in my soul. A mix of such strange emotions, awe, wonder, terror, suspense, deep sadness, the feeling of victory, all at the same time wondering 'what is happening here'?

Foreword

It is a journey. We could not ask for a better tour guide than Susan to take us all on this riveting, prophetic end time journey deep dive into Revelation.

In this book Susan will show us how we can understand more. Not everything. There are many mysteries that God will reveal at his good pleasure. But this book will take us on an incredible journey of discovery through all of the Bible showing how the mysteries of Revelation are being revealed in not only scripture but actual current events. This book is full of eye opening 'revelations' concisely written showing us how the entirety of God's word is not just chapters or ancient history but unfolding today. She takes no shortcuts, no glossing over the hard parts. A real, sometimes painful hard look at those who refuse to accept the truth and sorrowful journey for all creation ending in victory through Jesus Christ.

- *"But you, Daniel, shut up the words, and seal the book until the time of the end; many shall run to and from and knowledge shall increase".* Daniel 12:4

When Daniel wrote these words over 2000 years ago much of the scripture had yet to be written. The New Covenant was being foretold but had yet to be fulfilled. So many prophesies had not yet come to pass.

Today, we have the full armor of God. I believe this is what God was telling Daniel so long ago. Now we are ready to open up the words and increase our knowledge.

The best interpretation of scripture is scripture itself. The Bible from the Old Testament to the New Testament, from Genesis to Revelation, is vital to studying Revelation. Susan brings together scripture after scripture, showing us that the Bible is one complete history from Genesis to Revelation showing us 'Full Armor of God' telling one unified complete story.

Scripture tells us from the very beginning:

- *"And the Lord said, "My Spirit shall not strive with man forever, ….:"* (Genesis 6:3)

Yet:

So the Image Could Speak

- *"For this is good and acceptable in the sight of God our Savior, who desires all men to be saved and to come to the knowledge of truth"* (1 Timothy 2:3)

Susan has a gift for taking us through Revelation. She has a way of not only taking us through the depth of scripture but making it come alive with meaning and context for today. It is like seeing things with fresh new eyes through Susan's perspective of deep and abiding faith. In 'So the Image could speak' she shows us how the entire bible has to be used to understand much of what seems disconnected or hidden. But Susan shows us how Scripture interprets Scripture, how other verses fit so perfectly into unlocking verses in Revelation. *"And God will wipe away every tear from their eyes; there shall be no more death, nor sorrow, nor crying. There shall be no more pain, for the former things have passed away."* (Revelation 21:4)

I know this book will be a blessing as will reading Revelation as promised in the word. We know we serve a good and loving God who is faithful and keeps his promises. He sent his only son to reconcile man to himself a sacrifice I cannot even comprehend. The message is urgent and it is clear. Now is the time. Don't wait.

- *"He who testifies to these things says, "Surely, I am coming quickly. Amen. Even so, come Lord Jesus!"* (Revelation 22:20)

I highly recommend reading her other books. A set of 3 books in 'the Beginning of Sorrows' series. Go Set a Watchman, As in the Days of Noah, and Convergence. These books look at current events with a biblical world view. The details will leap off the page and you too will look up...

- *"Now when these things begin to happen, look up and lift your heads, because your redemption draws near."* (Luke 21:28)

Ronda McPherson, a fellow Christian on this journey, urgently praying that you to take up this study being equipped to continue your journey, standing on a firm foundation, understanding all the coming groanings of all creation saying Even So, Come Lord Jesus.

Preface

The crowd gathered around the raised platform, set up with a table and eight chairs along one side, as the whole world watched the events unfold. They had been anxiously awaiting this day since the first promises of peace. At first, the world didn't believe the one who made those promises and, in fact, mocked him; "Who is this man who can bring this peace? Who does he think he is when so many have tried and failed?" The world was in chaos with wars erupting all over. If there wasn't a war, then the impact of those wars was felt in even the most remote locations, with people dying because they couldn't find anything to eat. When this man first made those promises of peace, there was hardly one family world-wide that had not been impacted by the worldwide losses.

Those who lived in Jerusalem, where this event was to occur, were especially eager for this day. The signing of the covenant between these countries, who had been enemies for so long, promised their land would experience the peace and safety for which they longed.

With great pomp and solemn attitude appropriate for the occasion, each of the countries' leaders took their assigned seats. Then the Israel Prime Minister entered, stepped up on the platform and took his place in the center. Behind the table were the various bodyguards and entourages of each of the countries represented by those kings, prime ministers, and presidents of those who had been, so recently, enemies of Israel.

In front of the platform, various newscasters from around the world spoke into their microphones and emphasized what a remarkable and historic event this was - the signing and reconfirming of an old and broken peace treaty between these nations. Israel and her enemies had been brought together by one charismatic man and the world stood amazed at what he had accomplished.

Each one took their time signing the document. Not because of indecision or because of lack of knowledge of what they were signing, but because they gloried in their moment in the spotlight and desired that moment to last. Finally, the peace agreement was placed before the Prime Minister of Israel and, with a smile and a small wave to the crowd, he lifted the gold pen in front of him, leaned forward, and placed his signature. The newscasters' excited voices proclaimed, "It is done!" and "Peace, at last!".

So the Image Could Speak

The crowd erupted in cheers and applause, believing this would call a cease-fire for all the battles, destroy the secret weapons stashes, halt the nuclear armament building, and end the sacrifice of their youth sent into battle.

In the midst of this jubilant celebration, another man quietly walked out on the platform. When the crowd noticed his arrival, silence fell like a heavy curtain. This is him - the one who brought this to pass! The miracle worker, the diplomat, the deliverer of peace! They watched in awe as he strode to the middle of the platform, picked up the pages of the treaty, and turning around, waved it in front of the cameras and the crowd.

The eruption of applause, cheering and hallelujahs filled the air in that room and in nearly every home where this was being watched. The newscasters even turned their backs to their cameras, so they could look upon this mighty man – this savior of the world.

This day marked the beginning of a new era and he had promised it would be a time of peace and security. It wasn't long before the whole world realized he lied.

***

The event portrayed above is a fictional account. It hasn't happened yet and probably won't happen exactly as presented above, but it is coming and I believe sooner rather than later. This event, the confirmation of that covenant between Israel and her enemies, as written in Daniel, marks the beginning of the end.

"*[27]Then he shall confirm a covenant with many for one week*" (Daniel 9:27a)

In my previous books in the Beginning of Sorrows series; Go Set A Watchman, As In the Days of Noah, and Convergence, the focus was on modern events that pave the way to that which occurs during the Tribulation.

This book looks at the book of Revelation and attempts to unravel this last book of the canonical Bible – the devastation poured out in God's wrath and the Glorious Hope for all who have placed their faith in our

Preface

Lord, Jesus Christ. We'll explore how the events depicted in Revelation could actually happen in the current time, such as when the image of the AntiChrist is made to speak at the midpoint of the Tribulation.

There are some presuppositions here: 1) this writer believes in a Pre-Tribulation rapture of the Bride of Christ, or the Church and 2) the events portrayed in Revelation have not yet happened, but we are drawing ever closer to the time known as "Jacob's Trouble" as each day passes.

You may not agree with either or both of those presuppositions and that is ok – this book is not a "sales pitch" for what I believe, but rather an invitation for you to study and delve into God's Word on your own and come to your own conclusions, with the guidance of the Holy Spirit.

So, let's dive in...

So the Image Could Speak

Chapter 1 – Revelation or Mystery?

The Revelation of Jesus Christ is the last book in the canonical Bible and perhaps the most controversial. The book that brings to culmination God's plan for humanity and His Creation yet is the least taught book in many seminaries and least preached from many pulpits. The book that gives us a glimpse into the spiritual world in which we live, yet is often deemed allegory and/or even fiction. The only book in the canonical Bible that promises a blessing to those who read it, yet may be the least often read of all 66 books of the canonical Bible.

Is the Revelation of Jesus Christ a mystery we are not meant to understand or is it an unveiling of the future? We'll let the scripture translate itself.

"¹The Revelation of Jesus Christ, which God gave Him to show His servants—things which must shortly take place. And He sent and signified it by His angel to His servant John, ²who bore witness to the word of God, and to the testimony of Jesus Christ, to all things that he saw." (Revelation 1:1-2)

The Greek word for revelation is apokalupsis[1] which means an uncovering or unveiling. This book of The Revelation of Jesus Christ is given by God to show His servants – we who believe – things which must "shortly" (note – this doesn't mean what we think it means) take place – an unveiling or revelation of the future.

While there has been some contention over who wrote the Book of Revelation, John identifies himself, *"⁹I, John, both your brother and companion in the tribulation and kingdom and patience of Jesus Christ, was on the island that is called Patmos for the word of God and for the testimony of Jesus Christ."* (Revelation 1:9)

---

[1] Strong's Greek.602. apokalupsis, noun,feminine, "an unveiling, uncovering, revealing, revelation"

Chapter 1 – Revelation or Mystery?

Understanding who this John is, which is an interesting study in itself, would take an entire volume to fully explore. If you are interested in learning more about that history, there is an Appendix, titled "Who Wrote Revelation?" at the end of this book. That Appendix is not a full study but gives an overview of the pros and cons of the various theories and offers some additional references for those who want to take a deeper dive into that subject.

For our purposes here, we'll accept the following:

1. The John identified in the passage above is John the Apostle, son of Zebedee and brother of James the Apostle.
2. The book was written while John was exiled to Patmos.
3. It was written sometime after 81AD, when Emperor Domitian came to power, and before 96AD, when Emperor Domitian died and John was released from Patmos, though most historians believe it was written in the later part of that era – around 95-96AD.

*"[1]The Revelation of Jesus Christ, which God gave Him to show His servants—things which must **shortly** take place."* (Revelation 1:1a) (emphasis added)

The word "shortly" in this passage has caused consternation among the scholars over the years; with some believing it means the things John saw and recorded in the Revelation of Jesus Christ happened soon after the writing of the book and are, therefore, past history.

So the Image Could Speak

But when we look at the original Greek, that interpretation – that the things happened soon after the writing of this passage, doesn't compute. The phrase "shortly take place" is translated from the original Greek; "genesthai[2] en[3] tachei[4]" or "to take place in quickness" or, to put it in our vernacular, "happens quickly". In other words, the events recorded by John will happen in quick succession once they begin and not shortly after the writing of this text. That phrase is used again in Revelation 22:6, with the same meaning. We know the events depicted by John in Revelation 22:6 have not yet happened – there is no River of Life flowing from the Throne of God here on earth and, as far as I know, there is not a tree on earth that produces twelve different kinds of fruit and a fresh crop appears every month. Therefore, it is safe to presume that John is writing about future events; events he doesn't know when will happen, but he is assured will happen just as he has written them.

And therein lies the conundrum – "just as he has written them." So will those who live during the times of these events see a stranger riding up on a white horse, carrying a bow (Revelation 6:1), or a mountain burning with fire thrown into the sea (Revelation 8:8), or a star fallen from heaven holding a key (Revelation 9:1)?

The Revelation of Jesus Christ is full of symbolism, so many of those descriptions are representative of something else. It is also important to remember that John, in the first century AD, is writing of things that will take place in the future. In fact, since they have not yet occurred, they happen very far in the future – nearly two thousand years later.

If Roman soldiers had seen a vision of warfare in the mid 19th century, how would they describe the tanks or battleships used in World War II? Perhaps as great beasts?

If soldiers of the Revolutionary War in the United States (1775AD – 1783AD) had seen a vision of modern warfare, how would they describe the modern drones carrying missiles? Maybe as some type of deadly flying insect?

---

[2] Strong's Greek.1096.ginomai, verb, "to come into being, to happen, to become"
[3] Strong's Greek.1722.en, preposition, "in, on, at, by, with"
[4] Strong's Greek.5034.tachei, root word tachos, noun, "speed"

Chapter 1 – Revelation or Mystery?

Of course, we serve the Creator Who created all things and could, if He chose, create exactly what John is describing. However, I think we also want to look at the other possibilities – the modern tools that John would not have been able to describe in the first century. We'll explore those possibilities as we go through the book of Revelation, including, as the title of this book suggests, how the image could speak in chapter thirteen.

If we accept it was John the Apostle while he was exiled to Patmos, writing these things, then the next question is to whom is he writing? The first part of that answer is revealed within the text: *"⁴John, **to the seven churches which are in Asia**: Grace to you and peace from Him who is and who was and who is to come, and from the seven Spirits who are before His throne, ⁵and from Jesus Christ, the faithful witness, the firstborn from the dead, and the ruler over the kings of the earth. To Him who loved us and washed us from our sins in His own blood, ⁶and has made us kings and priests to His God and Father, to Him be glory and dominion forever and ever. Amen. ⁷Behold, He is coming with clouds, and every eye will see Him, even they who pierced Him. And all the tribes of the earth will mourn because of Him. Even so, Amen. ⁸'I am the Alpha and the Omega, the Beginning and the End,' says the Lord, 'who is and who was and who is to come, the Almighty.' "* (Revelation 1:4-8) (emphasis added)

So John is to write to the seven churches which are specifically named in the following verses. But before we look at who those specific churches are, there is a part of this passage that bears closer inspection. The Bible is its own translator, as we see in verse 4, *"from the seven Spirits who are before His throne."*

Who are those seven Spirits before the throne? If we go to Isaiah, we see the fullness of the Holy Spirit, *"²The Spirit of the Lord shall rest upon Him, The Spirit of wisdom and understanding, The Spirit of counsel and might, The Spirit of knowledge and of the fear of the Lord."* (Isaiah 11:2)

The message John is sending to those seven churches is coming from the Lord Jesus Christ and the fullness of the Holy Spirit.

So the Image Could Speak

"⁹I, John, both your brother and companion in the tribulation and kingdom and patience of Jesus Christ, was on the island that is called Patmos for the word of God and for the testimony of Jesus Christ. ¹⁰I was in the Spirit on the Lord's Day, and I heard behind me a loud voice, as of a trumpet, ¹¹saying, 'I am the Alpha and the Omega, the First and the Last,' and, 'What you see, write in a book and send it to the seven churches which are in Asia: to Ephesus, to Smyrna, to Pergamos, to Thyatira, to Sardis, to Philadelphia, and to Laodicea.'" (Revelation 1:9-11)

John is told twelve times in Revelation to write what he sees and once, he is forbidden to write – but more on that later.

"Which are in Asia: to Ephesus, to Smyrna, to Pergamos, to Thyatira, to Sardis, to Philadelphia, and to Laodicea."

Why these seven churches? We'll explore that further in the next chapter, but we know these seven churches in these cities represent key cities for each of the seven postal districts in which Asia Minor (modern Turkey) was divided. Sending the letters to these seven churches would ensure they would be further disseminated. They are listed in the order a messenger would travel on the circular road that connected these seven cities.

But John is not writing to just those seven churches, just as Paul was not just writing to the church at Thessalonica or Corinth. *"¹⁶All Scripture is given by inspiration of God, and is profitable for doctrine, for reproof, for correction, for instruction in righteousness, ¹⁷that the man of God may be complete, thoroughly equipped for every good work."* (2 Timothy 3:16)

So this message John is told to write is for all of us, even now…perhaps especially now, as the times depicted in this last book of the Bible draw nearer.

The book of The Revelation of Jesus Christ is divided into three parts, clearly outlined in this first chapter, *"¹⁹Write the things which you have seen, and the things which are, and the things which will take place after this."* (Revelation 1:19)

Chapter 1 – Revelation or Mystery?

- *"The things which you have seen"* – the vision John had of Jesus Christ and shared in verses 10-16 and the command given to him by Jesus.
- *"The things which are"* – the seven churches, which existed at that time and to whom John is to write a letter.
- *"The things which will take place after this"* – the future events which John will see and record in chapters 4-22.

The book of The Revelation of Jesus Christ is the only book in the canonical Bible that promises a blessing to those *"who reads and those who hear the words of this prophecy, and keep those things which are written in it; for the time is near."* (Revelation 1:3)

Let us remember that blessing as we continue through this book. Before we delve into the letters to those seven churches, take a moment and read the description of Jesus Christ, as he appeared to John, in verses 12-16. It is breathtaking.

So the Image Could Speak

Chapter 2 – The Seven Churches

The word church in the Greek is ekklésia[5] – a noun, a combination of the Greek word ek, "out from and to" and kaléō, "to call". So the church is a body of people called out from the world and to God.

Why these seven churches? These letters were written about 60 years after Pentecost when the Church began, and there were approximately 100+ churches. Of course, there were no church buildings – that didn't begin until around the 3rd century. Some of them would meet in the local synagogue, some met in rented halls and some met in their homes. Many of them had to be very secretive as they were considered an illegal sect in many places and the members could be imprisoned or put to death (and many were) just for meeting and proclaiming the Word of God. Each of these seven are major postal centers for the rest of Asia Minor and surrounding areas, so any information sent to them would certainly be disseminated further. Each of these seven churches would receive not just the letter addressed to them, but all seven letters. There are other reasons these seven churches were chosen than just the probability of spreading the Word, but we'll get to those in a minute.

There are four levels of understanding, or interpreting, for each of these seven churches and we'll look at each one. Those four levels are:

---

[5] Strong's Greek.1577.ekklésia, "an assembly, a (religious) congregation"

Chapter 2 – The Seven Churches

1. Local – these are all actual churches. Sir William Mitchell Ramsay (1851-1939), a Scottish theologian and historian, did a great deal of research and visited each of the locations for these seven churches and verified their authenticity.
2. Admonishment – while these seven letters were addressed specifically to these seven churches, the warnings were for all churches, even to this day. More about that further on.
3. Personal – "he that hath an ear" the words written to each of these churches apply to us individually, if we will listen.
4. Prophetic – there is a reason these seven churches were chosen and the order in which the letters are presented and we'll delve into that before the end of this chapter.

The letters have seven components with a couple of exceptions. Those components are:

1. Name of the church.
2. Title that Christ gives Himself – each is different and relevant to that church.
3. Commendation – what the church has done well. Not all churches have a commendation.
4. Concern – "Nevertheless" – where the church needs work. Not all churches have a concern.
5. Admonishment – Repent.
6. Promise to the Overcomer. This is for the individuals – both those individuals in those churches at that time who heeded the warning and obeyed, and for all of us since that time. Who are the overcomers?

    "^{1}Whoever believes that Jesus is the Christ is born of God, and everyone who loves Him who begot also loves him who is begotten of Him. ^{2}By this we know that we love the children of God, when we love God and keep His commandments. ^{3}For this is the love of God, that we keep His commandments. And His commandments are not burdensome. ^{4}For whatever is born of God overcomes the world. And this is the victory that has overcome the world—our faith. ^{5}Who is he who overcomes the world, but he who believes that Jesus is the Son of God?" (1 John 5:1-5)

7. *"He who has an ear, let him hear what the Spirit says to the churches."* This statement is near, or at, the end of each of the letters to the seven churches. It is either just before, or just after, the promise to the overcomer.

There are two churches where there is no concern – no "Nevertheless", and there are two churches where there is no commendation, or what the church has done right.

All seven churches have the statement from Jesus, *"I know your works..."* He sees all, knows all and that hasn't changed.

1. The Letter to the church at Ephesus

   "¹'To the angel of the church of Ephesus write, 'These things says He who holds the seven stars in His right hand, who walks in the midst of the seven golden lampstands: ²'I know your works, your labor, your patience, and that you cannot bear those who are evil. And you have tested those who say they are apostles and are not, and have found them liars; ³and you have persevered and have patience, and have labored for My name's sake and have not become weary. ⁴Nevertheless I have this against you, that you have left your first love. ⁵Remember therefore from where you have fallen; repent and do the first works, or else I will come to you quickly and remove your lampstand from its place—unless you repent. ⁶But this you have, that you hate the deeds of the Nicolaitans, which I also hate.⁷'He who has an ear, let him hear what the Spirit says to the churches. To him who overcomes I will give to eat from the tree of life, which is in the midst of the Paradise of God.' " (Revelation 2:1-7)

   At the time of this letter, Ephesus was a thriving port city of commerce and the Roman capital of that province. It was called "Queen of Asia" – a beautiful city. This is where one of the ancient wonders of the world, the temple of Diana, was, with the "Marble Way" – a marble street lined with statues and fountains that led from the temple of Artemis through the city to the Magnesia Gate. It also had a large theatre measuring 495' in diameter and could hold 25,000 people. (There is a brief mention

Chapter 2 – The Seven Churches

of this theatre in Acts 19:28-41). There was also the Arcadian Way - another main road from the theater to the harbor, 1735' long and 70' wide, lined with columns and shops and illuminated at night. And we can't leave out the huge library with over 200,000 volumes, though we should also note there was a tunnel from the library to the brothels along the Main Way. It was the largest city of its day! A center for study of arts and magic, Ephesus was world renowned for talismans, incantations, books, charms, etc. And, of course, they had a lot of visitors to that library.

Ephesus later became the center for missionary operations throughout Asia Minor.

Today, Ephesus is just an archeological dig site. Due to the erosion caused by the Roman destruction of all the trees, the once prized port city now sits about 6 miles inland. It is no longer "beach front property."

   a. Name – Ephesus. Some have claimed that the name, in the original Greek, means "desired one", a term of endearment. It is the church without devotion.
   b. Title of Christ. *"He who holds the seven stars in His right hand, who walks in the midst of the seven golden lampstands"*. This is a reference to that verse in chapter 1: *"[20]The mystery of the seven stars which you saw in My right hand, and the seven golden lampstands: The seven stars are the angels of the seven churches, and the seven lampstands which you saw are the seven churches."* (Revelation 1:20) Meaning – He is with us at all times and protects us.
   c. Commendation. *"[2]I know your works, your labor, your patience, and that you cannot bear those who are evil. And you have tested those who say they are apostles and are not, and have found them liars; [3]and you have persevered and have patience, and have labored for My name's sake and have not become weary.'"* (Revelation 2:2-3)

So the Image Could Speak

Paul, in his last letter to the elders of the church at Ephesus, warned them about this very thing and they had, apparently, heeded that warning. Jesus is commending them for the job they have done. Reference – Acts 20:25-31

Then they have a second commendation, of sorts: *"⁶But this you have, that you hate the deeds of the Nicolaitans, which I also hate."* (Revelation 2:6) There is a lot of contention about who the Nicolaitans were, with some saying they were an actual sect, led by Nicholas (mentioned briefly in Acts 6), who believed church elders were not just in authority over the church, but sovereign over the church. They were in charge of what you could do, say, wear, how you could act, or do business – everything. This is, of course, in contrast to what Jesus taught and the example He gave when he washed the feet of the Apostles at the Last Supper. The name Nicholas means "one who conquers the people."

Others say this was not a sect led by a particular man, but a group who encouraged others to eat that which was offered to idols and sexual immorality. The Greek word Nicolah means "let us eat."

Whichever it was, it was certainly an abomination to God and the church and elders of Ephesus had done a commendable job of repelling them.

d. Concern – *"⁴Nevertheless I have this against you, that you have left your first love."* What does this mean? Well, "first" in this verse is the Greek word prótos: which means first in priority. So Jesus is not referring to first in time, but first in priority or importance. What Jesus is telling this church is that they have become too busy in the business of the church and everyday life to have time for God. They

Chapter 2 – The Seven Churches

       have left out time for devotion to God. I wonder how many of us, in the daily busyness of our lives, have left our first love?

  e. Admonishment – *"⁵Remember therefore from where you have fallen; repent and do the first works, or else I will come to you quickly and remove your lampstand from its place—unless you repent."* It is interesting to note that Ephesus exists no more. The Goths destroyed both the temple and the city in 262 AD and it has never regained its prior prominence.

  f. *"⁷"He who has an ear, let him hear what the Spirit says to the churches."*

  g. Promise to the overcomer: *" 'To him who overcomes I will give to eat from the tree of life, which is in the midst of the Paradise of God.' "* The tree of life – in other words, He will grant them immortality, everlasting life. It is interesting that the tree of life echoes through many false religions: Persians - homa-tree, growing at the spring Arduisur which comes from throne of God; Hindus - halpasoma-tree, which supplied water of immortality; Arab's tuba-tree, and Greek's lotus-tree, and then there was the Assyrian tree with royal figures and guarded by genii. There is also an interesting correlation to the tree mentioned in the first half of Ezekiel 47.

2. The letter to the church at Smyrna. The persecuted church.

So the Image Could Speak

"⁸And to the angel of the church in Smyrna write, 'These things says the First and the Last, who was dead, and came to life: ⁹I know your works, tribulation, and poverty (but you are rich); and I know the blasphemy of those who say they are Jews and are not, but are a synagogue of Satan. ¹⁰Do not fear any of those things which you are about to suffer. Indeed, the devil is about to throw some of you into prison, that you may be tested, and you will have tribulation ten days. Be faithful until death, and I will give you the crown of life. ¹¹'He who has an ear, let him hear what the Spirit says to the churches. He who overcomes shall not be hurt by the second death.'" (Revelation 2:8-11)

Smyrna was also a port city at that time. In fact it had two ports and was located about 40 miles north of Ephesus. Today it is a thriving city, Izmir, and the 3rd largest city in Turkey with a population of nearly 3 million. It was a major exporter of various goods, as it sat at the entrance to the broad fertile valley of Mermus at the mouth of the river Meles and on the sheltered gulf of Smyrna. The city of Smyrna ceased to exist for about 300 years until Alexander the Great ordered it rebuilt during the Hellenistic era. It was where the poet, Homer, lived. But Smyrna was not very friendly towards, or tolerant of, its Christian residents.

At the foot of the mountain was the temple of Zeus, and along Golden Street there was a row of shrines to Apollo, Aphrodite, Aesculapius (god of medicine), Cybele (nature goddess). At the marketplace were more statues and shrines to Poseidon and Demeter. The primary deity of Smyrna was Cybele, whose devotion was in the form of wild unbridled worship. She was considered to be the giver of wealth. Smyrna was also one of the earliest to worship Caesar. In 196 BC they erected a temple to Dea Roma.

Chapter 2 – The Seven Churches

Smyrna later won a contest to build a temple to Emperor Tiberius in 26 AD. Emperor worship was compulsory. Once a year every Roman citizen was required to burn a pinch of incense on the altar and proclaim publicly that Caesar was lord. They would then receive a formal certificate which permitted them to buy and sell in the marketplace. This became a trial for the Christians and those who refused were burned at the stake or killed by wild beasts in the arena. So the Christians in Smyrna were heavily persecuted.

a. Name – Smryna. The name is derived from the Greek word, myrrh. Myrrh was used in embalming and was highly valued. But it also is an idiom for death. Myrrh was one of the gifts the Magi brought to the baby Jesus (Matthew 2:11) and it was also used by Nicodemus and Joseph of Arimathea in preparing the body of Jesus for burial (John 19:38-39).

b. Title of Jesus. *"the First and the Last, who was dead, and came to life"* Reference – Revelation 1:17-18. A reminder to the faithful of Smyrna that death is temporary and just a transition for those who believe.

c. Commendation. *"[9]'I know your works, tribulation, and poverty (but you are rich); and I know the blasphemy of those who say they are Jews and are not, but are a synagogue of Satan. [10]Do not fear any of those things which you are about to suffer. Indeed, the devil is about to throw some of you into prison, that you may be tested, and you will have tribulation ten days. Be faithful until death, and I will give you the crown of life.'* "

The word for tribulation here is thlipsis[6], not apokalypsis. Jesus is telling the church at Smyrna they will suffer persecution, even unto death, but it is not the Tribulation yet to come. He tells them He knows about their poverty, because without that certificate from the annual offering of incense, they could not buy and sell. But He tells them, *"(but you are rich)"*. This is completely opposite to the church of Laodicea, which was rich, but spiritually poor.

What is this "synagogue of Satan?" This is mentioned again in the letter to the church of Philadelphia. These were Jews who attacked and persecuted the Christians in both these cities. They slandered the church in Smyrna to get people to turn away from it.

What is meant by the *"ten days?"* We see this in Genesis 24:55 and Daniel 1:12 and in both passages it is interpreted as "a short time."

"Be faithful until death, and I will give you the crown of life." We will learn more about the many crowns in the Bible later in Revelation, but here is a short list of five mentioned in the New Testament.

- Crown of Life - James 1:12, for those who suffered for His sake.
- Crown of Righteousness - 2 Timothy 4:8, for those who loved His appearing.
- Crown of Glory - 1 Peter 5:4, for those who fed the flock.
- Crown Incorruptible - 1 Corinthians 9:25, for those who press on steadfastly.
- Crown of Rejoicing - 1 Thessalonians 2:19, for those who win souls.

d. Concern – none

---

[6] Strong's Greek.2347.thlipsis, noun feminine, "persecution, affliction, distress, tribulation"

Chapter 2 – The Seven Churches

      e. Admonishment – none
      f. *"7"He who has an ear, let him hear what the Spirit says to the churches."*
      g. Promise to the overcomer: They are all overcomers and all will receive the crown of life if they remain steadfast.

3. The letter to the church at Pergamos. The compromising church.

"12And to the angel of the church in Pergamos write, 'These things says He who has the sharp two-edged sword: 13'I know your works, and where you dwell, where Satan's throne is. And you hold fast to My name, and did not deny My faith even in the days in which Antipas was My faithful martyr, who was killed among you, where Satan dwells. 14But I have a few things against you, because you have there those who hold the doctrine of Balaam, who taught Balak to put a stumbling block before the children of Israel, to eat things sacrificed to idols, and to commit sexual immorality. 15Thus you also have those who hold the doctrine of the Nicolaitans, which thing I hate. 16Repent, or else I will come to you quickly and will fight against them with the sword of My mouth. 17'He who has an ear, let him hear what the Spirit says to the churches. To him who overcomes I will give some of the hidden manna to eat. And I will give him a white stone, and on the stone a new name written which no one knows except him who receives it.' " (Revelation 2:12-17)

Pergamos was the city on the hill. In fact, prior to Alexander the Great's time – that's all it was – just a castle on the hill. Alexander the Great had it rebuilt into the city it was at the time of John's letter. Pergamos was the great religious center. Zeus was said to have been born there and there was a huge altar to him. The official emblem of the city of Pergamos was the caduceus – the two-headed serpent entwined around a rod.

In order to understand this symbol, we have to go back to the

So the Image Could Speak

Old Testament book of Numbers. Moses had led the Israelites out of Egypt, but they had become greatly discouraged and disgruntled. The Lord sent fiery serpents among them to bite them and many died. They then repented and begged for forgiveness for their prior complaining and pleaded with Moses to save them from these serpents. When Moses prayed, the Lord told him to cast a bronze serpent and set it upon a pole and when someone was bitten, if they looked upon the pole, they would be healed. (Numbers 21:4-9) This casting of a serpent on a pole became the symbol of healing.

It is interesting to note that this bronze serpent that Moses had created, still stood until it was destroyed by Hezekiah in 2 Kings 18:4, because the people were still burning incense to it and worshipping it. Nearly 1,000 years passed before it was destroyed.

Jesus used this as an example in John 3:14 when talking to Nicodemus. He said, *"^{14}And as Moses lifted up the serpent in the wilderness, even so must the Son of Man be lifted up, ^{15}that whoever believes in Him should not perish but have eternal life."* which leads to, arguably, the best known and most oft-quoted verse in the Bible – John 3:16.

The Greeks then used that same symbol – the one headed snake on a pole – as the symbol of the god Aesculapius – the primary god of Pergamum. Hermes, the god of commerce, also had the symbol of the snake on the pole, but his was two-headed and it was his symbol that later became the world-wide symbol for medicine.

Chapter 2 – The Seven Churches

Figure 1 Rod of Aesculapius and the Caduceus[7]

The snake, going all the way back to the Garden of Eden is the symbol for sin – evil.

When Cyrus conquered Babylon in 539BC, the Chaldean priests moved to Pergamum. As Rome grew, they migrated further and infiltrated Rome and the Roman church. We'll talk more about that with the next church, Thyatira.

    a. Name – Pergamos. In the Greek, it simply means tower, or city, from the root word purgos. If you break it down, the per, or pur means mixed and gamos is marriage, so the mixed marriage. We'll see how that fits further on.

    b. Title of Jesus. *"He who has the sharp two-edged sword"* or He who will judge by the Word of God. Hebrews 4:12 states that the Word of God is sharper than any two-edged sword.

    c. Commendation: *"[13]'I know your works, and where you dwell, where Satan's throne is. And you hold fast to My name, and did not deny My faith even in the days in which Antipas was My faithful martyr, who was killed among you, where Satan dwells.' "*

---

[7] The Biblical Caduceus - Symbol of Medicine, Sandra Sweeny Silver, date unknown, https://earlychurchhistory.org/medicine/the-biblical-caduceus-symbol-of-medicine/

So the Image Could Speak

"Where Satan's throne is." What or where is Satan's throne? Many today believe the altar to Zeus, or the "Great Altar of Pergamos" is what is referred to here as Satan's throne. Interestingly, this altar still survives today, although it was relocated to Berlin in the 19th century.

Antipas was a Christian martyr, but we're not sure when he was martyred or by whom. It is widely believed he was martyred near the end of the first century, which would place it under the rule of Emperor Domitian. This would add further weight to when the book of Revelation was written. Simeon Metaphrastes has a story that Antipas, during Domitian's reign, was shut up in a red-hot brazen bull and was heard singing worship songs and praying until he died. No confirmation that this is the same Antipas but it is possible, as the timing would be right.

Others suggest it is symbolic. Antipas in the Greek means "against all" - those who serve Christ stand out against all for His Sake. Antipas was not an uncommon name at that time, so it is difficult to firmly establish whether this Antipas is the same mentioned in the letter to Pergamos.

But the church at Pergamos did not deny Him, even under threat of death. They held fast.

d. Concern. *"14'But I have a few things against you, because you have there those who hold the doctrine of Balaam, who taught Balak to put a stumbling block before the children of Israel, to eat things sacrificed to idols, and to commit sexual immorality. 15Thus you also have those who hold the doctrine of the Nicolaitans, which thing I hate.'"* Here are those Nicolaitans again and this time, it would seem to support the theory that these were a loosely held

Chapter 2 – The Seven Churches

group of those within the church that encouraged others to eat food sacrificed to idols and practice sexual immorality.

What is the "doctrine of Balaam?" This gets interesting. We know Balaam was a "soothsayer" (Joshua 13:22), he was from Mesopotamia (Deuteronomy 23:4-5), around the Euphrates (Numbers 22:5). He was hired by Balak, the King of the Moabites to curse Israel. You will want to read that whole story starting in Numbers 22, if you haven't already, for it is quite interesting and, at times, entertaining, especially when the donkey speaks to Balaam. Balaam refuses to curse Israel, but what he does do is show Balak how to conquer the Israelites.

How? By putting his most attractive young maidens around the camp of the Israelites and tempting the young men to intermingle with the Moabite women, even marrying them – which was forbidden. These were "mixed" marriages and the beginning of one of the times the Lord's anger was turned against Israel.

But what is the Lord referring to here? This all happened many many years earlier and the Lord had forgiven them, so what has it to do with this church? Apparently they had not all repented of their evil ways and the many pagan traditions of the Moabites had wormed their way into the practice of Christianity. The marriage of Christianity and the world had begun, a true "mixed marriage."

e. Admonishment. *"^{16}Repent, or else I will come to you quickly and will fight against them with the sword of My mouth."* Again, the sword of My mouth – the Word of God.

f. *"^{17}'He who has an ear, let him hear what the Spirit says to the churches.' "*

g. Promise to the overcomer. *"To him who overcomes I will give some of the hidden manna to eat. And I will give him a white stone, and on the stone a new name written which no one knows except him who receives it."*

What is manna? We know from Exodus 16 that it was collected from Heaven daily, except for the 7th day. The Israelites ate manna morning, noon, and night for 40 years. It was called *"food from heaven and bread of mighty"* (Psalms 78:24) and *"bread of heaven"* (Psalms 105:40). But the real source of this "hidden manna" is Jesus Christ Himself, *"^{35}And Jesus said to them, 'I am the bread of life. He who comes to Me shall never hunger, and he who believes in Me shall never thirst.' "* (John 6:35)

The white stone is interesting. Although there is little validation, it is believed the Romans gave a stone with the name of the carrier engraved upon it as a "ticket" to the games and events. This gave the owner of that stone access to those games and to the food served there. Could it be that Jesus is symbolically promising the overcomer something that will give that person access to life everlasting and into Heaven?

4. The letter to the church at Thyatira. The corrupt church

"^{18}And to the angel of the church in Thyatira write, 'These things says the Son of God, who has eyes like a flame of fire, and His feet like fine brass: ^{19}I know your works, love, service, faith, and your patience; and as for your works, the last are more than the first. ^{20}Nevertheless I have a few things against you, because you allow that woman Jezebel, who calls herself a prophetess, to teach and seduce My servants to commit sexual immorality and eat things sacrificed to idols. ^{21}And I gave her time to repent of her sexual immorality, and she did not repent. ^{22}Indeed I will cast her into a sickbed, and those who commit adultery with her into great tribulation, unless they repent of their deeds. ^{23}I will kill her

Chapter 2 – The Seven Churches

children with death, and all the churches shall know that I am He who searches the minds and hearts. And I will give to each one of you according to your works. ²⁴'Now to you I say, and to the rest in Thyatira, as many as do not have this doctrine, who have not known the depths of Satan, as they say, I will put on you no other burden. ²⁵But hold fast what you have till I come. ²⁶And he who overcomes, and keeps My works until the end, to him I will give power over the nations—²⁷'He shall rule them with a rod of iron; They shall be dashed to pieces like the potter's vessels'— as I also have received from My Father; ²⁸and I will give him the morning star. ²⁹'He who has an ear, let him hear what the Spirit says to the churches.' " (Revelation 2:18-29)

Thyatira was located about 42 miles southwest of Pergamos and was used as a "line of first defense" for Pergamos. The invading armies would have to capture Thyatira first, which gave Pergamos time to get their defenses ready. It sat at the juncture of three roads – to Pergamos, Sardis, and Smyrna. One of Thyatira's main products was dyed wool. It was well-known for those dyes, especially purple. Lydia, a sales rep for the Thyatira purple dye, is mentioned in Acts 16:14-15. Paul and Silas stayed at her house while in Phillipi. The purple dye, made from plant roots and the blood of a small snail (murex trunculus), was also used in the priest's robes for the Temple in Jerusalem. That snail was believed to have gone extinct but has recently been rediscovered. The city was also known for its trade guilds, which were compulsory and each one under the patronage of a pagan deity. Unfortunately for the Christians, this meant they could not join the trade guilds (and worship a pagan god). This is the basis for the message from Jesus to the church at Thyatira.

    a. Name – Thyatira. The name means "unceasing sacrifice."
    b. Title of Jesus. *"the Son of God, who has eyes like a flame of fire, and His feet like fine brass."* This is the only place in Revelation where *"the Son of God"* is mentioned. *"Who has eyes like a flame of fire"* – those piercing eyes that see straight to the heart and knows not just our outward actions, but the true motive inside, and *"the feet of brass"* – He Who will sit in judgment.

c. Commendation. *"¹⁹"I know your works, love, service, faith, and your patience; and as for your works, the last are more than the first."* Of those churches that received a commendation, this is the shortest one. The church at Thyatira was doing good works, serving others, growing their faith – doing everything right, it would seem. And they're doing more now than they did at first, so those good works, service, and growth in faith is expanding – as it should in a growing church.

d. Concern. *"²⁰Nevertheless I have a few things against you, because you allow that woman Jezebel, who calls herself a prophetess, to teach and seduce My servants to commit sexual immorality and eat things sacrificed to idols. ²¹And I gave her time to repent of her sexual immorality, and she did not repent. ²²Indeed I will cast her into a sickbed, and those who commit adultery with her into great tribulation, unless they repent of their deeds. ²³I will kill her children with death, and all the churches shall know that I am He who searches the minds and hearts. And I will give to each one of you according to your works." ²⁴'Now to you I say, and to the rest in Thyatira, as many as do not have this doctrine, who have not known the depths of Satan, as they say, I will put on you no other burden. ²⁵But hold fast what you have till I come.' "*

This is not the Jezebel of the Old Testament as she was long gone by this time. But whoever this "prophetess" is that this church was allowing to influence its practices must be similar to that Jezebel, i.e. – one who cares only for herself and her power and doesn't care what destruction she brings to get what she wants. The Old Testament Jezebel, who married King Ahab of Israel, introduced Baal worship, which includes sexual fornication, to Israel. This new Jezebel seems to be using that as a model and is, as stated in Jesus' concern, inducing those in the church to indulge in sexual

Chapter 2 – The Seven Churches

immorality and to eat things sacrificed to idols. She had been given the chance to repent, but she would not.

But why was this temptation so strong, and so successful, among the Christians in Thyatira? Remember the church at Smyrna – they were surrounded by temptation but were able to hold fast to their faith. Apparently, there were those at Thyatira who had not been so steadfast and gave in to the sacrifice to and worship of idols. Perhaps it was because that was the only way they could make a living in Thyatira. Whatever the reason, Jesus Christ is letting them know He knows what they are doing and is not happy about it.

e. Admonishment. *"^{22}Indeed I will cast her into a sickbed, and those who commit adultery with her into great tribulation, unless they repent of their deeds. ^{23}I will kill her children with death, and all the churches shall know that I am He who searches the minds and hearts. And I will give to each one of you according to your works."*

While this, at first glance, seems to apply only to this Jezebel, it also applies to all who follow her – *"and those who commit adultery with her."* And what is their punishment if they do not repent? *"^{22}Indeed I will cast her…. into great tribulation."* This is the Greek word thlipsis again, not the Tribulation or Apokalypsis. *"All the churches shall know that I am He who searches the minds and hearts."* The message here is pretty clear; all will see the judgment on those who follow this woman and all will know He is God. *"And I will give to each one of you according to your works."* We have to be careful here because while our salvation is not dependent on our works, our rewards are – remember those crowns?

"*²³I will kill her children with death"* Jesus is not talking about the "first death", but the second death – the one that separates us from God for all eternity – the death that casts those who do not follow Him into the lake of fire. Her children are not just those who came from her womb, but those who follow her example, even into the current age.

This is one of the longest concerns and admonishments in the letters to the churches and it tells us much more about this church, and the churches of today, than we see at first glance.

They justified their sin – after all, as Tertullian the apologist stated a century later – they had to join the trade guilds and participate in drunkenness and sexual idolatry to survive. There are churches today that are justifying their acceptance of homosexuality, abortion, and all these other practices becoming common in the world around us, by saying they have to do this to survive. It was wrong then and it is wrong today.

    f. Promise to the overcomer. *"²⁵But hold fast what you have till I come. ²⁶And he who overcomes, and keeps My works until the end, to him I will give power over the nations—²⁷'He shall rule them with a rod of iron; They shall be dashed to pieces like the potter's vessels'— as I also have received from My Father; ²⁸and I will give him the morning star."*

Those who overcome this idolatry will rule with Jesus in the millennium and He will give them the morning star – *"¹⁶"I, Jesus, have sent My angel to testify to you these things in the churches. I am the Root and the Offspring of David, the Bright and Morning Star."* (Revelation 22:16)

    g. *"²⁹'He who has an ear, let him hear what the Spirit says to the churches.' "*

5. The letter to the church at Sardis. The dead church.

"¹And to the angel of the church in Sardis write, 'These things says

Chapter 2 – The Seven Churches

He who has the seven Spirits of God and the seven stars: 'I know your works, that you have a name that you are alive, but you are dead. ²Be watchful, and strengthen the things which remain, that are ready to die, for I have not found your works perfect before God. ³Remember therefore how you have received and heard; hold fast and repent. Therefore if you will not watch, I will come upon you as a thief, and you will not know what hour I will come upon you. ⁴You have a few names even in Sardis who have not defiled their garments; and they shall walk with Me in white, for they are worthy. ⁵He who overcomes shall be clothed in white garments, and I will not blot out his name from the Book of Life; but I will confess his name before My Father and before His angels. ⁶'He who has an ear, let him hear what the Spirit says to the churches.' " (Revelation 3:1-6)

Sardis is a very interesting church. There are Bible scholars who compare Thyatira to the medieval church and the growth of the Roman Catholic church. If Thyatira represents the medieval church, then what does that make Sardis? What period in church history followed the medieval church and lessened the power of the Roman Catholic church? The Reformation.

Sardis was one of the oldest cities, founded around 2000 BC, or possibly even earlier. Are you familiar with the name, King Midas? He was the king of Phrygia in the Hellenistic period and the son of Cybele, the patron deity of Sardis. He was granted one wish by the god of wine, Dionysius. He wished for everything he touched to turn into gold and his wish was granted. But then he couldn't eat or drink because everything he touched turned to gold. It is said he was told to remove the curse by bathing in the river Pactolus, which he did.

Sardis sat at the intersection of all the roads to the other churches and provinces, which made it a very wealthy city. Then gold was discovered in the river Pactolus (remember King Midas's cure?) – which led to a massive influx of people. The gold and silver "Lydian Staters" were the first coins minted – and they were minted at Sardis. Have you ever heard the saying, "rich as Croesus"? King Croesus ruled Sardis from 585 BC until conquered by Cyrus the Great in 547-546 BC. Croesus and Sardis would

So the Image Could Speak

become synonymous with great wealth.

Sardis was thought to be impregnable because of its location. It sat 1000' high on a mountain with sheer cliffs on three sides and there was only one way in. The authorities thought they only had to be watchful of that one way and they were safe. They were wrong. Those cliffs were made of clay and suffered continuous erosion. What they thought was impregnable proved not to be. Their greatest failure was in not being watchful. Cyrus conquered the city in 549 BC by watching one of Sardis's soldiers entering through a secret path up the mountain side. Cyrus waited until dark when everyone was sleeping, followed the secret path, and conquered Sardis.

You would think they would have learned their lesson and stayed watchful, but they didn't. It happened again in 214 BC when Antiochus crept up the mountain side, like a thief in the night, and conquered the city for the Seleucid empire. Their failure? Again, they did not remain watchful.

   a. Name. Sardis – a once-precious jewel that became common and without value. It is also said to be the stone which occupied the first place in the first row of the high priest's breastplate. (Exodus 28:27), but we have to be careful here, because the names of semi-precious stones in the Old Testament and in the New Testament were not always consistent. There is still some debate about what the Sardis stone actually was.
   b. Title of Jesus. *"He who has the seven Spirits of God and the seven stars"* Remember the fullness of the Holy Spirit as listed in Isaiah 11:2.
   c. Commendation. none
   d. Concern. *"I know your works, that you have a name that you are alive, but you are dead."* What is going on with the church at Sardis? At the time, they had a reputation as a good church with lots of good works, ministries, and activity going on. Does this remind you of some churches today? As Paul put it in 2 Timothy 3:5, *"*[5]*having a form of*

godliness but denying its power." They were acting the part, or role, of Christians, but they had no real relationship with the Savior. Socially, they were alive and had the reputation of being "god-like", but spiritually, they were dead.

e. Admonishment. *"²Be watchful, and strengthen the things which remain, that are ready to die, for I have not found your works perfect before God. ³Remember therefore how you have received and heard; hold fast and repent. Therefore if you will not watch, I will come upon you as a thief, and you will not know what hour I will come upon you."*

Given their history, the people of Sardis would have well understood, *"I will come upon you as a thief."*

Strengthen is a verb which means "to strengthen, make stable, firm." The aspect of the verb (an aorist, or future, imperative in the Greek) carries the idea of urgency, e.g. do it now, before it is too late. This is basically a command to get with God's plan for spiritual stabilization and strength. And what is that plan? A life in the Word and in obedience to Him.

f. Promise to the overcomer. *"⁴You have a few names even in Sardis who have not defiled their garments; and they shall walk with Me in white, for they are worthy. ⁵He who overcomes shall be clothed in white garments, and I will not blot out his name from the Book of Life; but I will confess his name before My Father and before His angels."*

The people of Sardis would have understood this well, for the patron god of Sardis, Cybele, required clean clothes to enter in her temple. But Jesus is promising them everlasting purity in those white garments and their name will never be blotted out from the Book of Life.

Jesus Himself will confirm their purity before His Father and before the angels.

    g. *"⁵"He who has an ear, let him hear what the Spirit says to the churches."'*

6. The letter to the church in Philadelphia.

"⁷And to the angel of the church in Philadelphia write, 'These things says He who is holy, He who is true, 'He who has the key of David, He who opens and no one shuts, and shuts and no one opens': ⁸'I know your works. See, I have set before you an open door, and no one can shut it; for you have a little strength, have kept My word, and have not denied My name. ⁹Indeed I will make those of the synagogue of Satan, who say they are Jews and are not, but lie—indeed I will make them come and worship before your feet, and to know that I have loved you. ¹⁰Because you have kept My command to persevere, I also will keep you from the hour of trial which shall come upon the whole world, to test those who dwell on the earth. ¹¹Behold, I am coming quickly! Hold fast what you have, that no one may take your crown. ¹²He who overcomes, I will make him a pillar in the temple of My God, and he shall go out no more. I will write on him the name of My God and the name of the city of My God, the New Jerusalem, which comes down out of heaven from My God. And I will write on him My new name. ¹³'He who has an ear, let him hear what the Spirit says to the churches.' " (Revelation 3:7-13)

Philadelphia was the youngest of these 7 cities, founded about 189 BC. It was known for its vineyards and wine. In fact, Dionysius, the god of wine, was its principal deity.

Today it is "Allah-Shehu" - city of God in western Turkey.

    a. Name. Philadelphia. Combination of "phile" - friendly toward and delphia – city. "Friendly city."

    b. Title of Jesus. *"He who is holy, He who is true, "He who has the key of David, He who opens and no one shuts, and shuts and no one opens."*

    Holy and true. Each time we see the angels around the

Chapter 2 – The Seven Churches

throne of heaven, they cry "Holy Holy Holy". Reference Exodus 15:11, Isaiah 6:1-3, Isaiah 46:9, Revelation 4:8. Why three times? For the triune spirit of God: God the Father, God the Son, and God the Holy Spirit. The Greek word for true used here is alethinos, meaning real or genuine (John 17:3, 1 John 5:20).

Let's talk about those keys. First, the key of David. We have to go back to Isaiah 22:20-23. Shebna, the treasurer under King Hezekiah is about to exit stage right, due to his failings and Eliakim is called to replace him.

"[20]'Then it shall be in that day, That I will call My servant Eliakim the son of Hilkiah; [21]I will clothe him with your robe and strengthen him with your belt; I will commit your responsibility into his hand. He shall be a father to the inhabitants of Jerusalem And to the house of Judah. [22]The key of the house of David I will lay on his shoulder; So he shall open, and no one shall shut; And he shall shut, and no one shall open. [23]I will fasten him as a peg in a secure place, And he will become a glorious throne to his father's house.' " (Isaiah 22:20-23)

A messianic prophecy or prototype?

Whoever held the key to the House of David was fairly powerful as no one could access the King without going through whoever held the key, in this case, Eliakim.

Jesus Christ, of course, holds the real key. *"[6]Jesus said to him, 'I am the way, the truth, and the life. No one comes to the Father except through Me.' "* (John 14:6)

c. Commendation. *"[8]'I know your works. See, I have set before you an open door, and no one can shut it; for you have a little strength, have kept My word, and have not denied My name. [9]Indeed I will make those of the synagogue of Satan, who say they are Jews and are not, but lie—indeed I will make them come and worship before your feet, and to know that I have loved you.*

[10]Because you have kept My command to persevere, I also will keep you from the hour of trial which shall come upon the whole world, to test those who dwell on the earth. [11]Behold, I am coming quickly! Hold fast what you have, that no one may take your crown."

So they have an open door to the throne room! *"For you have a little strength, have kept My word, and have not denied My name."*

This is not a large congregation, so their strength is not equal to the larger gatherings in Ephesus and the previous cities mentioned. Yet, they have remained steadfast and loyal in their faith in the One True God. That synagogue of Satan we first read about with the church of Smyrna is also mentioned here.

"[10]'Because you have kept My command to persevere, I also will keep you from the hour of trial which shall come upon the whole world, to test those who dwell on the earth.' " *"From the hour of trial"*, but the Greek word used here is ek, which means out of. It is also in the word for church – ekklésia, which means to separate "out from and to" – out of the world and to God. You can't build a whole pre-Tribulation rapture doctrine around just this verse, but it would seem to be saying that those who hold steadfast to the faith, no matter what is going on around them, will be kept out of that hour, or season, of trial coming to the whole world.

"[11]'Behold, I am coming quickly! Hold fast what you have, that no one may take your crown.' "

    d. Concern. None
    e. Admonishment. None
    f. Promise to the overcomer. *"[12]'He who overcomes, I will make him a pillar in the temple of My God, and he shall go out no more. I will write on him the name of My God and the name of the city of My God, the New Jerusalem,*

Chapter 2 – The Seven Churches

which comes down out of heaven from My God. And I will write on him My new name.' "

Remember Sardis had a name, but was dead? Well, those who overcome will get a new name and it is the name of God. This letter was written to the church in Philadelphia, but there can be no question it was meant to be prophetic.

    a.   "*¹³'He who has an ear, let him hear what the Spirit says to the churches.' "*

7. The letter to the church at Laodicea. The luke-warm church.

"¹⁴'And to the angel of the church of the Laodiceans write, 'These things says the Amen, the Faithful and True Witness, the Beginning of the creation of God: ¹⁵'I know your works, that you are neither cold nor hot. I could wish you were cold or hot. ¹⁶So then, because you are lukewarm, and neither cold nor hot, I will vomit you out of My mouth. ¹⁷Because you say, 'I am rich, have become wealthy, and have need of nothing'—and do not know that you are wretched, miserable, poor, blind, and naked— ¹⁸I counsel you to buy from Me gold refined in the fire, that you may be rich; and white garments, that you may be clothed, that the shame of your nakedness may not be revealed; and anoint your eyes with eye salve, that you may see. ¹⁹As many as I love, I rebuke and chasten. Therefore be zealous and repent. ²⁰Behold, I stand at the door and knock. If anyone hears My voice and opens the door, I will come in to him and dine with him, and he with Me. ²¹To him who overcomes I will grant to sit with Me on My throne, as I also overcame and sat down with My Father on His throne. ²²He who has an ear, let him hear what the Spirit says to the churches.' " (Revelation 3:14-22)

Laodicea got its name from Antiochus when he conquered the city in 250BC and named it after his wife, Laodice. We know from Josephus there was a large Jewish settlement in Laodicea. A lot of wealth would go through Laodicea, as it sat at the crossroads to Ephesus and Smyrna. Cicero did his banking there. It was a major trading post, with caravan trade coming from as far east as the Yellow River in Punjab, China.

So the Image Could Speak

Laodicea was a part of a triad of cities, all very close together. That triad was made up of the cities of Colossae, Laodicea, and Hierapolis. At some point in time they decided to share the water supply and they built aqueducts between each of the three cities. Laodicea was in the middle, so got its water supply from two places – Hierapolis and Colossae.

The water that came from Hieropolis came from their hot springs but, by the time it reached Laodicea, it would be lukewarm. The water that came from Colossae was very cold. It is said Laodicea also had a waterfall; however, it is rumored that water had a high concentration of sulfur in it with the accompanying smell and taste. The water in Hieropolis was also not good, which was probably why they joined together with these other two cities to exchange water.

Laodicea suffered a severe earthquake in 62AD, destroying the city. The wealth of its citizens was so great that they rebuilt the city themselves without any assistance – financial or otherwise – from Rome. So it was a very rich city and quite prideful – they were wealthy and had need of nothing. Many professing Christians today rely on their wealth, or social position, or political authority and therefore do not actively pursue their relationship with Christ.

The city of Laodicea was not militarily defendable, so they maintained an attitude of compromise – "come trade with us and we will give you riches."

It was a city of merchants, bankers and gold refiners and the city was well known for a breed of black wool sheep bred in the Lycus valley. A sheep with wool so soft and so glossy, it was highly desired for use in textiles and carpets. They also had a very well-known medical school in Laodicea that was known for an ophthalmic ointment. This eye salve, Phrygian salve, was very well known – Aristotle even mentions it.

    a. Name. Laodicea

Chapter 2 – The Seven Churches

    b. Title of Jesus Christ. *"the Amen, the Faithful and True Witness, the Beginning of the creation of God."* There are multiple Scripture references to the *"Amen"* and the *"Faithful and True"*. The Amen means true; we see this in such passages as Isaiah 65:16, and John 14:6. We'll see it again in Revelation in chapters 7 and 18. We see reference to the *"Faithful and True"* in Psalms 89:34-37 and John 18:37. And we see the witness in Isaiah 55:4.

But the *"Beginning of the creation of God"*, we only see one other time – in Colossians 1:15. *"^{15}He is the image of the invisible God, the firstborn over all creation."* Firstborn – the one who inherits all from the Father and who is in authority overall.

    c. Commendation. None

    d. Concern. *"^{15}'I know your works, that you are neither cold nor hot. I could wish you were cold or hot. ^{16}So then, because you are lukewarm, and neither cold nor hot, I will vomit you out of My mouth. ^{17}Because you say, 'I am rich, have become wealthy, and have need of nothing'—and do not know that you are wretched, miserable, poor, blind, and naked— ^{18}I counsel you to buy from Me gold refined in the fire, that you may be rich; and white garments, that you may be clothed, that the shame of your nakedness may not be revealed; and anoint your eyes with eye salve, that you may see.' "*

How many times have you been working outside, in the hot sun and someone brought you a glass of ice-cold water? How good did that water taste? Or, in the cold of winter, you put a pot of water on to boil, immerse some tea or coffee into that hot water and then sit back and enjoy the warmth of that first sip?

But lukewarm water? Blah! Lukewarm water is an emetic and may cause you to "spew it out of" your mouth. Jesus is telling the church at Laodicea it isn't only their water that is lukewarm.

Then He tells them "you think you're rich, but you're poor and you need to get gold refined in the fire – not that gold they are using to trade and grow rich, but the real stuff, and clothing from One who will give them a white robe, signifying their purity. And He tells them they need to be anointed with eye salve, not the Phrygian salve for which they are known, but the real stuff that will open their eyes, so they may see real redemption.

e. Admonishment. *"[19]'As many as I love, I rebuke and chasten. Therefore be zealous and repent. [20]Behold, I stand at the door and knock. If anyone hears My voice and opens the door, I will come in to him and dine with him, and he with Me.' "*

Jesus loves His church! Even when they falter, He still loves them and yearns for them to turn back. He loves us enough to chasten us when we've faltered and turned away. But here's the real key – He says *"[20]Behold, I stand at the door and knock. If anyone hears My voice and opens the door, I will come in to him and dine with him, and he with Me."* If He is standing at the door and knocking, then He is not in the church! He's standing outside and waiting for someone to let Him in! But when, and if, they do open the door to Him – look what happens.

f. Promise to the overcomer. *"[21]'To him who overcomes I will grant to sit with Me on My throne, as I also overcame and sat down with My Father on His throne.' "* Jesus is telling us He is not sitting on His throne...yet. He is sitting on His Father's throne. So where is Jesus' throne? During the millennium it will be in Jerusalem. So where will those who overcome sit? With Jesus, on His Throne – the Throne of David – in Jerusalem.

g. *[22]'He who has an ear, let him hear what the Spirit says to the churches.' "*

Chapter 2 – The Seven Churches

We have completed an overview of the seven churches, but we're not done yet. There is a chart in the Appendix (Appendix II – The Letters to the Churches) that gives an overview of these seven churches and the commendation and concerns for each. Smyrna and Philadelphia had no concern and no exhortation. Sardis and Laodicea had no commendation.

At the beginning of this chapter, I mentioned there were four levels of interpretation for these two chapters:

1. Local – we can see within each letter the message was unique to that church and what it was dealing with in the environment they were in.
2. Admonishment – while these seven letters were addressed specifically to these seven churches, the warnings were for all churches, even to this day.
3. Personal – *"he that hath an ear"* the words written to each of these churches apply to us individually. Let's just take a quick look at what we can learn from these seven churches.
    - Ephesus – neglected priorities. They were too busy with the business of the church to give time to God.
    - Smyrna – Satanic opposition. They were surrounded by pagan worship, but they held fast.
    - Pergamos – Worldly compromise. A "mixed marriage" of the church and the world.
    - Thyatira – pagan practices.
    - Sardis – Be watchful! Sardis failed because they thought they were safe and failed to keep watch.
    - Philadelphia – Faithfulness.
    - Laodicea – Lukewarm. Having the appearance, but not the depth of a true relationship with Christ.
4. Prophetic – There are those who say these churches were chosen and presented in a specific order and that order represents the order of Church history since the beginning of the Church. This is highly controversial, but I believe there are no coincidences in the Bible and there are some clear indications that the actions of one church did, in fact, lead to the concerns or admonishments of the next church – just as the failure in one church age led to the next

church age – think of the years of Roman Catholic dominance and how that led to the Reformation. Let's take a look at these seven churches and how they may apply to the history of the church, even to the current time.

1. Ephesus – The Apostolic Church. 33AD - 100AD. This one is self-explanatory. While they were very active and serious about the doctrine, they had left their first love. They had the doctrine down pat but left no time for devotion to God. I recently read a saying that I would like to share. Anyone who has spent time either in or around the military have heard the phrase, "boots on the ground." In a battle, those in charge want to know how many "boots on the ground", or warriors, they have ready to fight and how many the opposition has. Well, in the times we're in, we need to know how many "knees on the ground" we have. How many of us are prayer warriors, spending time in daily devotions to and with God?
2. Smyrna – The Persecuted, or Martyr, Church. 100AD - 313AD. The early church was illegal and heavily persecuted – first by the Jews and then by the Romans. A study of the history of the Roman emperors during this time will reveal the depth of persecution and the horrible deaths of the martyrs during this time.
3. Pergamos – The Compromising Church or Worldly church. 313AD - 590AD. The church at Pergamos had a problem – there were those within the church who were still worshipping pagan gods – particularly Balaam. It is interesting to learn that when Cyrus the Great conquered Babylon, the Chaldean priests and their many followers moved to Pergamos and set up shop. Many of the rituals they practiced were "adopted" into the church and just given a new name. Some of those practices continue to this day. At the Council of Nicea (June 19, 325 AD) under Constantine, then again on Feb 27, 380 AD, under Emperor Theodosius I (347 – 395 AD) a decree was issued that made Christianity

Chapter 2 – The Seven Churches

the religion of the state and punished the practice of pagan rituals.

4. Thyatira – The Corrupt Church (Roman Catholic Church). 590AD - 1517AD. Remember those Chaldeans who left Babylon and set up shop in Pergamos? Well, when the Romans took over, many of them moved to Rome. That influence on the church in Pergamos continued to spread – to the church in Rome and beyond. It is interesting to note the title "Pontifex Maximum" was originally the name given to the high priest of that pagan religion and was originally coined by Nimrod, the founder of Babylon. It was later adopted as the title for the highest position in the Roman Catholic church. The Inquisition began during this period and continued for almost 200 years.

5. Sardis – The Reformation Church. 1517AD - 1700AD. The Reformation church did a lot of good, obviously. It stopped the overwhelming, and, in many cases, oppressive power of the Roman Catholic church. While it began long before Martin Luther nailed those 95 theses to the church door in Germany, it reached fulfillment during this time. However, there were some issues. Luther, Calvin and many others we consider to be founders of the Protestant movement were believers in the "Replacement Theology", or the church replaced Israel in God's heart. It was this replacement theology that was used as justification for the many horrific things that happened to the Jews, particularly by Hitler before and during World War II. At least one scholar calls this period of time a period of "soft hermeneutics" – what the Bible says, but with a few adjustments to meet the perception of the reader. That "soft hermeneutics" still exists today in many churches. This was legalism run rampant.

6. Philadelphia – The Revival, or Missionary, Church. 1700AD – 1900AD. There were several periods of revival in this time, with John Wesley perhaps leading the charge. He and George Whitefield led a period of revival in the early to mid 1700s that led to the creation of over 150 new churches in the New England area alone. Charles Finney, the well-known

revivalist, led another such growth in the early 1800s. He followed the example of those before but went about it in a more organized manner. His <u>Lectures on Systematic Theology</u>, written in 1846 was the go-to book for revivalists through the years and may still be taught in seminaries today.

7. Laodicea – The Lukewarm Church. 1900AD – Today. We have churches ordaining gay ministers and performing gay weddings. We have churches accepting, if not outright encouraging, abortion. The marriage of the church to the world is glaringly obvious and becoming more prevalent the closer we get to the things we see presented in the book of Revelation.

Chapter 2 – The Seven Churches

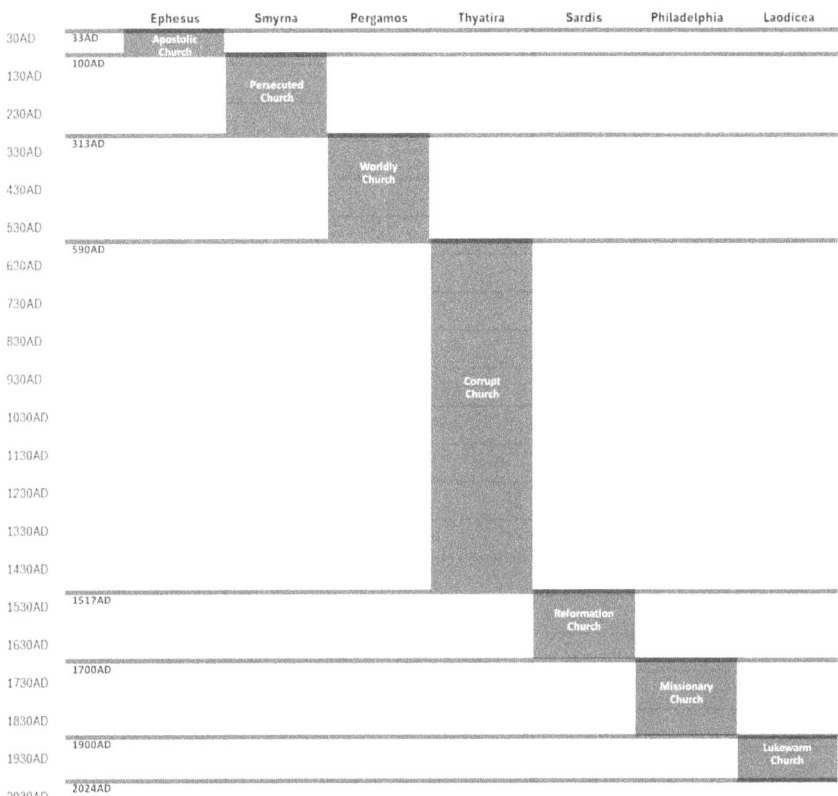

Figure 2 The Seven Churches and the Church Ages

What we can definitively say is that the characteristics – both good and bad – of each of these seven churches do exist in churches today, to various degrees within each church. I dare say all seven exist in every church, at different levels, today. The degree of each in each church would depend on first - the leadership within that church, and second - how many of those in the church are spending time daily with the Bible and in devotion to our Lord Jesus Christ. There can be no question, in comparison to what we read in the Gospels and the book of Acts, that many of the churches of today are lukewarm.

Suggestion - read the Kingdom Parables in Matthew 17 and see how they seem to match not only these seven churches in Asia Minor, but also the church today. Fascinating reading.

So the Image Could Speak

Chapter 3 – The Door to Heaven is Opened

John is instructed by Jesus to " *'[19]Write the things which you have seen, and the things which are, and the things which will take place after this.'* "(Revelation 1:19) The first chapter in the Book of the Revelation of Jesus Christ makes up those *"things which you have seen"*. He is on the Isle of Patmos, exiled for his testimony by Emperor Domitian and he is visited by Jesus Christ.

John is then told to write to those seven churches in what we now call Asia Minor. Those seven churches existed at the time Jesus Christ told John what to write and that makes up the second part of that passage, *"and the things which are."*

The focus shifts as we move into Chapter Four and beyond. In fact, even the location of those visions changes.

"[1]After these things I looked, and behold, a door standing open in heaven. And the first voice which I heard was like a trumpet speaking with me, saying, "Come up here, and I will show you things which must take place after this." [2]Immediately I was in the Spirit; and behold, a throne set in heaven, and One sat on the throne." (Revelation 4:1-2)

Remember what Jesus said to the church at Philadelphia – *"[8]'I know your works. See, I have set before you an open door, and no one can shut it; for you have a little strength, have kept My word, and have not denied My name.'* "(Revelation 3:8)

Jesus opened the way to the very throne of God, when the temple curtain was torn from the top to the bottom (opening the way to the Holy of Holies), when He died on the cross: *"[51]Then, behold, the veil of the temple was torn in two from top to bottom; and the earth quaked, and the rocks were split, [52]and the graves were opened; and many bodies of the saints who had fallen asleep were raised; [53]and coming out of the graves after His resurrection, they went into the holy city and appeared to many."* (Matthew 27:51-53)

Before we dig too deep into those visions given to John in Heaven, we must understand this crucial shift that begins in chapter four, along with the change in focus to what will happen in the future. Remember the

Chapter 3 – The Door to Heaven is Opened

Greek word for church – ekklésia. This word is used a couple of times in Matthew, throughout the book of Acts and the rest of the New Testament. We've seen it already 18 times in the first three chapters of this book (4 times in chapter 1, 8 times in chapter 2, and 6 times in chapter 3), but we won't see it again until chapter 22. We will, however, see some references to it. We'll explore those as we get to them. While you can't build a Pre-Tribulation rapture doctrine on just the fact that the Church – the Bride of Christ – is not mentioned again until the Glorious Second Coming, it does add to the growing evidence that the Church is raptured before the Tribulation begins.

"¹After these things I looked, and behold, a door standing open in heaven. And the first voice which I heard was like a trumpet speaking with me, saying, "Come up here, and I will show you things which must take place after this." (Revelation 4:1)

This verse begins and ends with similar phrasing – *"after these things"*, and *"after this"*. The phrase in the Greek is the same in both places – meta[8] touto[9].

Strong's defines meta as "with, among, or after. (1) behind, beyond, after, of place, (2) after, of time". You'll see it used throughout the New Testament, in relation to a place (with or among and in relation to time (after or following). In fact, you'll see it used both ways (with, among) and (after) throughout the Gospels and all through the New Testament. The word is found 473 times in the New Testament.

Strong's defines touto as, simply, "this". John is using it here, just as translated – after this, or these things. After what? What preceded this chapter? The seven churches.

"¹After these things I looked, and behold, a door standing open in heaven." (Revelation 4:1)

"²Immediately I was in the Spirit; and behold, a throne set in heaven, and One sat on the throne. ³And He who sat there was like a jasper and a sardius stone in appearance; and there was a rainbow around the throne,

---

[8] Strong's Greek.3326, meta, preposition, "with, among, after"
[9] Strong's Greek.3778, houtos, hauté, touto, demonstrative pronoun, "this"

So the Image Could Speak

in appearance like an emerald." (Revelation 3:2-3)

Remember when we see a comparison using the words "like", or "as", it is a simile. The use of the word "rainbow" is interesting here, especially given the current connotation for rainbow. The word in the Greek is iris[10] and can mean rainbow or halo. John is not saying God is made of these jewels; he is using words in his vocabulary to explain something which is outside of his, and our, comprehension.

"⁴Around the throne were twenty-four thrones, and on the thrones I saw twenty-four elders sitting, clothed in white robes; and they had crowns of gold on their heads. ⁵And from the throne proceeded lightnings, thunderings, and voices. Seven lamps of fire were burning before the throne, which are the seven Spirits of God." (Revelation 4:4-5)

Who are these elders? We are given some hints here: they are sitting on thrones, so in a position of authority; they are wearing white robes, so are pure; and they are wearing crowns. These three hints eliminate some of the identities used to describe these twenty-four: tribulation saints, angels, nation of Israel.

They can't be tribulation saints because we see them in chapter 7 standing before the throne. It is one of these twenty-four elders who tells John who that multitude standing before the throne are.

They can't be angels for the same reason. They are standing before the throne in chapter 7 and there isn't any place in the Bible where angels are referred to as "elders", nor are they given crowns or thrones.

They can't be the nation of Israel, or some representation of Israel, as Israel has not yet been redeemed and therefore they can't be in heaven. Israel is not redeemed until chapter 12, which we'll explore when we get to that chapter.

So, who are they?

The hints we have:

---

[10] Strong's Greek.2463, iris, noun feminine, "a rainbow"

Chapter 3 – The Door to Heaven is Opened

1. *"⁴Around the throne were twenty-four thrones, and on the thrones I saw twenty-four elders sitting"*. Elders are mentioned throughout the Bible. We see the 70 elders of the Israelites throughout Exodus, and the elders of each of the various churches are mentioned throughout the New Testament. The title of "elders" is fairly common, so we need to narrow it down a bit.

2. *"Clothed in white robes"* Remember the church in Sardis, the dead church? Even in Sardis are a few who *"⁴have not defiled their garments; and they shall walk with Me in white, for they are worthy."* (Revelation 3:4) We'll see those who are clothed in white as a symbol of their purity, further on in chapter 7, but we can discern that those who are given the white robes are those who have been purified by the blood of Jesus. But, as we'll see in chapter 7, this could either be 1) those who died in Christ prior to the 70th week of Daniel, or 2) those who were martyred during the 70th week of Daniel. We'll explore that further when we get to chapter 7.

3. *"And they had crowns of gold on their heads."* Now we're getting somewhere. The faithful at the church of Smyrna were told, *"Be faithful until death, and I will give you the crown of life."* As previously mentioned there are four other crowns referenced in the New Testament:

    - Crown of Life - James 1:12, for those who suffered for His sake.
    - Crown of Righteousness - 2 Timothy 4:8, for those who loved His appearing.
    - Crown of Glory - 1 Peter 5:4, for those who fed the flock.
    - Crown Incorruptible - 1 Corinthians 9:25, for those who press on steadfastly.
    - Crown of Rejoicing - 1 Thessalonians 2:19, for those who win souls.

    In each of these, only those who are saved by the blood of Jesus Christ can receive those crowns.

4. We have one more clue, not mentioned here, but in Revelation 20: *"⁴And I saw thrones, and they sat on them, and judgment was*

committed to them. Then I saw the souls of those who had been beheaded for their witness to Jesus and for the word of God, who had not worshiped the beast or his image, and had not received his mark on their foreheads or on their hands. And they lived and reigned with Christ for a thousand years." (Revelation 20:4)

Those sitting on these thrones will be judging those who were martyred during the 70th week of Daniel, or who are what we call the Tribulation Saints – those who are martyred during the Tribulation for their faith.

From these clues, we can put a picture together of who those elders are. They represent the raptured Church. In fact, they represent a resurrected Church, as Stephen Armstrong from Verse by Verse Ministries pointed out – you can't put crowns on a spirit.

"⁶Before the throne there was a sea of glass, like crystal. And in the midst of the throne, and around the throne, were four living creatures full of eyes in front and in back. ⁷The first living creature was like a lion, the second living creature like a calf, the third living creature had a face like a man, and the fourth living creature was like a flying eagle. ⁸The four living creatures, each having six wings, were full of eyes around and within. And they do not rest day or night, saying:
'Holy, holy, holy,
Lord God Almighty,
Who was and is and is to come!' " (Revelation 4:6-8)

The sea of glass has often been compared to the laver that was in front of the temple. Anyone entering the temple was required to wash prior to entering, but if we're in Heaven, we're already cleansed and purified through the blood of Jesus Christ.

Who are these four living creatures? If we go back to Isaiah 6, we see something similar. Isaiah sees the throne of God, *"¹In the year that King Uzziah died, I saw the Lord sitting on a throne, high and lifted up, and the train of His robe filled the temple. ²Above it stood seraphim; each one had six wings: with two he covered his face, with two he covered his feet, and with two he flew. ³And one cried to another and said:*
'Holy, holy, holy is the Lord of hosts;
The whole earth is full of His glory!' " (Isaiah 6:1-3)

Chapter 3 – The Door to Heaven is Opened

In the book of Ezekiel, Ezekiel sees a vision of God and four living creatures: *"⁵Also from within it came the likeness of four living creatures. And this was their appearance: they had the likeness of a man. ⁶Each one had four faces, and each one had four wings."* (Ezekiel 1:5-6)

"¹⁰As for the likeness of their faces, each had the face of a man; each of the four had the face of a lion on the right side, each of the four had the face of an ox on the left side, and each of the four had the face of an eagle." (Ezekiel 1:10)

The description in Ezekiel states, *"the face of an ox"*, while the one in Revelation states, *"like a calf"*, but that is a difference of age, not necessarily species. I think we can safely say these living creatures are seraphim – highly placed angels worshipping before the throne of God.

We're going to hear about these four living creatures a lot in the book of Revelation.

"⁹Whenever the living creatures give glory and honor and thanks to Him who sits on the throne, who lives forever and ever, ¹⁰the twenty-four elders fall down before Him who sits on the throne and worship Him who lives forever and ever, and cast their crowns before the throne, saying: ¹¹'You are worthy, O Lord, To receive glory and honor and power; For You created all things, And by Your will they exist and were created.' " (Revelation 4:9-10)

There is one more interesting fact that deserves mentioning here. In Numbers 2, the Lord gives very specific instructions on how the tribes are to set up camp around the tabernacle.

So the Image Could Speak

Of course, each tribe has their own standard and emblem and it is interesting to note that the first tribe for each side's emblem is:
- Judah – the lion
- Reuben – the man
- Ephraim – the ox
- Dan – the eagle

In the same chapter in Numbers, chapter 2, the numbers of the army for each tribe are also given. It gets even more interesting when you look at those numbers and put together an image. For the image following, each individual tribe's graphic is the same width (originally 400 pixels but scaled down for this book) and then adjusted proportionately for the number of the army.

For example, the army of Judah was 74,600 men. Divide 74,600 by 400 (the width of each graphic) and you get 187 (rounded to the nearest whole number). So the graphic representing the army of Judah is 400 pixels wide by 187 pixels high.

The size of the tabernacle shown is proportionate according to the dimensions given in Exodus 25-27.

Chapter 3 – The Door to Heaven is Opened

What do you see?

So the Image Could Speak

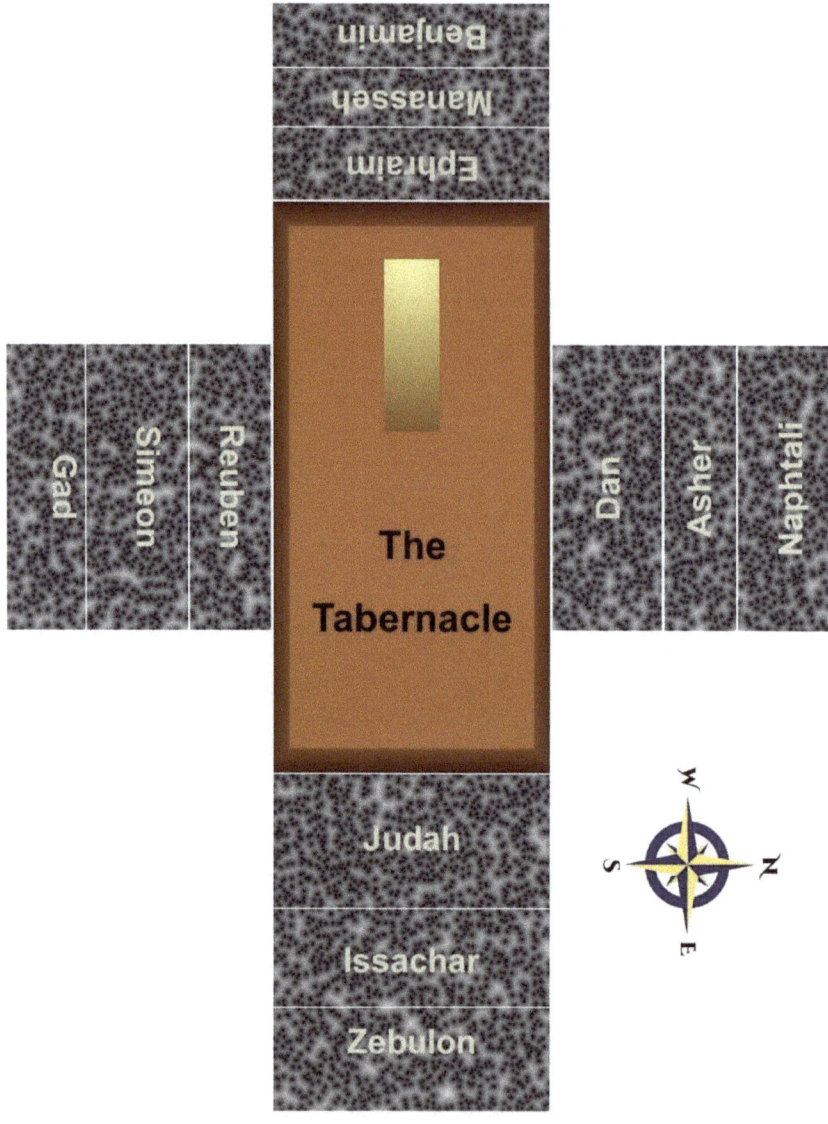

Reminds me of something I heard long ago, *"The New Testament is in the Old Testament concealed. The Old Testament is in the New Testament revealed."* I can't recall the original source of the quote, but I believe it was Augustine.

Chapter 4 – Who is Worthy?

"¹And I saw in the right hand of Him who sat on the throne a scroll written inside and on the back, sealed with seven seals. ²Then I saw a strong angel proclaiming with a loud voice, 'Who is worthy to open the scroll and to loose its seals?' ³And no one in heaven or on the earth or under the earth was able to open the scroll, or to look at it." (Revelation 5:1-3)

Before we take a look at that scroll, or document, and what it may be, there is one very important observation that is often overlooked. Who is holding the scroll in verse 1? *"Him who sat on the throne"*, that is, God. And to whom is the scroll given? *"⁷Then He (Jesus) came and took the scroll out of the right hand of Him (God) who sat on the throne."* Jesus Christ takes the scroll – the Lamb who was slain, the Lion of the tribe of Judah.

If judgment is poured out when those seals are loosed, (and we will soon see it is), then who is unleashing that judgment? Jesus Christ is opening the scroll and the judgment is coming from the Throne of God. We'll see more references to the source of the wrath that takes place during the Tribulation as those seals are opened, but there can be no question this is God's wrath. This is important because there are those who say the first half of the 70th week of Daniel, or the tribulation, is not God's wrath, but man's, or Satan's wrath. But these first 7 verses of chapter 5 would refute that.

What is this scroll? If you've ever been to a closing, or settlement, of property, such as when you're buying or selling real property – like buying a house or land, then you are probably familiar with title deeds and mortgages. Of course, today those title deeds are no longer in the form of scrolls, but the legitimacy of that document has not changed. You sit at a table and, as each document from the seemingly hundreds stacked on the table is passed over to you, you sign your name. This is, of course, after you've handed over that certified check which may well represent your life's savings. And when all the paperwork is done and the funds transferred, you are handed a title deed to the property...or a mortgage, depending on whose money you used to buy the property.

This scroll is "written inside and on the back", which is unusual. Rarely was a scroll written on both the front and the back. The fact that this one

So the Image Could Speak

is signifies its importance as well as the depth of information contained within that scroll.

This event recorded in chapter five is somewhat like a property transfer, though much more powerful and all-encompassing than what we experience at a real estate closing. However at this "settlement", there is no exchange of certified funds as the price was already paid...at Calvary.

In the first chapter of the first book of the Bible, Genesis 1, we read about God creating man and then giving him dominion over the earth; in effect – the title deed: *"^{26}Then God said, 'Let Us make man in Our image, according to Our likeness; let them have dominion over the fish of the sea, over the birds of the air, and over the cattle, over all the earth and over every creeping thing that creeps on the earth.' ^{27}So God created man in His own image; in the image of God He created him; male and female He created them. ^{28}Then God blessed them, and God said to them, 'Be fruitful and multiply; fill the earth and subdue it; have dominion over the fish of the sea, over the birds of the air, and over every living thing that moves on the earth.' "* (Genesis 1:26-28)

However, man's dominion over the earth was conditional: it was dependent on man obeying God's command in Genesis 2:17: *"You must not eat from the tree of the knowledge of good and evil, for when you eat from it, you will certainly die."*

Just two chapters later, we read about Adam's disobedience and fall and how sin was brought into the world. That earthly dominion changed hands once again and Satan was granted dominion over the earth. God was still supreme, but man had lost his authority. Please note, while Satan may have gained dominion over the earth and her governments, the Lord God is still holding that scroll! He is still the Supreme Authority overall. Man gave up his authority, not God's.

That man lost his authority and dominion over the earth, and that it was given to Satan, is further shown in Luke 4, when Jesus goes off into the wilderness for 40 days. Satan tempts Him, saying, *"^{5}Then the devil, taking Him up on a high mountain, showed Him all the kingdoms of the world in a moment of time. ^{6}And the devil said to Him, 'All this authority I will give You, and their glory; for this has been delivered to me, and I give it to whomever I wish. ^{7}Therefore, if You will worship before me, all will be Yours.' "* (Luke 4:5-7)

Chapter 4 – Who is Worthy?

This offer, or temptation, would be meaningless if it was not Satan's to offer. I can walk up to someone and say, "if you give me all your riches, I will give you the Statue of Liberty." That offer only has value, or validity, if I own the Statue of Liberty and it is mine to give. Satan couldn't tempt Jesus with something that wasn't his to give. Jesus didn't deny Satan had that authority. He just told him, *"⁸And Jesus answered and said to him, 'Get behind Me, Satan! For it is written, 'You shall worship the Lord your God, and Him only you shall serve.' "* (Luke 4:8)

It should be noted that Satan does not have ultimate authority as he is still restricted by God, who is the Supreme Authority. Satan only has the authority permitted by God, the Ultimate and Supreme Authority. When Jesus died on the cross, was resurrected, and ascended into heaven, Satan's authority was even further restricted. But his authority will not be completely vanquished until Jesus Christ binds him and throws him into the abyss at the end of the 70th week of Daniel. Even then it is only for a period of a thousand years as he is released at the end of the millennium for a short period of time. We'll see how that ends for him when we get to the end of Revelation.

"³And no one in heaven or on the earth or under the earth was able to open the scroll, or to look at it. ⁴So I wept much, because no one was found worthy to open and read the scroll, or to look at it." (Revelation 5:3-4)

There is a crisis! If this scroll represents the transfer of that authority and the salvation of man from Satan's grasp, then someone needs to be able to open it – someone who has the authority to reveal the contents of that scroll. But it seems there is no one worthy and John weeps.

"⁵But one of the elders said to me, 'Do not weep. Behold, the Lion of the tribe of Judah, the Root of David, has prevailed to open the scroll and to loose its seven seals.' ⁶And I looked, and behold, in the midst of the throne and of the four living creatures, and in the midst of the elders, stood a Lamb as though it had been slain, having seven horns and seven eyes, which are the seven Spirits of God sent out into all the earth. ⁷Then He came and took the scroll out of the right hand of Him who sat on the throne." (Revelation 5:5-7)

Crisis averted! Jesus Christ, the Lamb of God is the only one found worthy

So the Image Could Speak

to open the scroll.

"*[6]And I looked, and behold, in the midst of the throne and of the four living creatures, and in the midst of the elders, stood a Lamb as though it had been slain, having seven horns and seven eyes, which are the seven Spirits of God sent out into all the earth.*" The number seven is symbolic for perfection and completion, the horns are used throughout scripture to represent authority or omnipotence, and the eyes represent knowledge and wisdom or omniscience. So the Lamb with perfect authority "seven horns" and perfect knowledge "seven eyes" takes the scroll from His Father on the throne.

And Heaven rejoices, "*[8]Now when He had taken the scroll, the four living creatures and the twenty-four elders fell down before the Lamb, each having a harp, and golden bowls full of incense, which are the prayers of the saints. [9]And they sang a new song, saying:*
'You are worthy to take the scroll, and to open its seals;
For You were slain, and have redeemed us to God by Your blood
Out of every tribe and tongue and people and nation,
[10]And have made us kings and priests to our God;
And we shall reign on the earth.'
[11]Then I looked, and I heard the voice of many angels around the throne, the living creatures, and the elders; and the number of them was ten thousand times ten thousand, and thousands of thousands, [12]saying with a loud voice:
'Worthy is the Lamb who was slain to receive power and riches and wisdom,
And strength and honor and glory and blessing!'
[13]And every creature which is in heaven and on the earth and under the earth and such as are in the sea, and all that are in them, I heard saying:
'Blessing and honor and glory and power Be to Him who sits on the throne,
And to the Lamb, forever and ever!'
[14]Then the four living creatures said, 'Amen!' And the twenty-four elders fell down and worshiped Him who lives forever and ever." (Revelation 5:8-14)

Chapter 5 – Jacob's Trouble

Chapter 5 – Jacob's Trouble

At the end of chapter five in the book of Revelation, Jesus Christ, the Lamb who was slain, is the only one found worthy to take the scroll with the seven seals from His Father on the throne. Opening the first seal on that scroll releases the first event in the seven year Tribulation.

Why seven years? Why not three and a half years, or five years or even ten years? For the answer, we must go back to the book of Daniel.

Daniel is one of those books that can be a challenge to read, but the wealth of information contained therein is well worth the struggle. It is in Daniel we read about the angel Gabriel who appears to Daniel and delivers God's promise to the people of Israel of seventy weeks.

"[24]'Seventy weeks are determined for your people and for your holy city, to finish the transgression, to make an end of sins, to make reconciliation for iniquity, to bring in everlasting righteousness, to seal up vision and prophecy, and to anoint the Most Holy.'" (Daniel 9:24)

The word translated to "weeks" in this verse is the Hebrew word "shebuim[11]", the plural of the root word shabua, which means a group of seven – sometimes a group of seven days or a week, as in Deuteronomy 16:9 and sometimes a group of seven years, as in Genesis 29:18-30. The literal translation of the first part of this verse would be "Seventy sevens are determined..."

This system of calculating and translating days into years and weeks into a grouping of seven years began with Moses and what is called the "Jubilee calendar." They were told to farm for 6 years, and in the 7th year, let their land rest. (see Leviticus 25:1-7) They referred to those rotating periods of seven years in much the same way we refer to rotating periods of 10 years, or decades, today. At the end of seven of these seven year periods, or forty-nine years, they were told to proclaim a Jubilee, which was heralded in with the sound of a trumpet.

"[8]'And you shall count seven sabbaths of years for yourself, seven times

---

[11] Strong's Hebrew.7620.shabua, noun, masculine, " a period of seven (days, years), heptad, week"

So the Image Could Speak

seven years; and the time of the seven sabbaths of years shall be to you forty-nine years. ⁹Then you shall cause the trumpet of the Jubilee to sound on the tenth day of the seventh month; on the Day of Atonement you shall make the trumpet to sound throughout all your land. ¹⁰And you shall consecrate the fiftieth year, and proclaim liberty throughout all the land to all its inhabitants. It shall be a Jubilee for you; and each of you shall return to his possession, and each of you shall return to his family. ¹¹That fiftieth year shall be a Jubilee to you; in it you shall neither sow nor reap what grows of its own accord, nor gather the grapes of your untended vine. ¹²For it is the Jubilee; it shall be holy to you; you shall eat its produce from the field.' " (Leviticus 25:8-12)

Just as a side note, the next Jubilee Year is in 2025.

The Israelites, upon reaching the Promised Land, were instructed on how to live, how to farm, and how to worship the Lord God. And, for a while, they listened and obeyed. However, there was a period of 490 years when they didn't. They did not follow the Jubilee Calendar; they didn't follow the six years of farming and let the land rest in the seventh year. At the end of that period, they owed the Lord God 70 years of rest for the land. So they were captured by King Nebuchadnezzar and lived as slaves in Babylon for 70 years as punishment for their lapse.

Daniel was one of the captive slaves brought back from Jerusalem to King Nebuchadnezzar. Nebuchadnezzar was particular about the type of captives he wanted, "³Then the king instructed Ashpenaz, the master of his eunuchs, to bring some of the children of Israel and some of the king's descendants and some of the nobles, ⁴young men in whom there was no blemish, but good-looking, gifted in all wisdom, possessing knowledge and quick to understand, who had ability to serve in the king's palace, and whom they might teach the language and literature of the Chaldeans. ⁵And the king appointed for them a daily provision of the king's delicacies and of the wine which he drank, and three years of training for them, so that at the end of that time they might serve before the king. ⁶Now from among those of the sons of Judah were Daniel, Hananiah, Mishael, and Azariah. ⁷To them the chief of the eunuchs gave names: he gave Daniel the name Belteshazzar; to Hananiah, Shadrach; to Mishael, Meshach; and to Azariah, Abed-Nego." (Daniel 1:3-7)

All four of these young men have a story to tell in the book of Daniel and

Chapter 5 – Jacob's Trouble

all four attained some status, as it is written, *"17As for these four young men, God gave them knowledge and skill in all literature and wisdom; and Daniel had understanding in all visions and dreams."* (Daniel 1:17)

Their knowledge and wisdom were also recognized by King Nebuchadnezzar, *"19Then the king interviewed them, and among them all none was found like Daniel, Hananiah, Mishael, and Azariah; therefore they served before the king. 20And in all matters of wisdom and understanding about which the king examined them, he found them ten times better than all the magicians and astrologers who were in all his realm."* (Daniel 1:19-20)

Daniel was gifted by God for his role as a prophet of God and he grows in power and authority, not only under King Nebuchadnezzar, but through the remainder of the Babylonian empire and into the reigns of King Cyrus and Darius, who conquered Babylon and ended the Babylonian empire. Nearly 70 years had passed since Daniel was first brought, as a slave, from Jerusalem to Babylon.

Daniel was well-versed in the Scriptures and knew the promise from God that the nation of Israel would be held captive for 70 years, from the writings of the prophet, Jeremiah.

"8Therefore thus says the Lord of hosts: 'Because you have not heard My words, 9behold, I will send and take all the families of the north,' says the Lord, 'and Nebuchadnezzar the king of Babylon, My servant, and will bring them against this land, against its inhabitants, and against these nations all around, and will utterly destroy them, and make them an astonishment, a hissing, and perpetual desolations. 10Moreover I will take from them the voice of mirth and the voice of gladness, the voice of the bridegroom and the voice of the bride, the sound of the millstones and the light of the lamp. 11And this whole land shall be a desolation and an astonishment, and these nations shall serve the king of Babylon seventy years.' " (Jeremiah 25:8-11)

Daniel knew these seventy years of slavery for Israel was drawing to a close and He goes to the Lord God in prayer. While he was praying, the angel Gabriel appears before him to give him a message, *"21yes, while I was speaking in prayer, the man Gabriel, whom I had seen in the vision at the beginning, being caused to fly swiftly, reached me about the time of*

So the Image Could Speak

the evening offering. ^{22}And he informed me, and talked with me, and said, 'O Daniel, I have now come forth to give you skill to understand. ^{23}At the beginning of your supplications the command went out, and I have come to tell you, for you are greatly beloved; therefore consider the matter, and understand the vision: ^{24}'Seventy weeks are determined for your people and for your holy city, to finish the transgression, to make an end of sins, to make reconciliation for iniquity, to bring in everlasting righteousness, to seal up vision and prophecy, and to anoint the Most Holy.' " (Daniel 9:21-24)

If the word "weeks" here is actually years, or a group of seven years each, then 70 weeks (or groups of 7) x 7 = 490 years. In this passage, God, through the angel Gabriel, is promising Israel and the city of Jerusalem 490 years. At the time this covenant was given, Jerusalem and that temple still lay in ruins as Cyrus had not yet freed the Israelites and they had not yet returned to Jerusalem.

The Israelites had sinned. They had turned away from God. They had stopped following the laws of Moses, even stopped following that Jubilee Calendar. *"^{11} Yes, all Israel has transgressed Your law, and has departed so as not to obey Your voice; therefore the curse and the oath written in the Law of Moses the servant of God have been poured out on us, because we have sinned against Him."* (Daniel 9:11)

Gabriel further defines this promised time:

*"$^{25'}$Know therefore and understand, that from the going forth of the command to restore and build Jerusalem until Messiah the Prince, There shall be **seven weeks** and **sixty-two weeks**; The street shall be built again, and the wall, Even in troublesome times.' "* (Daniel 9:25) (emphasis added)

- "seven weeks", or 7 x 7 = 49 years
- "three score and two weeks." A score is 20, so threescore is sixty, so this refers to a period of 62 "weeks" x 7 = 434 years. If we add these two together, we have 434 + 49 = 483 years.

Josephus tells us of their freedom and the rebuilding of Jerusalem, granted by Cyrus the Great, in his writing, The Antiquities of the Jews:

Chapter 5 – Jacob's Trouble

"In the first year of the reign of Cyrus which was the seventieth from the day that our people were removed out of their own land into Babylon, God commiserated the captivity and calamity of these poor people, according as he had foretold to them by Jeremiah the prophet, before the destruction of the city, that after they had served Nebuchadnezzar and his posterity, and after they had undergone that servitude seventy years, he would restore them again to the land of their fathers, and they should build their temple, and enjoy their ancient prosperity. And these things God did afford them; for he stirred up the mind of Cyrus, and made him write this throughout all Asia: 'Thus saith Cyrus the king: Since God Almighty hath appointed me to be king of the habitable earth, I believe that he is that God which the nation of the Israelites worship; for indeed he foretold my name by the prophets, and that I should build him a house at Jerusalem, in the country of Judea.' (<u>Antiquities of the Jews</u>, Josephus, Book XI, Chapter 1.1)

When Gabriel states, *"[25]'Know therefore and understand, that from the going forth of the command to restore and build Jerusalem until Messiah the Prince' "* he is referring to the release of the Israelites back to Jerusalem and the rebuilding of the temple in Jerusalem and the time that will elapse until Jesus Christ ("Messiah the Prince").

When Jesus rode into Jerusalem on a donkey, on what we now call Palm Sunday, it was the first time Jesus allowed himself to be publicly recognized as the Messiah. That event, the entry into Jerusalem by Christ and showing himself to be the promised Messiah, ended the first 69 weeks of the 70 weeks Gabriel said was determined upon the Jewish nation. So one week, or seven years in prophetic terms, remains. That 70th week, promised to Daniel for the appointed time of the Israelites, is the week, or 7 years, of the Tribulation.

Who is the Tribulation for and why is it called "Jacob's Trouble?" That comes from Jeremiah 30:7: *"[7] Alas! For that day is great, So that none is like it; And it is the time of Jacob's trouble, But he shall be saved out of it."* (Jeremiah 30:7)

Jesus referred to this period, as well: *"[8]'All these are the beginning of sorrows. [9]'Then they will deliver you up to tribulation and kill you, and you will be hated by all nations for My name's sake. [10]And then many will be offended, will betray one another, and will hate one another. [11]Then many*

So the Image Could Speak

false prophets will rise up and deceive many. ^{12}*And because lawlessness will abound, the love of many will grow cold.* ^{13}*But he who endures to the end shall be saved.* ^{14}*And this gospel of the kingdom will be preached in all the world as a witness to all the nations, and then the end will come.'* " (Matthew 24:8-14)

To whom is Jesus speaking? His Apostles and, along with the entire context of Matthew, chapter 24, to the Jews.

To whom did Gabriel address his message, from God to Daniel? "^{24}'*Seventy weeks are determined **for your people and for your holy city**, to finish the transgression, to make an end of sins, to make reconciliation for iniquity, to bring in everlasting righteousness, to seal up vision and prophecy, and to anoint the Most Holy.'* " (Daniel 9:24) (emphasis added)

What is this period of Tribulation and to whom is it directed? God made a promise to Daniel for His people the Israelites for an appointed time of 70 weeks, or 490 years in prophetic terms. Only 483 of that promised 490 years, or sixty-nine of the seventy weeks, have elapsed. That promised 70 weeks has not yet been completed as one week, or seven years, remains and we know God does not break His promises. Is God done with Israel? Not yet, but I think we're getting closer.

For a more detailed look at those first 483 years, I have included a graphic in the Appendix, '**70 Weeks Timeline**'.

Chapter 6 – Our Eyes Deceive Us

In April 1983, CBS offered a special presentation featuring the magician, David Copperfield. David Copperfield performed various magic tricks in front of a live audience of about twenty people and a virtual uncounted audience of those watching on their television sets. The climactic event of the evening was the disappearance of the Statue of Liberty. Those twenty or so people watching from a specially constructed platform in the harbor, about 200' from the iconic statue, and all those glued to their TV screens saw the Statue of Liberty disappear on live television and were amazed or dumbfounded or, maybe just confused by what they saw.

It wasn't until 2017 that the secret behind the seemingly impossible act was revealed. We need not go into all the details of it; suffice it to say it involved a moving platform, some specially constructed towers, and a well-placed sheet. In fact, the entire trick was based on the principle of perspective – changing the perspective equals changing the perception. David Copperfield used a slow-moving platform and a sheet to create an illusion. He knew he could deceive millions simply by changing their perspective, which he accomplished with that slowly rotating platform. David Copperfield knew that most people would accept the impossible if they saw it happen. Most people, in fact, will believe the impossible even without seeing it, if they are told it happened – especially if they are told repeatedly it happened. Many of those who didn't watch the event on live television heard about it over the following days as the TV news stations replayed the event.

What David Copperfield knew then, Satan has known for thousands of years – we humans tend to be somewhat gullible. Of course, with all the fantastic graphics effects in movies today, we would not be as easily fooled as we were in 1983, right?

Well, maybe and maybe not. As recently as 2000, a series of chain emails were sent out warning people about "flesh-eating bananas."[12] The threat was taken so seriously that the US Centers for Disease Control and

---

[12] Bananas and Flesh-Eating Disease, David Mikkelson, June 25, 2001, https://www.snopes.com/fact-check/banana-fits/

So the Image Could Speak

Prevention issued a statement about the false nature of the rumors.[13] However, instead of calming the storm, the statement by the CDC only seemed to give it more credence – to the point where the CDC actually created a "banana hotline" to field the massive number of phone calls about the disease. The panic did eventually fade into obscurity, only to be revived in 2011 with much the same effect and panic as previously.

I'm not a psychologist and cannot delve into all the reasons why, and how, we can be so easily fooled. One of the writers at the BBC wrote an interesting article about that very subject a few years ago, "Why are people so incredibly gullible?"[14]. It is a good read if this subject interests you.

But the simple answer is because God made us this way. He wants us to be trusting, but with that trust placed in Him. We are told, *"⁵Trust in the LORD with all your heart, and lean not on your own understanding; ⁶in all your ways acknowledge Him, and He will make your paths straight."* (Proverbs 3:5-6)

"Lean not on your own understanding." So we are not to trust in the things of this world, even when seen with our own eyes, but to trust, fully and completely, in Him alone. If we do not do this – place our trust in Him and His Word – then we leave ourselves open for the deceit of this world and we leave an open door for Satan to lead us down the path of destruction.

That open door is how Satan gets millions, across the globe, to believe he, and his emissary the AntiChrist, are the answer to the world's problems at the beginning of the Tribulation. Satan has many tools in his toolbox to convince the world he has all the answers at a time when the world is in chaos – with his greatest tool being the art of deception. A tool he has honed and sharpened through the ages until he can deceive nearly everyone, *"²²For false Christs and false prophets will appear and perform signs and wonders that would deceive even the elect, if that were possible."* (Mark 13:22)

---

[13] Flesh-Eating Bananas From Costa Rica?, EricT_Culinarylore, January 3, 2018, https://culinarylore.com/food-history:flesh-eating-bananas-from-costa-rica/
[14] Why are people so incredibly gullible?, David Robson, March 24, 2016, https://www.bbc.com/future/article/20160323-why-are-people-so-incredibly-gullible

Chapter 6 – Our Eyes Deceive Us

At the beginning of chapter 6 of the Revelation of Jesus Christ, Jesus begins the process of opening the seals on the scroll He was given by His Father on the throne.

"¹Now I saw when the Lamb opened one of the seals; and I heard one of the four living creatures saying with a voice like thunder, 'Come and see.' ²And I looked, and behold, a white horse. He who sat on it had a bow; and a crown was given to him, and he went out conquering and to conquer." (Revelation 6:1-2)

This person, or being, on this white horse is described as a conqueror; he carries a bow like a warrior. But he has no arrows. How is he to conquer without any arrows. Isn't that like expecting Israel to protect herself from the armies and weapons of her enemies without any missiles?

The rider on this white horse is the AntiChrist and he carries no arrows because he conquers not by violence or aggressive action – though there will be plenty of both in this period. He conquers by deceit. The imaginary depiction of a peace treaty being signed in the Preface of this book is arranged by him, the AntiChrist, just as Gabriel told Daniel. He promises peace, but he does not deliver it. His promises are false, yet many will believe him.

"²⁷Then he shall confirm a covenant with many for one week; but in the middle of the week he shall bring an end to sacrifice and offering. And on the wing of abominations shall be one who makes desolate, even until the consummation, which is determined, is poured out on the desolate." (Daniel 9:27)

That one verse in Daniel gives us a high-level overview of the entire seven year Tribulation:

- *"He shall confirm a covenant with many for one week"*. That confirmation of the peace treaty between Israel and her enemies marks the beginning of this period called the Tribulation, or time of Jacob's Trouble.
- *"In the middle of the week he shall bring an end to sacrifice and offering"*. We'll read more about this further on in Revelation,

but this event, which we call the Abomination of Desolation, marks the mid-way point through the Tribulation.

- *"Even until the consummation, which is determined, Is poured out on the desolate."* The Battle of Armageddon and the final event in this period.

If you believe in the rapture of the Church and believe it is a pre-Tribulation event, then you know the Church won't be here to see that deception or be subject to it. So why do we even need to study it? In fact, why even study the book of Revelation at all, if we believe (as I do) the Church won't be here to see any of the events depicted in Revelation take place – the seven seals or the seven trumpets, the Mark of the Beast, the Abomination of Desolation and all the rest of the judgment poured out on an unrepenting world?

In the second book in the Beginning of Sorrows series, <u>As In the Days of Noah</u>, I devote a chapter to why we should study prophecy, with perhaps the most important reason is how important it is to God. "Paul, in his second letter to Timothy, writes *"¹⁶All Scripture is God-breathed and is useful for instruction, for conviction, for correction, and for training in righteousness, ¹⁷so that the man of God may be complete, fully equipped for every good work."* (2 Timothy 3:16-17). So every word of God's Word to us is intentional and there for a reason: for us to learn doctrine, be corrected when we've gone off track, and for our instruction in righteousness, that we may be found perfect in Christ, our Redeemer."[15]

By studying the book of Revelation, and understanding the events which will take place, we can prepare ourselves and not be taken captive through empty deception, as Paul writes to the church at Colossus, *"⁸See to it that no one takes you captive through philosophy and empty deception, which are based on human tradition and the spiritual forces of the world rather than on Christ. ⁹For in Christ all the fullness of the Deity dwells in bodily form. ¹⁰And you have been made complete in Christ, who is the head over every ruler and authority."* (Colossians 2:8-10)

---

[15] As in the Days of Noah: Sequel to Go Set a Watchman, Mouw, Susan. n.d. Amazon. https://www.amazon.com/dp/B09NTZN9Y5..

Chapter 7 – The Seven Seals are Opened

Chapter 7 – The Seven Seals are Opened

Before we start digging into these seven seals and what follows, let's take a look at the chronology of these seven judgments, and the two sets of seven judgments each which follow. There are many who say these are not in chronological order, but I disagree. While there are some events, or interludes, depicted that do not happen in the order in which they are presented in Revelation, the seven seals are shown in order, as are the seven trumpets and the seven bowl, or vial, judgments. The first set of seven judgments are the seals, with a short interlude between the sixth and seventh seal. The next set of seven judgments are the trumpets, with an interlude between the sixth and seventh trumpets. The final set of seven judgments are the vials, or bowl, judgments, with a very short but quite powerful interlude between the sixth and seventh bowls.

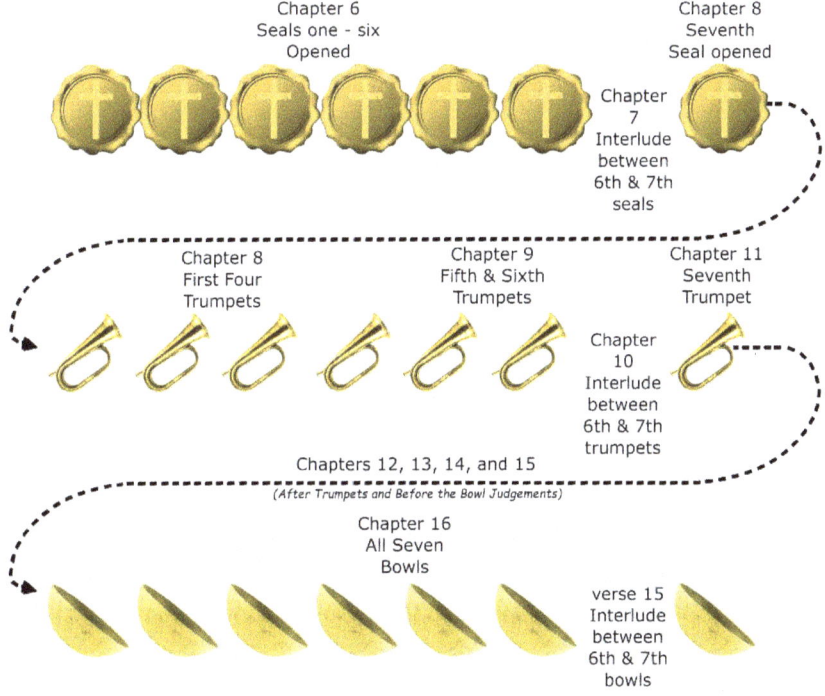

Many of the events that occur at the midpoint of the Tribulation, i.e. the Abomination of Desolation, the Mark of the Beast, the death and resurrection of the Two Witnesses, are revealed just after the seventh trumpet. This may be an indication of when the midpoint of the Tribulation occurs, but not necessarily. For example, the Two Witnesses aren't introduced until chapter 11, yet we know: 1) they are given 1,260 days, which according to the Jewish lunar calendar would be 42 months, or three and one-half years, to prophesy before the western wall in Jerusalem, and 2) they are killed by the AntiChrist at the midpoint of the 70th week of Daniel. In order for them to prophesy for the full 1,260 days before the midpoint of the 70th week of Daniel, they have to appear very early – perhaps simultaneous with the opening of the first seal.

There is an interesting timeline on David Jeremiah's website, www.davidjeremiah.org. You can request a free copy of it online but remember – we don't really know how long each of the seven seals, or seven trumpets, or seven bowls, last so it is difficult to assign an exact timeline to the events of the 70th week of Daniel.

So let's go through the seven seals; we'll dig into the seven trumpets and the seven bowls in later chapters.

1. The first seal – the Conqueror.

    "^{1}Now I saw when the Lamb opened one of the seals; and I heard one of the four living creatures saying with a voice like thunder, 'Come and see.' ^{2}And I looked, and behold, a white horse. He who sat on it had a bow; and a crown was given to him, and he went out conquering and to conquer." (Revelation 6:1-2)

    The white horse symbolizes 1) purity and 2) power. The rider of this horse carries a bow – or symbol of war, but he has no arrows. He is given a crown (stephanos) – a symbol of victory, and he goes out conquering and to conquer. The crown, stephanos, was given to conquering heroes on their return. It was a symbol of their victory, unlike the crown (diadema) that Jesus Christ wears, as a symbol of His complete authority.

    We know Satan tries, over and over again, to imitate Jesus and this is just a repeat of past performances. This is a counterfeit christ, the AntiChrist, and his mission, while he claims to desire and promote peace, is actually to conquer and gain world dominion. He is carrying a bow, which represents warfare, but he

Chapter 7 – The Seven Seals are Opened

has no arrows. He is given a crown, which symbolizes his many victories. He is a conqueror, but he does not conquer through warfare – he conquers through deception. Who is this AntiChrist and how will we know him?

We need to go back to Daniel chapter 9, specifically verses 26 and 27, for the answer: *"²⁶And after the sixty-two weeks Messiah shall be cut off, but not for Himself; and the people of the prince who is to come shall destroy the city and the sanctuary. The end of it shall be with a flood, and till the end of the war desolations are determined. ²⁷Then he shall confirm a covenant with many for one week; but in the middle of the week He shall bring an end to sacrifice and offering. And on the wing of abominations shall be one who makes desolate, Even until the consummation, which is determined, Is poured out on the desolate."* (Daniel 9:26-27)

"The people of the prince who is to come" who destroy the city and the sanctuary. Daniel could be prophesying about the destruction of Jerusalem in 70AD, led by General Titus, later Emperor Titus, of the Roman empire. Does that make General Titus the AntiChrist? If that were so, then we would have already seen the New Millenium with Jesus Christ reigning from a throne in Jerusalem. That has not yet happened. General Titus may have been an early prototype of the AntiChrist, but he wasn't the final AntiChrist. It would seem we have a huge time gap here, for the next verse refers to a covenant and an end to sacrifice and offering. But General Titus destroyed the temple – what sacrifice and offerings could there be?

It could only be in another temple: the Third Temple in Jerusalem and that has not yet been built. So that gap in time is at least nearly two thousand years.

"²⁷Then he shall confirm a covenant with many for one week." (Daniel 9:27)

Confirm – the Hebrew word used here is gabar[16], which means to be strong, or prevail. It is used multiple times in Genesis, in

---

[16] Strong's Hebrew.1396, gabar, verb, "to be strong, mighty"

relation to the flood waters, *"¹⁸The waters prevailed and greatly increased on the earth, and the ark moved about on the surface of the waters. ¹⁹And the waters prevailed exceedingly on the earth, and all the high hills under the whole heaven were covered. ²⁰The waters prevailed fifteen cubits upward, and the mountains were covered."* (Genesis 7:18-20)

We see it again in Exodus, and again in 1 and 2 Samuel, 1 Chronicles, Job, and in Psalms. The full definition in Strong's is "exceed, confirm, be great, be mighty, prevail, **put to more strength, strengthen, be stronger.**" (emphasis added) There are many who believe the covenant the AntiChrist confirms is not a new covenant, or treaty, but an existing one - such as the Abraham Accords, and he strengthens it, or makes it stronger. That is a possibility, but it could also be a new treaty. We do know that when this event takes place, the one who arranges it and brings Israel's enemies to the peace table is the AntiChrist.

There are a lot of various theories and conjectures about who the AntiChrist is, or will be, and many take this verse in Daniel to mean he must be from western Europe – or the remains of the Roman empire. But the Roman empire was split into two parts – remember the two legs on the statue Daniel saw? When Constantine came to power, in 306AD, he became fed up with the power plays and political maneuverings in Rome and moved the capital to Byzantine, later renamed Constantinople, now Istanbul, Turkey.

This AntiChrist appears at a time when the whole world is clamoring for peace and he is the great negotiator and great deceiver. He is able to bring Israel's enemies to the table and bring peace to a region that is been under attack for centuries. He is hailed as a hero and he is quickly elevated to global recognition. But as much as he claims to support peace, he has an ulterior motive and it becomes evident with the next seal.

2. The Second Seal – the Red Horse of War.

"³When He opened the second seal, I heard the second living creature saying, 'Come and see.' ⁴Another horse, fiery red, went

Chapter 7 – The Seven Seals are Opened

out. And it was granted to the one who sat on it to take peace from the earth, and that people should kill one another; and there was given to him a great sword." (Revelation 6:3-4)

In 1938, England's Prime Minister Neville Chamberlain met with Adolf Hitler in Munich. Even though Hitler's own Mein Kampf, written nearly a decade previously, detailed his desire for world domination, PM Chamberlain was desperate to placate Hitler and keep the peace. He returned from his meeting and waved the document wherein Hitler promised he, too, only wanted peace. PM Chamberlain proclaimed there would be "peace with honor…peace in our time."[17]

What followed was a period of peace, though it was a false peace. While those in the west were relaxing and celebrating their success in negotiating a peace, Hitler was planning complete subjugation of the countries around Germany. It was only when Germany invaded Poland in 1939 that the west realized just how serious, and dangerous, Hitler was. Similarly, all those promises of peace and safety made by the AntiChrist don't last very long. The war, and wars, which ensue make the devastation of WWII look like child's play. Even within his own cabal, as he brings to coalition that one world government, there is rebellion. Of those ten countries he brings together, three rebel.

Adolf Hitler was not the AntiChrist and the second World War was not the Tribulation, but that false promise of peace and Hitler's talent for deception and to conceal his real intentions are like that of the AntiChrist's deception and the false peace that will ensue between the first seal and the second seal.

"And it was granted to the one who sat on it to take peace from the earth." We are already seeing the stage set for this. The brutality of the attack on Israel in Gaza in October 2023 and the escalation since shows us a foreshadowing of what will come with this second seal. Remember what Jesus told the Disciples

---

[17] Neville Chamberlain's "Peace For Our Time" speech, Richard Hacken, European Studies Librarian, August 6, 2018,
https://eudocs.lib.byu.edu/index.php/Neville_Chamberlain%27s_%22Peace_For_Our_Time%22_speech

when they came to him and asked when these things would be. *"⁴And Jesus answered and said to them: 'Take heed that no one deceives you. ⁵For many will come in My name, saying, 'I am the Christ,' and will deceive many. ⁶And you will hear of wars and rumors of wars. See that you are not troubled; for all these things must come to pass, but the end is not yet. ⁷For nation will rise against nation, and kingdom against kingdom. And there will be famines, pestilences, and earthquakes in various places. ⁸All these are the beginning of sorrows.' "* (Matthew 24:4-8)

3. The Third Seal – The Black Horse of Famine.

   "⁵When He opened the third seal, I heard the third living creature say, 'Come and see. So I looked, and behold, a black horse, and he who sat on it had a pair of scales in his hand. ⁶And I heard a voice in the midst of the four living creatures saying, 'A quart of wheat for a denarius, and three quarts of barley for a denarius; and do not harm the oil and the wine.' " (Revelation 6:5-6)

   A denarius, in John's time, was about a day's wages, so it will take a full day's wages just to eat, but the rich (the oil and the wine) will still be wining and dining as though nothing has changed. In the late first century, it was common for a scale to be used in the marketplace for weighing out measures of produce, or, as in this verse, wheat, and barley. Wheat was used to make bread. Barley was the poor man's choice to replace wheat, but neither wheat nor barley were overly expensive at the time of John's writing about the black horseman of the third seal.

   While the actual cost of wheat and barley at the time of John's writing is difficult to estimate, some reports state this valuation is ten to twelve times the then-current price. Suffice it to say, when one must spend a whole day's wages just for a loaf of bread, times are hard.

4. The Fourth Seal – The Horseman of Death

Chapter 7 – The Seven Seals are Opened

"⁷When He opened the fourth seal, I heard the voice of the fourth living creature saying, 'Come and see.' ⁸So I looked, and behold, a pale horse. And the name of him who sat on it was Death, and Hades followed with him. And power was given to them over a fourth of the earth, to kill with sword, with hunger, with death, and by the beasts of the earth." (Revelation 6:7-8)

The Greek word used for pale in verse 8 is chlōros.[18] It is the color of plants, or grass, as used in Mark 6:39, but most scholars believe here it is used to represent the color of death. This is the only one of the four horsemen of the Apocalypse given a name and a companion, and that name is "Death." Hades, his companion, rides behind "Death" to clean up the after-effects.

This rider is given authority to kill one-fourth of the world's population. As I write these words, the Worldometer shows the world population at 8,109,702,100 and counting. We can't predict how big that population will be at the time of the ride of this fourth horseman, and we can't estimate how many will have already been raptured, but just for the sake of argument, let's say that one-quarter would be somewhere in the neighborhood of two billion people. Two billion people, worldwide, killed.

These people are killed by 1) sword (the second Horseman), 2) by famine, by plague (the third Horseman), and 3) by the beasts of the earth.

"The beasts of the earth"? Does this mean that people will be attacked in their offices, factories, homes, condos, and high-rise apartments by lions, and tigers, and bears?

The Greek word for beast is thērion[19] defined as "a wild beast." It is used in Mark, when Jesus is tempted by Satan, *"and He was there for forty days, being tempted by Satan. He was with the wild animals, and the angels ministered to Him."* (Mark 1:13)

---

[18] Strong's Greek.5515, chlóros, adjective, "pale green, pale"
[19] Strong's Greek.2342.thēriōn, noun neuter, "a wild beast"

It is also used in several other places in the New Testament (Acts, Titus, Hebrews, James) and is translated as an actual wild beast, or creature. It is also used in Revelation for the beast who comes up out of the abyss, or the AntiChrist. (see Revelation 13:1-4)

I don't think we can definitively say that this fourth Horseman causes people to die from attacks of wild beasts of nature – though that is entirely possible, but neither can we state conclusively that it is the AntiChrist (the Beast) who is the cause of the death of so many just based on the use of this one word. We do know the AntiChrist, that first Horseman, comes forward to conquer and we know that Satan's purpose is to steal, kill, and destroy.

"¹⁰The thief does not come except to steal, and to kill, and to destroy. I have come that they may have life, and that they may have it more abundantly." (John 10:10)

Regardless of how they are killed, one-quarter of the world's population at that time will die.

5. The Fifth Seal – The Martyrs.

"⁹When He opened the fifth seal, I saw under the altar the souls of those who had been slain for the word of God and for the testimony which they held. ¹⁰And they cried with a loud voice, saying, 'How long, O Lord, holy and true, until You judge and avenge our blood on those who dwell on the earth?' ¹¹Then a white robe was given to each of them; and it was said to them that they should rest a little while longer, until both the number of their fellow servants and their brethren, who would be killed as they were, was completed." (Revelation 6:9-11)

Chapter 7 – The Seven Seals are Opened

The Greek word translated to "souls" in this verse is psychas, from the root word psuche'.[20] It is used many times throughout the Gospels, especially in Matthew, to indicate the spirit, not the physical being of a person. For example, in Matthew 16, Jesus is speaking to his disciples, *"^{24}Then Jesus said to His disciples, 'If anyone desires to come after Me, let him deny himself, and take up his cross, and follow Me. ^{25}For whoever desires to save his life will lose it, but whoever loses his life for My sake will find it. ^{26}For what profit is it to a man if he gains the whole world, and loses his own soul? Or what will a man give in exchange for his soul?' "* (Matthew 16:24-26)

Jesus is not telling his disciples their physical body will never die in verse 25, but their spiritual body – their soul – will have eternal life if they follow Him.

These souls John sees under the altar are those who have been martyred during this 70th week of Daniel, not people with physically resurrected bodies. They cannot be those who were martyred prior to the 70th week of Daniel, as those have been Raptured and given their resurrection bodies. *"^{15}For this we say to you by the word of the Lord, that we who are alive and remain until the coming of the Lord will by no means precede those who are asleep. ^{16}For the Lord Himself will descend from heaven with a shout, with the voice of an archangel, and with the trumpet of God. And the dead in Christ will rise first. ^{17}Then we who are alive and remain shall be caught up together with them in the clouds to meet the Lord in the air. And thus we shall always be with the Lord."* (1 Thessalonians 4:15-17)

Nor are these the twenty-four elders who are sitting on thrones, for these souls are all under the altar.

The only conclusion that can be drawn is these are the souls of those who are martyred for their faith during the Tribulation. This would mean there are people who get saved during the Tribulation and scripture confirms that, as we'll see further on.

---

[20] Strong's Greek.5590.psuché, noun feminine, "breath, the soul"

So the Image Could Speak

> "¹³Then one of the elders answered, saying to me, 'Who are these arrayed in white robes, and where did they come from?' ¹⁴And I said to him, 'Sir, you know.' So he said to me, 'These are the ones who **come out of the great tribulation**, and washed their robes and made them white in the blood of the Lamb. ¹⁵Therefore they are before the throne of God, and serve Him day and night in His temple. And He who sits on the throne will dwell among them. ¹⁶They shall neither hunger anymore nor thirst anymore; the sun shall not strike them, nor any heat; ¹⁷for the Lamb who is in the midst of the throne will shepherd them and lead them to living fountains of waters. And God will wipe away every tear from their eyes.' " (Revelation 7:13-17) (emphasis added)

Those wearing the white robes are those who rejected the AntiChrist and turned to God during the Tribulation. These are those who refused the mark of the beast and did not fall down in worship of the AntiChrist but gave their life so their testimony would be heard and preserved. These are the Tribulation Saints.

6. The Sixth Seal – The Great Earthquake

> "¹²I looked when He opened the sixth seal, and behold, there was a great earthquake; and the sun became black as sackcloth of hair, and the moon became like blood. ¹³And the stars of heaven fell to the earth, as a fig tree drops its late figs when it is shaken by a mighty wind. ¹⁴Then the sky receded as a scroll when it is rolled up, and every mountain and island was moved out of its place. ¹⁵And the kings of the earth, the great men, the rich men, the commanders, the mighty men, every slave and every free man, hid themselves in the caves and in the rocks of the mountains, ¹⁶and said to the mountains and rocks, 'Fall on us and hide us from the face of Him who sits on the throne and from the wrath of the Lamb! ¹⁷For the great day of His wrath has come, and who is able to stand?' " (Revelation 6:12-17)

God has previously used earthquakes, or shaking of the earth, to get our attention. When He gave the law to Moses in Exodus, "¹⁸Now Mount Sinai was completely in smoke, because the Lord descended upon it in fire. Its smoke ascended like the smoke of a furnace, and the whole mountain quaked greatly."

Chapter 7 – The Seven Seals are Opened

(Exodus 19:18)

The Lord used an earthquake again in 1 Kings, *"¹¹Then He said, 'Go out, and stand on the mountain before the Lord.' And behold, the Lord passed by, and a great and strong wind tore into the mountains and broke the rocks in pieces before the Lord, but the Lord was not in the wind; and after the wind an earthquake, but the Lord was not in the earthquake; ¹²and after the earthquake a fire, but the Lord was not in the fire; and after the fire a still small voice."* (1 Kings 19:11-12)

God also used an earthquake to free Paul and Silas from prison, *"²⁶Suddenly there was a great earthquake, so that the foundations of the prison were shaken; and immediately all the doors were opened and everyone's chains were loosed."* (Acts 16:26)

Both Ezekiel and Isaiah prophesied about earthquakes as God's judgment. (Ezekiel 38:19 and Isaiah 29:6) This doesn't mean that every time the earth trembles, the Lord is giving judgment; it just means He can and does use earthquakes to impose judgment.

Most notably, God used an earthquake when Jesus died on the cross, *"⁵⁰And Jesus cried out again with a loud voice and yielded up His spirit. ⁵¹Then, behold, the veil of the temple was torn in two from top to bottom; and the earth quaked, and the rocks were split, ⁵²and the graves were opened; and many bodies of the saints who had fallen asleep were raised; ⁵³and coming out of the graves after His resurrection, they went into the holy city and appeared to many."* (Matthew 27:50-53)

But this earthquake will be like none before it. Even the heavens will shake, causing the stars to fall from the sky. The moon will turn blood red and the sky will roll back like a scroll.

*"¹⁶And said to the mountains and rocks, 'Fall on us and hide us from the face of Him who sits on the throne and from the **wrath of the Lamb!** ¹⁷For the great day of His wrath has come, and who is able to stand?' "*

Whose wrath? The Wrath of the Lamb. This confirms what we already know from chapter 4, when God the Father hands the document with the seals to the Lamb, Jesus Christ. The wrath that is poured out during the Tribulation; beginning with the first seal, is the wrath of God.

7. The Seventh Seal – Silence in Heaven

"¹When He opened the seventh seal, there was silence in heaven for about half an hour." (Revelation 8:1)

When I was a child, growing up in the Southern Baptist church, I pictured Heaven as this quiet, sedate place. Where the angels sat around on soft clouds, gently playing their harps, while we listened and smiled and gave gratitude that we were "here" and not "there."

But that's not the Heaven that John portrays in Revelation!

"⁵And from the throne proceeded lightnings, thunderings, and voices. Seven lamps of fire were burning before the throne, which are the seven Spirits of God. ⁶Before the throne there was a sea of glass, like crystal. And in the midst of the throne, and around the throne, were four living creatures full of eyes in front and in back. ⁷The first living creature was like a lion, the second living creature like a calf, the third living creature had a face like a man, and the fourth living creature was like a flying eagle. ⁸The four living creatures, each having six wings, were full of eyes around and within. And they do not rest day or night, saying:
'Holy, holy, holy,
Lord God Almighty,
Who was and is and is to come!'
⁹Whenever the living creatures give glory and honor and thanks to Him who sits on the throne, who lives forever and ever, ¹⁰the twenty-four elders fall down before Him who sits on the throne and worship Him who lives forever and ever, and cast their crowns before the throne, saying:
¹¹'You are worthy, O Lord,
To receive glory and honor and power;
For You created all things,

Chapter 7 – The Seven Seals are Opened

And by Your will they exist and were created.' " (Revelation 4:5-11)

John sees these four creatures giving praise unto He who sits on the throne, as well as the twenty-four elders giving praise. From the throne are flashes of lightning and the sound of thunder.

But it isn't just those four living creatures and the elders who are giving praise. In Revelation 5, after Jesus is found to be worthy of opening those scrolls, *"[11]Then I looked, and I heard the voice of many angels around the throne, the living creatures, and the elders; and the number of them was ten thousand times ten thousand, and thousands of thousands, [12]saying with a loud voice:*
'Worthy is the Lamb who was slain to receive power and riches and wisdom, And strength and honor and glory and blessing!"
[13]And every creature which is in heaven and on the earth and under the earth and such as are in the sea, and all that are in them, I heard saying:
"Blessing and honor and glory and power
Be to Him who sits on the throne,
And to the Lamb, forever and ever!' " (Revelation 5:11-13)

So much for my idea of a quiet and sedate Heaven!

Whatever your concept of Heaven is, there is only one time in all of scripture where there is quiet in Heaven and it happens at the seventh seal and it lasts for thirty minutes.

Theologians have debated about the purpose of this quiet for years, and there are many theories about why there is thirty minutes of silence around the Throne of God. I can only speculate, but I imagine something like the following.

Let's say you are in school and the final grades are about to be published. You've been waiting for this day, as those final grades may determine the course of your education, and perhaps, your life. The hallway where the grades will be published is noisy with students and teachers striding purposefully to their destination. The noise can reach deafening levels as some traveling down this hallway are playful, some are studious, and some are loudly complaining about this teacher or that class. But when those grades are published, there is silence as each student focuses on each sheet as it is placed to see their grades.

Or you're at a staff meeting at work where the much anticipated announcement for an upcoming promotion will be heard. You and the other staff members are sitting in the chairs, leaning over and whispering in each other's ears, or talking loudly about how your dog got out that morning and made you late, or how horrible the coffee in the break room has been. Until your boss enters the room and walks to his or her seat at the front of the room. Then, there is silence.

Neither of the two above scenarios come close to what is happening in Heaven, but you can get an idea of why the silence. The last of the seven seals is open and, for the first time, those around the throne see the full weight, majesty, and glory, of God's plan for this world revealed on that scroll.

Chapter 8 – God's Mercy Revealed

Chapter 8 – God's Mercy Revealed

The next set of seven of God's judgment poured out on the earth are announced with seven trumpets, but before the last seal is opened and the first trumpet is heard, there is a pause, an interlude, recorded in chapter 7.

Six of the seven seals are opened in Revelation chapter 6 and the final one is opened in chapter 8. So, what happens in chapter 7?

"¹After these things I saw four angels standing at the four corners of the earth, holding the four winds of the earth, that the wind should not blow on the earth, on the sea, or on any tree. ²Then I saw another angel ascending from the east, having the seal of the living God. And he cried with a loud voice to the four angels to whom it was granted to harm the earth and the sea, ³saying, 'Do not harm the earth, the sea, or the trees till we have sealed the servants of our God on their foreheads.' " (Revelation 7:1-4)

The "four winds" are often used in the Bible to symbolize 1) God's complete authority over the whole world and all four points of the compass – North, South, East, and West and 2) God's judgment upon the earth.

For example, in Jeremiah, God uses the four winds to bring judgment on the inhabitants of Hazor:

"³⁰'Flee, get far away! Dwell in the depths, O inhabitants of Hazor!' says the Lord. 'For Nebuchadnezzar king of Babylon has taken counsel against you, and has conceived a plan against you. ³¹'Arise, go up to the wealthy nation that dwells securely,' says the Lord, 'which has neither gates nor bars, dwelling alone. ³²Their camels shall be for booty, and the multitude of their cattle for plunder. **I will scatter to all winds** *those in the farthest corners, and I will bring their calamity from all its sides,' says the Lord. ³³'Hazor shall be a dwelling for jackals, a desolation forever; No one shall reside there, nor son of man dwell in it.' "* (Jeremiah 49:30-33) (emphasis added)

With this pause, God is telling these four angels to halt destruction upon the earth until He has sealed His servants. As we saw with the seven seals

So the Image Could Speak

on the scroll, this process of "sealing" makes the document authentic and proclaims ownership.

This is not the first time God has "sealed" his people. We read about the seal on the foreheads of those chosen in Ezekiel who have expressed their grief over the abominations within the city, *"[3]Now the glory of the God of Israel had gone up from the cherub, where it had been, to the threshold of the temple. And He called to the man clothed with linen, who had the writer's inkhorn at his side; [4]and the Lord said to him, 'Go through the midst of the city, through the midst of Jerusalem, and put a mark on the foreheads of the men who sigh and cry over all the abominations that are done within it.' "* (Ezekiel 9:3-4)

While our seals are not visible to the world, except through how we live our lives, those who have accepted Jesus Christ as their Savior are also sealed, *"[21]Now He who establishes us with you in Christ and has anointed us is God, [22]who also has sealed us and given us the Spirit in our hearts as a guarantee."* (2 Corinthians 1:21-22)

Our Savior, the Lord Jesus Christ, was also sealed by His Father, *"[27]'Do not labor for the food which perishes, but for the food which endures to everlasting life, which the Son of Man will give you, because God the Father has set His seal on Him.' "* (John 6:27)

So, who are these servants God is placing His seal upon?

"[4]And I heard the number of those who were sealed. One hundred and forty-four thousand of all the tribes of the children of Israel were sealed:
[5]of the tribe of Judah twelve thousand were sealed;
of the tribe of Reuben twelve thousand were sealed;
of the tribe of Gad twelve thousand were sealed;
[6]of the tribe of Asher twelve thousand were sealed;
of the tribe of Naphtali twelve thousand were sealed;
of the tribe of Manasseh twelve thousand were sealed;
[7]of the tribe of Simeon twelve thousand were sealed;
of the tribe of Levi twelve thousand were sealed;
of the tribe of Issachar twelve thousand were sealed;
[8]of the tribe of Zebulun twelve thousand were sealed;
of the tribe of Joseph twelve thousand were sealed;

Chapter 8 – God's Mercy Revealed

of the tribe of Benjamin twelve thousand were sealed." (Revelation 7:5-8)

First, these are not Jehovah Witnesses. Jehovah Witnesses have built a whole cult around being "the chosen" 144K who are going to Heaven. Of course, they have a bit of a problem in that on their own website, they claim there are more than 8 million Jehovah Witnesses worldwide. According to their own doctrine, most of those are going to be very disappointed.

We know these 144,000 are from *"all the tribes of the children of Israel"*, so they are Jews and we know from chapter 14, *"⁴These are the ones who were not defiled with women, for they are virgins. These are the ones who follow the Lamb wherever He goes. These were redeemed from among men, being firstfruits to God and to the Lamb. ⁵And in their mouth was found no deceit, for they are without fault before the throne of God."* (Revelation 14:4-5)

So they 1) are Jews, 2) are virgins, 3) are sinless, or without fault (through the blood of Jesus, not through any effort or perfection of their own), and 4) have accepted Christ as the Messiah, for they "follow the Lamb wherever He goes." We also know they are "firstfruits" – but what does that mean?

The term firstfruits is used throughout the Old Testament referring to what our gift to God should be – the firstfruits, or the first and the best, not the leftovers. In the New Testament, all believers are the firstfruits of God, as we see in James 1:18, *"¹⁸Of His own will He brought us forth by the word of truth, that we might be a kind of firstfruits of His creatures."* In Romans 16:5, Paul refers to a recent convert as a firstfruit, *"⁵Likewise greet the church that is in their house. Greet my beloved Epaenetus, who is the firstfruits of Achaia to Christ."* Apparently, Epaenetus was the first to accept Jesus, after hearing the testimony of the new apostle, Achaia.

In Jeremiah, the prophet describes those who will accept Jesus Christ as their Messiah as God's firstfruits, *"³Israel was holiness to the Lord, The firstfruits of His increase. All that devour him will offend; Disaster will come upon them," says the Lord.' "* (Jeremiah 2:3)

These 144,000 are the first, of Jewish heritage, who accept Jesus Christ

So the Image Could Speak

as the Messiah during this period known as the 70th Week of Daniel, or the Tribulation, and they are given a mission – but more on that further down.

One of the recurring questions about this passage is concerning the "Lost Tribes of Israel", or that migration of the people of northern Israel after they were chased out by the Assyrians. I won't delve into that history here, but it is worth studying. Although history may have failed to record the details of that migration, God did not fail to record it. While many of the Jewish people worldwide may have forgotten who their original tribe is, God has not forgotten. Rest assured, the Lord God will be able to, accurately and efficiently, select His chosen servants when the time for this sealing has come.

What is the purpose of this 144,000? This is where the glory and mercy of God shines in all its brilliance.

Think about the time of this event; six of the seven seals have been opened and devastation has already been poured out upon the land. One-fourth of the global population have died after just one of those seals; the totality of the deaths worldwide from all of the seals is incalculable, but know it is a staggering number. All over the world, people are scared and wondering where to go for peace and safety.

There are no churches; or at least, none that preach a true Gospel, for whoever does preach a true Gospel risks their lives during this time of extreme persecution. The Church, the Bride of Christ, is already gone – raptured - and most of the buildings with a steeple have either been destroyed, recommissioned for a new purpose, or stand empty.

But even during this time of righteous judgment upon an earthly people that have turned their backs on their own Creator, God does not wish for any to perish. *"⁹The Lord is not slack concerning His promise, as some count slackness, but is longsuffering toward us, not willing that any should perish but that all should come to repentance."* (2 Peter 3:9)

So He halts everything to send these 144,000 out into the world with a mission and they are hugely successful!

Chapter 8 – God's Mercy Revealed

"*⁹After these things I looked, and behold, a **great multitude which no one could number**, of all nations, tribes, peoples, and tongues, standing before the throne and before the Lamb, clothed with white robes, with palm branches in their hands, ¹⁰and crying out with a loud voice, saying, 'Salvation belongs to our God who sits on the throne, and to the Lamb!' "* (Revelation 7:9-10) (emphasis added)

The results of the ministry of these 144,000 cannot be numbered and those who turn to Christ during this period come from all walks of life, all over the globe. A great awakening, indeed!

Remember that silence in Heaven? Well, Heaven is not silent now.
"*¹¹All the angels stood around the throne and the elders and the four living creatures, and fell on their faces before the throne and worshiped God, ¹²saying: 'Amen! Blessing and glory and wisdom, Thanksgiving and honor and power and might, Be to our God forever and ever. Amen.' "* (Revelation 7:11-12)

So there is no misunderstanding about who this great multitude of people are, one of the elders asks John, " *'Who are these arrayed in white robes, and where did they come from?'* " (Revelation 7:13b)

John wisely responds, "*¹⁴And I said to him, 'Sir, you know.'* " (Revelation 7:14a)

The elder tells John, and us, who these people are: "*So he said to me, 'These are the ones who come out of the great tribulation, and washed their robes and made them white in the blood of the Lamb. ¹⁵Therefore they are before the throne of God, and serve Him day and night in His temple. And He who sits on the throne will dwell among them. ¹⁶They shall neither hunger anymore nor thirst anymore; the sun shall not strike them, nor any heat; ¹⁷for the Lamb who is in the midst of the throne will shepherd them and lead them to living fountains of waters. And God will wipe away every tear from their eyes.'* " (Revelation 7:14b - 17)

That final verse in chapter seven grabs me every time I read it, "*And God will wipe away every tear from their eyes.*"

So the Image Could Speak

If you're old enough to read this text, you've cried. But these people – those who trusted in Him during the most difficult period in all of earth's history, will have their tears wiped away by God the Father Himself.

Chapter 9 – The Trumpets Sound

Chapter 9 – The Trumpets Sound

There are three sets of seven judgments in Revelation, with each set more devastating than the one before. The first set – the seven seals – looses the Four Horsemen, a devastating earthquake, and showed us the Tribulation Saints under the altar in Heaven. This second set, the set of Trumpets, are what is often called the "Judgment of Thirds" and we'll see why as we go through them.

Jesus Christ opened the seven seals on that scroll He received from His Father, but who is announcing these seven judgments? The seven angels who stand before God. There is much discussion about who those seven angels are, with some believing they are the same as the seven angels of the churches we read about in chapters two and three. Others go outside the canonical Bible and reference some of the ancient Jewish writings, such as those found about the Second Temple, which reference seven angels. "I am Raphael, one of the seven holy angels who present the prayers of the saints and enter into the presence of the glory of the Holy One" (Tobit 12:15) Seven angels are specifically named in the apocryphal work of I Enoch, "Uriel, Raphael, Raguel, Michael, Sariel, Gabriel, and Remeiel (missing in the Ethiopic text, see OTP 1:23–24)" (1 Enoch 20)

As interesting as it is to explore who those seven angels might be, they are not named in the reference in Revelation, so it is speculation at this point.

For those not familiar with the book of Tobit, also called the book of Tobias, it is one of the books of the Apocrypha and was written either late third century or early second century BC. While it is included in the Roman Catholic Bible, it is not a part of the accepted canon of Scripture by either the Jewish or the Protestant faiths. It is, however, interesting reading and, like the books of Enoch, can give a better understanding of the history of the Jewish people.

Before the first of the seven trumpets are announced, something else is happening in Heaven:

"³Then another angel, having a golden censer, came and stood at the altar. He was given much incense, that he should offer it with the prayers of all the saints upon the golden altar which was before the throne. ⁴And

So the Image Could Speak

the smoke of the incense, with the prayers of the saints, ascended before God from the angel's hand. ⁵Then the angel took the censer, filled it with fire from the altar, and threw it to the earth. And there were noises, thunderings, lightnings, and an earthquake." (Revelation 8:3-5)

There is an interesting corollary to this passage in the Gospel of Luke: *"⁸One day while Zechariah's division was on duty and he was serving as priest before God, ⁹he was chosen by lot, according to the custom of the priesthood, to enter the temple of the Lord and burn incense. ¹⁰And at the hour of the incense offering, the whole congregation was praying outside. ¹¹Just then an angel of the Lord appeared to Zechariah, standing at the right side of the altar of incense. ¹²When Zechariah saw him, he was startled and gripped with fear. ¹³But the angel said to him, 'Do not be afraid, Zechariah, because your prayer has been heard. Your wife Elizabeth will bear you a son, and you are to give him the name John.' "* (Luke 1:8-13)

Zechariah and his wife, Elizabeth, had been praying for a child. When Zechariah entered the temple and burned the incense, those outside the temple – the entire congregation, we are told - were praying. An angel, who we learn later is the angel Gabriel, tells Zechariah his prayers have been heard and will be answered and they will have a son. Who is this son of Zechariah and Elizabeth? John the Baptist – the voice in the wilderness.

So, our prayers – the prayers of the saints – are mingled with incense in heaven to make them pleasing to God and God hears our prayers.

There are a lot of commentaries written about these verses, with a lot of various ideas on how our prayers are made pleasing to God. Whatever happens to our prayers after they leave our lips, we know we have an intercessor – Jesus Christ. *"³³Who shall bring a charge against God's elect? It is God who justifies. ³⁴Who is he who condemns? It is Christ who died, and furthermore is also risen, who is even at the right hand of God, who also makes intercession for us."* (Romans 8:33-34)

What happens after our prayers are heard by God? *"⁵Then the angel took the censer, filled it with fire from the altar, and threw it to the earth. And there were noises, thunderings, lightnings, and an earthquake."* The answers to our prayers, of course.

Chapter 9 – The Trumpets Sound

As mentioned above, this group of the seven trumpets is often called the "judgment of thirds". In the first four and the sixth trumpets, there is a common denominator for, or limitation on, what areas can be impacted. That common denominator or limitation is one third, 1/3.

Just like the seven seals, the first four of the seven trumpets call upon specific judgments with specific targets:

1. The first trumpet brings devastation to the earth.
2. The second trumpet is targeted towards the seas.
3. The third trumpet affects the water supply.
4. The fourth trumpet attacks the sky affecting the sun, moon, and stars.

Land, sea, water, and sky – all the natural elements of the world around us are affected, but the damage is restricted to only one third of that element.

1. The first trumpet – the vegetation. *"⁷The first angel sounded: And hail and fire followed, mingled with blood, and they were thrown to the earth. And a third of the trees were burned up, and all green grass was burned up."* (Revelation 8:7)

    Remember the plagues God brought upon Egypt because the pharaoh wouldn't let His people go? The seventh plague resembles this first trumpet judgment, *"¹⁸Behold, tomorrow about this time I will cause very heavy hail to rain down, such as has not been in Egypt since its founding until now. ¹⁹Therefore send now and gather your livestock and all that you have in the field, for the hail shall come down on every man and every animal which is found in the field and is not brought home; and they shall die.' "* (Exodus 9:18-19)

    Just as in Egypt, the devastation of this judgment will be terrible. But there is one major difference. In Exodus, the damage was localized to only Egypt. While that was devastating to those who lived in Egypt at that time, it did not impact other countries. This time, however, the entire world is affected. It is difficult to understand the severity of such a judgment and nothing like it has ever happened on earth before, so we have to go to the news reports of other, more localized, wildfires to understand the impact.

From a Harvard Gazette report in 2020:
"The recent massive wildfires in Australia have killed more than 30 people and an estimated 1 billion animals and burned 2,500 homes and millions of acres. And the human toll is expected to rise even after the blazes wind down. According to Harvard scientist Loretta Mickley, senior research fellow in atmospheric chemistry at the Harvard John A. Paulson School of Engineering (SEAS), long-term exposure to the smoke-filled air hanging over much of the country could lead to many premature deaths in Australia."[21]

In an article published in the Journalists Resources in 2023, journalist Naseem S. Miller quotes the CDC, "Exposure to wildfire smoke can irritate the lungs, cause inflammation, alter immune function, and increase susceptibility to respiratory infections, including COVID-19, according to the CDC. In June (2023), the agency issued an advisory to health professionals about the acute signs and symptoms of smoke exposure, as smoke from wildfires in Canada affected air quality in parts of the U.S."[22]

He also states, "A 2022 study, published in Science of the Total Environment, finds the Australian bushfires in 2019 and 2020 were associated with a 6% increase in emergency department visits for respiratory diseases and 10% increase for cardiovascular diseases."[23]

While the events listed above are not caused by the first trumpet of Revelation, they do paint a clear picture of the destruction this trumpet will bring upon the earth and its

---

[21] Australian wildfires will claim victims even after they're out, Colleen Walsh, January 27, 2020, https://news.harvard.edu/gazette/story/2020/01/the-long-term-effects-of-wildfires/
[22] Wildfires have long-term health effects, both direct and indirect, several studies show, Naseem S. Miller, July 26, 2023, https://journalistsresource.org/health/wildfires-longterm-impact-on-health/
[23] Ibid

Chapter 9 – The Trumpets Sound

inhabitants. Crops will be destroyed, the livestock industry will be crippled, the medical field will be overwhelmed, and this is just the first trumpet.

2. The second trumpet – the seas. *"⁸Then the second angel sounded: and something like a great mountain burning with fire was thrown into the sea, and a third of the sea became blood. ⁹And a third of the living creatures in the sea died, and a third of the ships were destroyed."* (Revelation 8:8-9)

As much as I take the Bible literally, we have to be careful and pay attention to the words that are used. In this verse, we see "something like a great mountain burning with fire". John is writing what he sees and compares it to a great mountain. That doesn't mean, necessarily, that it is a great mountain; John is just comparing it to what is familiar to him. The Greek word used here is oros[24], which means, simply, a mountain. It is used in Matthew when Satan tempts Jesus (Matthew 4:8-9) and in several other verses throughout the Four Gospels and also in Paul's letter to the Galatians.

Some scholars today say this is actually a giant meteor and they could be right. We don't know and won't know until it happens. But whatever it is, the impact of this judgment is immediate and significant.

The Smithsonian reports "The ocean, which we often break into five large ocean basins, covers 71 percent of the Earth's surface and holds over 1.3 billion cubic km of water."[25] National Geographic states that our earth is 70% ocean, and that 70% ocean is what we depend on for life, 'The sun's heat causes water to evaporate, adding moisture to the air. The oceans provide most of this evaporated water. The water vapor condenses to form clouds, which release their moisture as rain or other kinds of precipitation. All life on

---

[24] Strong's Greek.3735.oros, noun neuter, "a mountain"
[25] Just How Big is the Ocean?, Scott Grass, date unknown, https://ocean.si.edu/planet-ocean/seafloor/just-how-big-ocean

Earth depends on this process, called the water cycle.' " [26]

This mountain, or meteor or whatever it is, kills off one third of the sea creatures and turns one third of the seawater to blood. It is interesting to note that scientists have been seeing a trend of rising deaths of sea life over the past several years. A writer for the Washington Post reported in an article in 2023, "Dead fish in Florida. Beached whales in New Jersey. Sea urchins, starfish and crayfish washing ashore in New Zealand. Millions of rotting fish clogging up a river in the Australian outback. A mass fish die-off in Poland. Around the world, freshwater and marine creatures are dying in large numbers, leaving experts to puzzle over the cause."[27]

This doesn't mean the second trumpet has already sounded and we are already in the Tribulation, as I write this. It does, however, give us a hint of the devastation that will occur during the Tribulation.

One third of the ships will also be destroyed. If there is any food (particularly crops like wheat, barley, rye) to be transported after the first trumpet, the shipping of that food will be severely restricted, assuming the remaining ships can even maneuver through the water.

3. The Third Trumpet – the waters. *"10Then the third angel sounded: and a great star fell from heaven, burning like a torch, and it fell on a third of the rivers and on the springs of water. 11The name of the star is Wormwood. A third of the waters became wormwood, and many men died from the water, because it was made bitter."* (Revelation 8:10-11)

    Wormwood...many have heard this name and wondered "what is it?" Well, before we delve into this, just a side note – did you know the Great Lakes contain 1/5 of all the world's

---

[26] All About the Ocean, National Geographic, March 5, 2024, https://education.nationalgeographic.org/resource/all-about-the-ocean/
[27] Why sea creatures are washing up dead around the world, Rachel Pannett, March 29, 2023, https://www.washingtonpost.com/climate-environment/2023/03/29/dead-sea-creatures-washing-up-climate-change/

Chapter 9 – The Trumpets Sound

fresh water?

What is Wormwood? Wormwood as we know it, or Artemisia absinthium, is a plant that is grown naturally in north Africa and the more temperate areas of Eurasia. It is used in the making of the alcoholic drinks, absinthe and vermouth. It is also used medicinally for pain and as a digestive aid. But I don't think God is throwing plants down.

Many scholars believe this also is a meteorite and, in fact, there is a meteor nicknamed "Wormwood" that concerned scientists in 2004. It is officially called Apophis, or meteor 99942, and was originally thought to be a great threat to earth when it was first discovered. They have since revised their original tracking and now believe it will pass close to earth on Friday, April 13, 2029.[28]

Whatever this is, the devastation, again, will be earth-shattering.

This judgment resembles the first of the plagues on Egypt when the Lord instructs Moses to tell Aaron to stretch his rod out over the river and turn the water into blood. *"²⁰And Moses and Aaron did so, just as the Lord commanded. So, he lifted up the rod and struck the waters that were in the river, in the sight of Pharaoh and in the sight of his servants. And all the waters that were in the river were turned to blood. ²¹The fish that were in the river died, the river stank, and the Egyptians could not drink the water of the river. So, there was blood throughout all the land of Egypt."* (Exodus 7:20-21)

The waters are not turned to blood, as in the plague of Egypt, but they are turned bitter – either way, we can't drink the water. Our bodies are made up of about 60% water and without water, our bodies begin to break down and will die.

---

[28] Exactly 7 Years From Today A Massive Asteroid Will Get Closer To Earth Than Some Of Our Satellites. Should NASA Visit It?, Jamie Carter, April 12, 2022, https://www.forbes.com/sites/jamiecartereurope/2022/04/12/exactly-7-years-from-today-a-massive-asteroid-will-get-closer-to-earth-than-some-of-our-satellites-should-nasa-visit-it/?sh=1694753c40f6

So will our livestock, our plants and crops...

In fact, every living creature on earth requires water to live. The human body can live an estimated three days without water, though there are some reports of humans living longer. Some creatures can go much longer without water, such as the Desert Tortoise which can go a year without a sip of water.[29] But the tortoise is not the winner of the "who can go the longest without water" contest. That prize goes to the thorny devil of Australia which has been reported to go twenty years![30]

So, while the thorny devil of Australia is partying, the rest of us are dying from lack of water.

4. The fourth trumpet – the heavens. *"[12]Then the fourth angel sounded: and a third of the sun was struck, a third of the moon, and a third of the stars, so that a third of them were darkened. A third of the day did not shine, and likewise the night."* (Revelation 8:12)

One-third of the sun, the moon, and the stars are darkened. All those who bought solar-powered roof panels and generators will not be happy.

Jesus warned about this in Luke 21, *"[25]'And there will be signs in the sun, in the moon, and in the stars; and on the earth distress of nations, with perplexity, the sea and the waves roaring; [26]men's hearts failing them from fear and the expectation of those things which are coming on the earth, for the powers of the heavens will be shaken.' "* (Luke 21:25-26)

This could be the aftereffects of a nuclear blast, when the smoke from the nuclear blast blocks the sun, moon, and stars. I wrote about this in my book, Convergence, "In 2022,

---

[29] What Animals Can Go the Longest Without Drinking Water?, Drew Wood, January 1, 2024, https://a-z-animals.com/blog/what-animals-can-go-the-longest-without-drinking-water-up-to-20-years/
[30] Ibid

Chapter 9 – The Trumpets Sound

a group of scientists at Louisiana State University released a report on the global impact of just one nuclear bomb. As one of the listed after-effects, the report shows: "In all of the researchers' simulated scenarios, nuclear firestorms would release soot and smoke into the upper atmosphere that would block out the Sun resulting in crop failure around the world. In the first month following nuclear detonation, average global temperatures would plunge by about 13 degrees Fahrenheit, a larger temperature change than in the last Ice Age." [31]

Crop failure? Assuming there are any crops left after the first three trumpets.

Something remarkably interesting is that this has already happened, or very nearly. In April 1815, the ash cloud from a volcanic eruption in Indonesia blocked the sun over much of the Northern Hemisphere. In an article published by CBS News, journalist Michael Casey writes, "The Tambora volcano in what is now Indonesia blew its top in April 1815, killing more than 60,000 people and turning the summer into winter across much of the Northern Hemisphere. It is considered the largest eruption to have occurred in 750 years. 'Because Tambora ejected sulphurous gas that generated sulphate aerosols in the atmosphere, which block sunlight, the eruption created a year without a summer, leading to food shortages -- people were eating cats and rats -- and very general hardship throughout Europe and eastern North America,' said Stephen Self, an adjunct professor of earth and planetary science at the University of California, Berkeley and an expert on volcanoes."[32]

Whether from a nuclear explosion or volcanic eruption or any other climactic event, the devastation from this and the other three trumpet judgments to this point cannot be overstated, and they're not over yet!

---

[31] Convergence, Susan Mouw, https://www.amazon.com/dp/B0C6W6XM34

[32] 200 years ago: A volcano that blocked out the sun, Michael Casey, March 31, 2015, https://www.cbsnews.com/news/tambora-1815-volcanic-eruption/

Before the last three trumpet judgments are brought forward, there is a pause in Heaven, *"13And I looked, and I heard an angel flying through the midst of heaven, saying with a loud voice, "Woe, woe, woe to the inhabitants of the earth, because of the remaining blasts of the trumpet of the three angels who are about to sound!"* (Revelation 8:13)

The next three trumpets bring even more devastation upon the earth and God is warning everyone to repent now.

God, who is a Just and Righteous God, gives us opportunities, over and over again, to turn to Him and receive the gift of everlasting life. This verse is another example of that patience – it is a warning to those who have yet to repent that things are about to get worse, but there is an answer, and that answer will be found only in God the Father, through the sacrifice of His Son, Jesus Christ. But many will not heed the warning.

5. The fifth trumpet and the first woe – the locusts. *"1Then the fifth angel sounded: And I saw a star fallen from heaven to the earth. To him was given the key to the bottomless pit. 2And he opened the bottomless pit, and smoke arose out of the pit like the smoke of a great furnace. So, the sun and the air were darkened because of the smoke of the pit. 3Then out of the smoke locusts came upon the earth. And to them was given power, as the scorpions of the earth have power. 4They were commanded not to harm the grass of the earth, or any green thing, or any tree, but only those men who do not have the seal of God on their foreheads. 5And they were not given authority to kill them, but to torment them for five months. Their torment was like the torment of a scorpion when it strikes a man. 6In those days men will seek death and will not find it; they will desire to die, and death will flee from them. 7The shape of the locusts was like horses prepared for battle. On their heads were crowns of something like gold, and their faces were like the faces of men. 8They had hair like women's hair, and their teeth were like lions' teeth. 9And they had breastplates like breastplates of iron, and the sound of their*

Chapter 9 – The Trumpets Sound

wings was like the sound of chariots with many horses running into battle. ¹⁰They had tails like scorpions, and there were stings in their tails. Their power was to hurt men five months. ¹¹And they had as king over them the angel of the bottomless pit, whose name in Hebrew is Abaddon, but in Greek he has the name Apollyon." (Revelation 9:1-11)

This is a being, not just an inactive element. This would seem to indicate this is not another meteor, or a star, but a fallen angel, or demon.

In fact, there are many who say this is Satan, from the reference in Isaiah, *"¹²How you are fallen from heaven, O Lucifer, son of the morning! How you are cut down to the ground, You who weakened the nations! ¹³For you have said in your heart: 'I will ascend into heaven, I will exalt my throne above the stars of God; I will also sit on the mount of the congregation on the farthest sides of the north; ¹⁴I will ascend above the heights of the clouds, I will be like the Most High.' ¹⁵Yet you shall be brought down to Sheol, to the lowest depths of the Pit."* (Isaiah 14:12-15)

He is given the key to the bottomless pit – access he did not previously have. What he releases from that bottomless pit aren't just locusts.

Locusts are devastating. Agrilife Today reports, "The most recent locust outbreak occurred from 2019-2022 and caused more than $1.3 billion in crop damage in 23 countries across eastern Africa, the Middle East and Asia, from Ethiopia to Nepal."[33]

But these aren't your everyday locusts. These are, in fact, demonic. They are not given the authority to kill, but only to cause extreme pain and suffering for five months – to the point where those stung will want to die. And they have a king – Apollyon. I haven't given a lot of study to locusts of the

---

[33] Searching for a global solution to locust outbreaks, Adam Russell, April 27, 2023, https://agrilifetoday.tamu.edu/2023/04/27/locust-research/

earth, but I'm pretty sure they don't have a king and, even if they do, they don't call him by name.

That name – Apollyon or Abaddon in the Hebrew, means "the Destroyer." And who comes to destroy? Jesus, referring to Satan, tells us in John 10:10, *"¹⁰'The thief does not come except to steal, and to kill, and to destroy. I have come that they may have life, and that they may have it more abundantly.'"*

So, Satan and these hordes of demonic creatures are let loose upon the earth – but not to kill and they cannot sting those who have the seal of God.

There are many who have attempted to allegorize this trumpet judgment, and the one that follows, but I don't think we can allegorize it. I think it is literal. And it will be horrible for those who have not yet accepted Jesus Christ.

"¹²One woe is past. Behold, still two more woes are coming after these things." (Revelation 9:12) Remember those three "woes" the angel cried out? Well, the first is over and there are two remaining.

6. The sixth trumpet and the second woe – the army of 200,000,000. *"¹³Then the sixth angel sounded: And I heard a voice from the four horns of the golden altar which is before God, ¹⁴saying to the sixth angel who had the trumpet, 'Release the four angels who are bound at the great river Euphrates.' ¹⁵So the four angels, who had been prepared for the hour and day and month and year, were released to kill a third of mankind. ¹⁶Now the number of the army of the horsemen was two hundred million; I heard the number of them. ¹⁷And thus I saw the horses in the vision: those who sat on them had breastplates of fiery red, hyacinth blue, and sulfur yellow; and the heads of the horses were like the heads of lions; and out of their mouths came fire, smoke, and brimstone. ¹⁸By these three plagues a third of mankind was killed—by the fire and the smoke and the brimstone which came out of their mouths. ¹⁹For their power is in their mouth and in their tails; for their tails are like serpents, having*

Chapter 9 – The Trumpets Sound

heads; and with them they do harm." (Revelation 9:13-19)

These four angels, who have been bound by the Euphrates River, are fallen angels, or demons. And the horsemen they release are also demonic. I have spent much of my life around horses and, while I have handled a few that snorted and pawed the ground during training sessions, I've never had one with the head of a lion and breathing "fire, smoke, and brimstone." This army, and the horses they ride in on, are demonic. This is another judgment limited to a third as they can only kill a third of mankind. I can't imagine this is a pleasant death, either.

The Euphrates River was the ancient border between Assyria and Israel and is often used to represent the division between civil discourse and civil chaos. It was in this region where the first murder took place (Genesis 4:8) and near where Nimrod, the first prototype of the AntiChrist, built his tower of Babel (Genesis 10:8-12). It is also near where it is believed the Garden of Eden was.

Are these actual creatures or is this another example of the spiritual war we wage, as stated in Ephesians? *"[12]For we do not wrestle against flesh and blood, but against principalities, against powers, against the rulers of the darkness of this age, against spiritual hosts of wickedness in the heavenly places. [13]Therefore take up the whole armor of God, that you may be able to withstand in the evil day, and having done all, to stand."* (Ephesians 6:12-13)

As horrible as these six trumpets are, many still do not repent, *"[20]But the rest of mankind, who were not killed by these plagues, did not repent of the works of their hands, that they should not worship demons, and idols of gold, silver, brass, stone, and wood, which can neither see nor hear nor walk. [21]And they did not repent of their murders or their sorceries or their sexual immorality or their thefts."* (Revelation 9:20-21)

It is interesting to see the difference between this verse, at this point in the Tribulation, and the verses in chapter 7 that describe the masses that come to repentance through the testimony of the 144,000. *"[9]After these* *things I looked, and behold, a great multitude which no one could number, of all nations, tribes, peoples, and tongues, standing before the throne and before the Lamb, clothed with white robes, with palm branches in their hands, ¹⁰and crying out with a loud voice, saying, 'Salvation belongs to our God who sits on the throne, and to the Lamb!' "* (Revelation 7:9-10)

This isn't the last time we'll see mankind unrepentant – we'll see it again in Revelation chapter 16. Instead of turning to God during these judgments, many have their hearts hardened against Him, even blaspheming God. But, as we've seen in chapter 7 and will again further on, there are also those who do turn to God and accept the greatest gift – that of salvation, offered to us by the sacrifice of our Risen Lord.

7. The seventh trumpet and the third woe – the Kingdom proclaimed.

> *"¹⁵Then the seventh angel sounded: And there were loud voices in heaven, saying, 'The kingdoms of this world have become the kingdoms of our Lord and of His Christ, and He shall reign forever and ever!' ¹⁶And the twenty-four elders who sat before God on their thrones fell on their faces and worshiped God, ¹⁷saying:*
> *'We give You thanks, O Lord God Almighty, The One who is and who was and who is to come, because You have taken Your great power and reigned. ¹⁸The nations were angry, and Your wrath has come, and the time of the dead, that they should be judged, and that You should reward Your servants the prophets and the saints,*
> *and those who fear Your name, small and great, and should destroy those who destroy the earth.' ¹⁹Then the temple of God was opened in heaven, and the ark of His covenant was seen in His temple. And there were lightnings, noises, thunderings, an earthquake, and great hail.* (Revelation 11:15-19)

This passage is a clear reference to the book in chapter 10 that John is told to eat, which we'll see further on.

"The kingdoms of this world have become the kingdoms of

Chapter 9 – The Trumpets Sound

our Lord and of His Christ, and He shall reign forever and ever!" This verse is where many get the concept that God's wrath starts at the midpoint of the 70th week of Daniel, but when you look at the original Greek, it tells you something different. In the original Greek, the phrasing is, "and came the wrath of You" and the verb used is ēlthen (Strong's. 2064.erchomai, verb, to come or to go), the past tense of the verb erchomai. At this point in the Tribulation, God's wrath is already present.

The title-deed to earth has been reclaimed and will never again be given to another. This is the seventh trumpet, and things are about to get serious.

Remember after the sixth seal, we had a pause and had to skip ahead by one chapter to finish out the seals? This is similar with an interlude in Revelation chapter 10 and most of Revelation chapter 11 before we hear the seventh trumpet. We'll cover that interlude in the following chapters in this book.

But we need to step back for just a second and look at where we are in these events. We know the first seal, the white horseman, represents the AntiChrist and we know, from Daniel 9, that the covenant he confirms with Israel is the opening scene of the 70th week of Daniel.

From that first seal in Chapter 6, we've gone through all seven seals – with the last one revealing the seven angels with the seven trumpets. We had a pause, as stated in Chapter 7, where the 144,000 are sealed and given protection from the events in the 70th week of Daniel.

We have completed the seven trumpets – the second of three sets of judgment upon the earth. The devastation upon the earth cannot be overstated and, except for the restriction to one third of mankind killed with the sixth trumpet, the loss of life is incalculable. Will there be any remaining for the next set of judgments?

One quick note before we close out this section on the seven trumpets about the word "sorceries" in Revelation 9:21. *"21And they did not repent of their murders or their sorceries or their sexual immorality or their*

So the Image Could Speak

thefts." (Revelation 9:21) The Greek word is phármakos[34], or pharmakeus and it is defined as "a drug, i.e. Spell-giving potion); a druggist ("pharmacist") or poisoner, i.e. (by extension) a magician -- sorcerer." It is the word from which we get pharmacy.

I have to wonder what this means and what "sorcery", or drugs, the people do not give up. Is it the rising trend of illegal drug use? The National Center for Drug Abuse Statistics reports that drug abuse among 8th graders rose 61% between 2016 and 2020.[35] An alarming graph of drug overdose deaths for those between 15 and 24 years old is shown on the site and will give you pause.

But is that to what this verse is referring? Or is it something even more prevalent...perhaps even government sanctioned? We've seen how the COVID-19 vaccines have changed lives and not always in a good way. Many lost their jobs because they refused to take the vaccine. After President Biden's vaccine mandate was announced for health care facilities and government employees in 2021, a journalist for the ABC News reports, "Hundreds of health care workers across the country are being fired or suspended in droves for not complying with COVID-19 vaccine mandates."[36] This is just one report among many listed on the internet. But this isn't about that mandate, or the pros and cons of the vaccine, but about setting a pattern.

Many of us in the West believe in a prophecy model of prediction and fulfillment, but the Hebrews believe it is in repeating patterns that prophecy is revealed.

Is this vaccine mandate a pattern that will be repeated during the Tribulation?

---

[34] Strong's Greek.5333.pharmakos, noun masculine, "a poisoner, sorcerer, magician
[35] Drug Use Among Youth: Facts & Statistics, https://drugabusestatistics.org/teen-drug-use/
[36] Hundreds of hospital staffers fired or suspended for refusing COVID-19 vaccine mandate, Marlene Lenthang, September 30, 2021, https://abcnews.go.com/US/hundreds-hospital-staffers-fired-suspended-refusing-covid-19/story?id=80303408

Chapter 10 – The Angel and the Scroll

Chapter 10 – The Angel and the Scroll

Remember that interlude between the sixth and seventh trumpets? This is similar with chapter 10 and most of chapter 11 in the Book of Revelation, an interlude between the sixth trumpet and seventh trumpet.

"¹I saw still another mighty angel coming down from heaven, clothed with a cloud. And a rainbow was on his head, his face was like the sun, and his feet like pillars of fire. ²He had a little book open in his hand. And he set his right foot on the sea and his left foot on the land, ³and cried with a loud voice, as when a lion roars. When he cried out, seven thunders uttered their voices. ⁴Now when the seven thunders uttered their voices, I was about to write; but I heard a voice from heaven saying to me, 'Seal up the things which the seven thunders uttered, and do not write them.'" (Revelation 10:1-4)

Who is this mighty angel? He is clothed with a cloud and a rainbow, or aura or halo, was on his head. This is not Jesus Christ. For one thing, while Jesus Christ is referred to many times in the Old Testament as "The Angel of the Lord", He is never referred to that way in the New Testament. Many believe this is Gabriel, whose name means "Mighty", and that could be. We really don't know who this angel is and I'm not sure it is significant. What is significant is how he is standing. In verse 2, we read *"And he set his right foot on the sea and his left foot on the land"*. We'll see the significance of that in chapter 13, when the two beasts appear – one from the sea and the second one from the earth. God is demonstrating His sovereignty over both.

We're going to come back to the little book he is holding in his right hand, but let's look at those seven thunders. This sounds a bit like the "the voice of the Lord" in Psalms 29; *"³The voice of the Lord is over the waters; The God of glory thunders; The Lord is over many waters. ⁴The voice of the Lord is powerful; The voice of the Lord is full of majesty. ⁵The voice of the Lord breaks the cedars, Yes, the Lord splinters the cedars of Lebanon. ⁶He makes them also skip like a calf, Lebanon and Sirion like a young wild ox. ⁷The voice of the Lord divides the flames of fire. ⁸The voice of the Lord shakes the wilderness; The Lord shakes the Wilderness of Kadesh. ⁹The voice of the Lord makes the deer give birth, and strips the forests bare; and in His temple everyone says, 'Glory!'"* (Psalms 29:3-9)

So the Image Could Speak

When those seven thunders speak, John gets ready to write down what they say, but is told *"Seal up the things which the seven thunders uttered, and do not write them."* This verse has frustrated theologians and scholars for nearly two millennium! If John can't write what they say, why even include this in the book? Why make us wonder about what was said for nearly 2000 years? Why not just leave it out all together, so we aren't left to wonder? After all, we are told in Amos, *"⁷Surely the Lord God does nothing, unless He reveals His secret to His servants the prophets."* (Amos 3:7)

Well, perhaps God determined that man is not yet ready to hear the words spoken by those seven thunders. Many generations prior to John writing this, Daniel was told to shut up the words of his book, *"⁴'But you, Daniel, shut up the words, and seal the book until the time of the end; many shall run to and fro, and knowledge shall increase.' "* (Daniel 12:4). Presumably because Israel wasn't ready to hear or understand the words written yet. This could be similar – we're just not ready – or weren't at the time of John's writing to hear what the angel says. But remember that verse in Daniel – *"many shall run to and fro, and knowledge shall increase."* We may now be in the times when that knowledge, and understanding of God's Word, is increasing.

"⁵The angel whom I saw standing on the sea and on the land raised up his hand to heaven ⁶and swore by Him who lives forever and ever, who created heaven and the things that are in it, the earth and the things that are in it, and the sea and the things that are in it, that there should be delay no longer, ⁷but in the days of the sounding of the seventh angel, when he is about to sound, the mystery of God would be finished, as He declared to His servants the prophets." (Revelation 10:5-7)

This is a serious oath – this angel is swearing by *"Him who lives forever and ever, who created heaven and the things that are in it, the earth and the things that are in it, and the sea and the things that are in it."* He is swearing that there *"should be delay no longer."* In other words, the plan has been set in motion, there can be no turning back, and the *"mystery of God would be finished."*

Remember those martyrs, or Tribulation Saints, under the altar in Revelation chapter 6? They cried out for vengeance, but were told, *"they should rest a little while longer, until both the number of their fellow*

Chapter 10 – The Angel and the Scroll

servants and their brethren, who would be killed as they were, was completed." (Revelation 6:11b)

The time for repentance is now past and, with the next set of seven judgments, God's righteousness will be seen in its fullness.
Let's look at that "mystery of God." There are a lot of mysteries in the Bible, some revealed and some not yet revealed:

- The ultimate conversion of the Jewish people is called a mystery (Romans 11:25).
- God's purpose for the church is called a mystery (Ephesians 3:3-11). Note: Paul goes into great detail revealing the mystery, so it is now not a mystery.
- The bringing in of the fullness of the Gentiles is called a mystery (Romans 11:25).
- The living presence of Jesus in the believer is called the mystery of God (Colossians 1:27-2:3). Note: also revealed now.
- The gospel itself is called the mystery of Christ (Colossians 4:3). Note: This mystery has also been revealed!

A mystery is something that can't be known by studying, or by intuition. It must be revealed. The mysteries of the Bible are revealed to those who God wishes to reveal them to and this one is no different. In this case, it is referring to the resolution of all things – the culmination of the plan God set in motion at the beginning of Genesis.

"⁸Then the voice which I heard from heaven spoke to me again and said, "Go, take the little book which is open in the hand of the angel who stands on the sea and on the earth." ⁹So I went to the angel and said to him, "Give me the little book." And he said to me, "Take and eat it; and it will make your stomach bitter, but it will be as sweet as honey in your mouth." ¹⁰Then I took the little book out of the angel's hand and ate it, and it was as sweet as honey in my mouth. But when I had eaten it, my stomach became bitter. ¹¹And he said to me, "You must prophesy again about many peoples, nations, tongues, and kings." (Revelation 10:8-11)

This is very similar to when Ezekiel is told to take a scroll and eat it in Ezekiel: *"¹Moreover He said to me, 'Son of man, eat what you find; eat this scroll, and go, speak to the house of Israel.' ²So I opened my mouth, and He caused me to eat that scroll. ³And He said to me, 'Son of man, feed*

So the Image Could Speak

your belly, and fill your stomach with this scroll that I give you.' So I ate, and it was in my mouth like honey in sweetness." (Ezekiel 3:1-3) Ezekiel is then told, after absorbing the scroll, " 'Son of man, go to the house of Israel and speak with My words to them.' " (Ezekiel 3:4a)

In other words, Ezekiel was not properly prepared to go preach God's Word to those in Israel who had turned away from God until he was filled with God's Word. The same is true of these verses in Revelation, but it is now John who is being prepared.

But what is this book and why is it bitter in the stomach?

The allegory of the sweetness of the scroll at first and then causing bitterness in the stomach is symbolic. It isn't the fiber in the scroll or the ink on the paper that makes it bitter in Ezekiel's or John's stomach; it is the nature of what is being absorbed. God's Word, to those of us who have accepted it, is a sweetness to our soul and a spiritual filling. But for those who have not accepted it, it is indeed bitter. Our God is a loving and merciful God who sent His Son in payment for our sins, but He is also a Righteous God and His condemnation for those who refuse Him is irrefutable. Ezekiel and John both are made to fully understand how His Word will be felt by those they are to teach - both those who accept it and those who reject it.

There are a lot of theories about what this little book, or scroll is, but let's narrow it down. Remember the seven seals on the scroll? The scroll that God held in His right hand and gave to His Son, who was found worthy to open the scroll? It is quite possible that this scroll, which John takes from the angel, is that same scroll – the seals are now opened and those judgments have been poured out, so it is no longer needed. There is another reason it is not needed, as well, which we'll see further on.

In Genesis, God gave dominion over the earth to man, *"[26]Then God said, "Let Us make man in Our image, according to Our likeness; let them have dominion over the fish of the sea, over the birds of the air, and over the cattle, over all the earth and over every creeping thing that creeps on the earth." [27]So God created man in His own image; in the image of God He created him; male and female He created them. [28]Then God blessed them, and God said to them, "Be fruitful and multiply; fill the earth and subdue*

Chapter 10 – The Angel and the Scroll

it; have dominion over the fish of the sea, over the birds of the air, and over every living thing that moves on the earth." (Genesis 1:26-30)

In effect, He gave title to, or authority over, the earth to man. Remember that scroll handed to Jesus was written on both sides, *"[1]And I saw in the right hand of Him who sat on the throne a scroll written inside and on the back, sealed with seven seals."* (Revelation 5:1) At that time, it was not common for scrolls to be written on both sides, with the exception of legal documents – such as wills and property titles or deeds. It is also notable that Romans typically sealed certain legal documents, specifically wills, with seven seals.

So Adam, and all his descendants, were given title to the earth, but then Satan usurped Adam's authority and caused him to lose that authority over earth. That is further confirmed in Luke, when Satan tempts Jesus with authority over the earth in the Gospel of Luke. Again, this would be an empty temptation if Satan did not actually have that authority to give away. Note that Jesus did not disagree or argue with him, either, as He knew what Satan offered was his to offer.

In Revelation chapter 5, *"[2]Then I saw a strong angel proclaiming with a loud voice, 'Who is worthy to open the scroll and to loose its seals?' [3]And no one in heaven or on the earth or under the earth was able to open the scroll, or to look at it."* (Revelation 5:2-3) Only Jesus Christ was found worthy to open the scroll – to claim back that which was lost in the Garden of Eden – and now He's ready to lay claim to that which is His.

I believe that is what this scroll is – the title deed to earth that Jesus Christ, through His Sacrifice and purity was entitled to open. But why is John told to eat it?

For one simple reason; because it won't be needed ever again. As Daniel tells us, *"[13]I was watching in the night visions, and behold, One like the Son of Man, Coming with the clouds of heaven! He came to the Ancient of Days, and they brought Him near before Him. [14]Then to Him was given dominion and glory and a kingdom, that all peoples, nations, and languages should serve Him. His dominion is an everlasting dominion, which shall not pass away, and His kingdom the one which shall not be destroyed."* (Daniel 7:13-14)

So the Image Could Speak

When does/did Jesus' recovered dominion begin? Mid Trib? At the beginning of the thousand-year reign? After Satan is eternally locked up?

That's a very good question. Probably a deeper question than most of us would ask, but one to which those of us who desire a better understanding of God's working in and with this world will appreciate an answer.

First, we need to understand that God (in three persons) is still in control of all things both in heaven and on earth. It is this earth over which dominion was given to Adam who then lost that dominion to Satan. (Jesus didn't refute that when tempted.) Therefore, it is the dominion of this earth we are talking about here.

Remember that God has and will use evil forces to punish His people. For example, He used Nebuchadnezzar to punish Israel for 70 years etc. During the seven year "time of Jacob's trouble" He will use the AntiChrist as well as other catastrophic means *"to finish the transgression, to put an end to sin, to atone for wickedness, to bring in everlasting righteousness, to seal up vision and prophecy and to anoint the Most Holy Place"*. (Daniel 9:24)

One of the reasons we understand that it is the entire seven year period we consider to be God's wrath is that it is Jesus who opens the first seal and releases the AntiChrist upon the world.

Jesus actually takes dominion over this world when He sets foot on earth at the end of that seven year Tribulation (our Glorious Hope!) and sets up the one thousand year reign during which He will rule "with a rod of iron". Dominion over the earth will never again be transferred, usurped, or given to anyone but Jesus Christ and He will rule until this heaven and earth are replaced with a new Heaven and Earth and we, who have accepted Him as our Lord and Savior, are made kings and priests with Him.

There is another, more subtle but no less vital, reason why John is told to eat it – the same reason Ezekiel is told to eat that scroll. To prepare us for the role our Lord has for our life. We can read, study, and memorize Scripture all day and every night, but until we absorb it – it has no meaning in our life. Anyone can learn the words as that is just head

Chapter 10 – The Angel and the Scroll

knowledge, but we need to absorb the Word of God and assimilate it into our lives for it to truly be a part of us. Of course, the only way that is possible is through the renewed heart given to us by God, and through the indwelling of the Holy Spirit who gives us that yearning to know more, learn more, and understand more about who our Heavenly Father is. It is the Holy Spirit that gives us understanding of His Word.

So the Image Could Speak

Chapter 11 – The Two Witnesses

Chapter eleven of the book of Revelation gives us two events: the measuring of the Temple and the appearance, death, and resurrection of the Two Witnesses. We'll cover both of these in the order in which they are presented in Revelation chapter eleven.

1. Measure the Temple

    The seventh trumpet is about to sound, but that interlude between the sixth and seventh trumpets isn't quite over yet. John has been an "innocent bystander" up to this point, not an active participant in the events he is recording. But that changes with the command he is given in the first verse of chapter eleven.

    "¹Then I was given a reed like a measuring rod. And the angel stood, saying, 'Rise and measure the temple of God, the altar, and those who worship there. ²But leave out the court which is outside the temple, and do not measure it, for it has been given to the Gentiles. And they will tread the holy city underfoot for forty-two months.' " (Revelation 11:1-3)

    First, we have to understand what John is told to measure and, as always, Scripture gives us the translation. The word translated to "temple" is the Greek word, naos[37] and is used to refer to the part of the temple where God resides – the Holy of Holies. John is then told to include the altar in his measurements but leave out the court outside the temple. He is also instructed to measure "those who worship there", but we'll take a closer look at that part further down.

    If we take a look at a sketch of the layout of the temple, we get an idea of what is included (the shaded areas) and what is excluded in his measurements.

---

[37] Strong's Greek.3485.naos, noun masculine, :a temple, a shrine, that part of the temple where God Himself resides"

Chapter 11 – The Two Witnesses

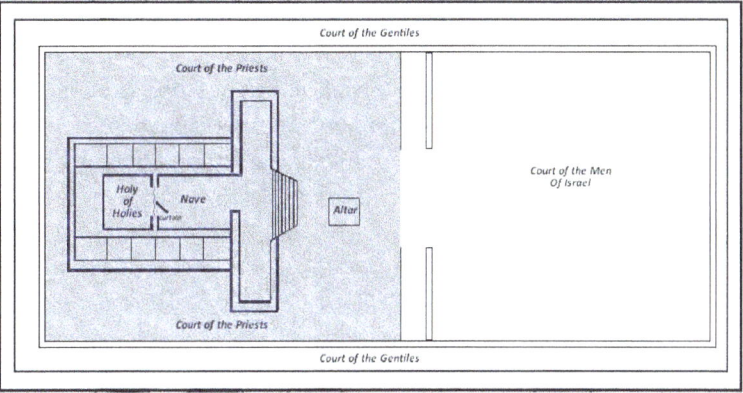

But how is John measuring a Temple that, at the time of this writing, no longer existed? The Temple in Jerusalem was destroyed in 70AD when General Titus (later Emperor Titus) led his armies into Jerusalem and destroyed the city. It was at this time the Ark of the Covenant disappeared, though history doesn't record whether it was destroyed by Titus and his army or saved by the Israelites before the destruction of the Temple. We'll discover the answer to this question in the (near?) future.

We have all heard about the two Temples in Jerusalem: the first temple, or Solomon's Temple, with all its gold and majestic glory, and the second temple, or Herod's Temple, which, while it didn't quite come up to the standards set by Solomon's Temple, was still quite impressive. Technically, Herod's Temple was the third temple, but since it was an expansion of the actual second temple, built by Zerubbabel (Ezra 3) after the release from Babylon, it is considered the second temple.

But that still begs the question, what temple is John measuring? If both the first temple and the second temple have been destroyed, what temple remains for him to measure? For that answer, we have to go back to the Old Testament. There is a similar event in Ezekiel, where he sees a temple being measured.

"[1]In the twenty-fifth year of our captivity, at the beginning of the year, on the tenth day of the month, in the fourteenth year after the city was captured, on the very same day the hand of the Lord was upon me; and He took me there. [2]In the visions of God He

> *took me into the land of Israel and set me on a very high mountain; on it toward the south was something like the structure of a city. ³He took me there, and behold, there was a man whose appearance was like the appearance of bronze. He had a line of flax and a measuring rod in his hand, and he stood in the gateway. ⁴And the man said to me, 'Son of man, look with your eyes and hear with your ears, and fix your mind on everything I show you; for you were brought here so that I might show them to you. Declare to the house of Israel everything you see.' ⁵Now there was a wall all around the outside of the temple. In the man's hand was a measuring rod six cubits long, each being a cubit and a handbreadth; and he measured the width of the wall structure, one rod; and the height, one rod."* (Ezekiel 40:1-5)

The temple measurements that are given in this passage do not match the temple built later – Herod's Temple. We know the Bible is never wrong, so what temple does Ezekiel see being measured? This is a temple that has not yet been built but will be and we'll see that further on in the book of Revelation. But there is another temple, the Third Temple, that will be built. There is a strong contingent of those in Israel now that have gone to great expense and effort to insure to prepare for that Third Temple. If you aren't familiar with their preparations, you might want to look at their website, https://templeinstitute.org/.

There is another reason we believe a Third Temple will be built and it is also found in Scripture. Remember the verse in Daniel when the angel is giving the covenant that God has made with Israel of their 70 weeks? We know that seventy weeks is a prophetic promise to Israel and we know those weeks are a group of seven years each, for a total of 490 years promised to Israel. We know that 483 years, or 69 of those "weeks", has elapsed and one week, or seven years, remains. The angel then tells Daniel what will happen in the middle of that last seven years, *"²⁷Then he shall confirm a covenant with many for one week; but in the middle of the week he shall bring an end to sacrifice and offering. And on the wing of abominations shall be one who makes desolate, even until the consummation, which is determined, is poured out on the desolate."* (Daniel 9:27)

Chapter 11 – The Two Witnesses

He who brings Israel and her enemies to the peace table and makes a covenant with them will break that covenant at the midpoint, or three and one-half years into that seven year covenant. He will bring an end to sacrifices and offerings. So, at the time the AntiChrist breaks that covenant with Israel, they are making sacrifices and taking offerings. There must be a temple for them to make these sacrifices and bring offerings.

"And on the wing of abominations shall be one who makes desolate" Daniel 11 reveals this abomination, *"So he shall return and show regard for those who forsake the holy covenant. ^{31}And forces shall be mustered by him, and they shall defile the sanctuary fortress; then they shall take away the daily sacrifices, and place there the abomination of desolation."* (Daniel 11:30b-31)

"Defile the sanctuary fortress" For the AntiChrist to defile the sanctuary fortress, there must be a sanctuary to be defiled.

At the midpoint of the Tribulation, there will be a Third Temple in Jerusalem. By the time of this abomination, it is well-established and the Jews will have been offering sacrifices at that temple for some time. How that third temple gets built, and when, is conjecture, though there is much discussion about it in the current times. But know that it will be built and it will be made desolate at the midpoint of the Tribulation.

It would seem, therefore, that it is this temple John is instructed to measure. But why is he told to measure *"those who worship there?"* What difference does it make how tall or short those who worship in the Temple are? Well, God doesn't look at the physical; He looks at the spiritual and what He sees, in the days even before the Abomination of Desolation, is a Temple that is being profaned and those who worship there are measured and found wanting. So He calls upon His Two Witnesses.

This passage, often overlooked, really shows us God's purpose for the Tribulation. *"^{2}But leave out the court which is outside the temple, and do not measure it, for it has been given to the Gentiles."* In other words, this isn't about the Gentiles (or the

Church), but about Israel. While many Gentiles are saved during the Tribulation, it is God's desire to turn Israel back to Him. It is God's primary purpose to fulfill all His promises to His chosen people.

2. The Two Witnesses

"³'And I will give power to my Two Witnesses, and they will prophesy one thousand two hundred and sixty days, clothed in sackcloth.' ⁴These are the two olive trees and the two lampstands standing before the God of the earth. ⁵and if anyone wants to harm them, fire proceeds from their mouth and devours their enemies. And if anyone wants to harm them, he must be killed in this manner. ⁶These have power to shut heaven, so that no rain falls in the days of their prophecy; and they have power over waters to turn them to blood, and to strike the earth with all plagues, as often as they desire.' " (Revelation 11:3-6)

The Two Witnesses are given the assignment to prophesy for 1,260 days. Using the Hebrew lunar calendar with 30-day months and 360 day years, 1,260 days is equal to exactly three and one half years – one half of the 70th week of Daniel. If we jump ahead a few verses, we see how the ministry of the Two Witnesses will end, *"⁷When they finish their testimony, the beast that ascends out of the bottomless pit will make war against them, overcome them, and kill them."* (Revelation 11:7)

They are likened to olive trees and lampstands; olive trees bear fruit and the ministry of these Two Witnesses will also bear fruit – while many mock them, many will also come to Christ during their ministry. And lampstands? Well, that seems pretty obvious, as Christ says, *"¹²Then Jesus spoke to them again, saying, 'I am the light of the world. He who follows Me shall not walk in darkness, but have the light of life.' "* (John 8:12) The Gospel of Christ brings light into a darkened world and His messengers are to shine His light into a very darkened and evil world.

So, the "beast that ascends out of the bottomless pit" kills the Two Witnesses – but that hasn't happened yet. The beast, and that possession of the AntiChrist, doesn't happen until the

Chapter 11 – The Two Witnesses

midpoint of the 70th week of Daniel, so for the Two Witnesses to fulfill their ministry of 1,260 days before they are killed by the beast, they had to start at the beginning – even as early as when that first seal is opened by Jesus Christ.

They are clothed in sackcloth. "Sackcloth" is sakkos[38], referring to a very coarse, dark cloth, usually made from goat hair and worn like a sack. It was used to express mourning, repentance and judgment, as shown in Genesis 37, when Jacob is shown the torn clothes of his son, Joseph, *"33And he recognized it and said, 'It is my son's tunic. A wild beast has devoured him. Without doubt Joseph is torn to pieces.' 34Then Jacob tore his clothes, put sackcloth on his waist, and mourned for his son many days."* (Genesis 37:33-34) The Two Witnesses' message will be similar to the message of John the Baptist, that of announcing the coming judgments and calling men to repent. Because of the truth of their message, they will be hated.

The big question – who are the Two Witnesses?

Let's start by examining the powers they are given. There are four:

- Fire from their mouths
- Shut Heaven for no rain
- Turn water into blood
- Smite the earth with plagues.

These look familiar. Let's look at who else in Bible history had these powers:

In 1 and 2 Kings, we read about Elijah calling down fire from heaven: first to consume the burnt offering and second to destroy those who had come against him.

"38Then the fire of the Lord fell and consumed the burnt sacrifice, and the wood and the stones and the dust, and it licked up the water that was in the trench." (1 Kings 18:37)

---

[38] Strong's Greek.4526.sakkos, noun masculine, "sackcloth, a sign of mourning"

So the Image Could Speak

"^{10}*So Elijah answered and said to the captain of fifty, 'If I am a man of God, then let fire come down from heaven and consume you and your fifty men.' And fire came down from heaven and consumed him and his fifty."* (2 Kings 1:10)

Both Jesus and James tell us how Elijah shut up the heavens and no rain fell in Israel for three and one half years:

Jesus had returned to Nazareth and, as was his custom, He went to the synagogue on the Sabbath. When the time was appropriate, He stood up to read. He had chosen a passage from Isaiah. *"*^{25}*'But I tell you truly, many widows were in Israel in the days of Elijah, when the heaven was shut up three years and six months, and there was a great famine throughout all the land;' "* (Luke 4:25) For some reason, his reading – whether it was of this passage or just the fact of Him, a carpenter's son, reading, those who heard Him were enraged, threw Him out of town, and even tried to throw Him off the cliff. But it was not yet His time, and He walked away.

"^{17}*Elijah was a man with a nature like ours, and he prayed earnestly that it would not rain; and it did not rain on the land for three years and six months.* ^{18}*And he prayed again, and the heaven gave rain, and the earth produced its fruit."* (James 5:17)

Moses was able to turn the water into blood and call up plagues upon Egypt:

"^{19}*Then the Lord spoke to Moses, 'Say to Aaron, 'Take your rod and stretch out your hand over the waters of Egypt, over their streams, over their rivers, over their ponds, and over all their pools of water, that they may become blood. And there shall be blood throughout all the land of Egypt, both in buckets of wood and pitchers of stone.' "* ^{20}*And Moses and Aaron did so, just as the Lord commanded. So he lifted up the rod and struck the waters that were in the river, in the sight of Pharaoh and in the sight of his servants. And all the waters that were in the river were turned to blood."* (Exodus 7:19-20)

Chapter 11 – The Two Witnesses

"⁵Then the Lord spoke to Moses, 'Say to Aaron, 'Stretch out your hand with your rod over the streams, over the rivers, and over the ponds, and cause frogs to come up on the land of Egypt.' ⁶So Aaron stretched out his hand over the waters of Egypt, and the frogs came up and covered the land of Egypt." (Exodus 8:5-6)

Another hint of who the Two Witnesses could be occurs in the account of Jesus on the Mount of Transfiguration. *"¹Now after six days Jesus took Peter, James, and John his brother, led them up on a high mountain by themselves; ²and He was transfigured before them. His face shone like the sun, and His clothes became as white as the light. ³And behold, Moses and Elijah appeared to them, talking with Him."* (Matthew 17:1-3)

While none of these passages are conclusive proof that these Two Witnesses are Moses and Elijah, because we know God can give anyone those powers whenever He chooses to do so, they do set a pattern. Remember the Jewish model for prophecy: that it is in repeating patterns that prophecy is revealed. If the Two Witnesses are Moses and Elijah, that model of a repeating pattern is certainly confirmed. And we are told in Malachi that Elijah would return: *"⁵Behold, I will send you Elijah the prophet before the coming of the great and dreadful day of the Lord. ⁶And he will turn the hearts of the fathers to the children, and the hearts of the children to their fathers, lest I come and strike the earth with a curse."* (Malachi 4:6-8)

Let's go back to the Revelation account of the Two Witnesses. *"⁷When they finish their testimony, the beast that ascends out of the bottomless pit will make war against them, overcome them, and kill them. ⁸And their dead bodies will lie in the street of the great city which spiritually is called Sodom and Egypt, where also our Lord was crucified. ⁹Then those from the peoples, tribes, tongues, and nations will see their dead bodies three-and-a-half days, and not allow their dead bodies to be put into graves. ¹⁰And those who dwell on the earth will rejoice over them, make merry, and send gifts to one another, because these two prophets tormented those who dwell on the earth."* (Revelation 11:7-10)

So those who hated the Two Witnesses celebrate when the beast kills them, but the party comes to a quick end when those Two Witnesses are resurrected and, with the current technology of livestreaming around the world, the whole world will see it. *"11Now after the three-and-a-half days the breath of life from God entered them, and they stood on their feet, and great fear fell on those who saw them. 12And they heard a loud voice from heaven saying to them, 'Come up here.' And they ascended to heaven in a cloud, and their enemies saw them. 13In the same hour there was a great earthquake, and a tenth of the city fell. In the earthquake seven thousand people were killed, and the rest were afraid and gave glory to the God of heaven."* (Revelation 11:11-13)

While the AntiChrist is not able to harm these Two Witnesses until their mission was accomplished – the mission ordained by God – at the end, he does kill them. Yet God uses even their death to show His power when He resurrects their dead bodies in the street, with everyone watching! Those who did not like the message of the Two Witnesses (and there will be many who don't) are rejoicing over their deaths. They won't even let the bodies be properly buried! But while they are rejoicing, the two bodies rise up and return to Heaven. Hallelujah! Their mission has been fulfilled and they return to be in the presence of the Lord for eternity. What greater gift could there be?

What is the connection between the temple and the Two Witnesses? God permits Israel to rebuild their temple and bring their sacrificial offerings. But those who worship at that temple are not followers of His Son, the ultimate sacrifice. So God introduces His Two Witnesses to prophesy against those who are not accepting of His Son and warns them of the judgments to come. He then turns that temple over to the non-believers for the remaining forty-two months of this last seven years. But there is an exception – He reserves for Himself the inner sanctum, the Holy of Holies, and the altar. Even in the judgments to come, God is preserving His people and will keep them through the remainder of the Tribulation.

The closing verses in Revelation chapter 11 are when the seventh trumpet is heard which we covered in the last chapter. The next four chapters in Revelation are about events that take place at the midpoint

Chapter 11 – The Two Witnesses

of the Tribulation and before the last of the sets of seven judgments – the bowls – are poured out.

So the Image Could Speak

Chapter 12 – The Woman and the Dragon

Revelation contains twenty-two chapters and with the completion of chapter eleven, we are halfway through the book. We've read the letters to the seven churches and saw where John is called up to Heaven and told to write what he sees. We've learned Who is worthy to open the scroll and then we read about the first of the three sets of seven judgments poured out on the earth, the seven seals, and then the second set, the seven trumpets. We've seen an amazing example of God's grace poured out on an unrepentant world when He sends 144,000 to evangelize. The next four chapters, before the beginning of the final set of seven judgments, reveal events at the midpoint of the Tribulation. While this doesn't necessarily indicate the order of events during the Tribulation, it is compelling.

This chapter, chapter twelve in Revelation, further opens the door on understanding what the book of Revelation is all about and may be the most symbolic of all the chapters in Revelation. John sees signs in Heaven and states these are signs; there isn't a woman flying through Heaven being chased by a red dragon. These are all symbolic, but if we let Scripture translate for us, we can figure out what is being represented by that symbolism.

We know from Daniel 9 that God is not done with Israel. He has made promises and covenants with Israel that have yet to be fulfilled. For example, when Gabriel appears to Mary, he gives her some wonderful news, *"^{30}Then the angel said to her, "Do not be afraid, Mary, for you have found favor with God. ^{31}And behold, you will conceive in your womb and bring forth a Son, and shall call His name Jesus. ^{32}He will be great, and will be called the Son of the Highest; and the Lord God will give Him the throne of His father David. ^{33}And He will reign over the house of Jacob forever, and of His kingdom there will be no end."* (Luke 1:30-33)

Jesus lived, died, and rose again, but He has yet to sit and reign from the throne of David – that doesn't happen until the millennium. But God is faithful and He always fulfills His promises.

"^{1}Now a great sign appeared in heaven: a woman clothed with the sun, with the moon under her feet, and on her head a garland of twelve stars. ^{2}Then being with child, she cried out in labor and in pain to give birth."

Chapter 12 – The Woman and the Dragon

(Revelation 12:1-2)

Who is this woman?

There are seven signs John sees in the heavens and this is the first of five revealed in this chapter in Revelation. We'll explore the last two in the next chapter, but just to summarize, he sees:

- The woman, representing Israel.
- The dragon, representing Satan.
- The man-child, representing Jesus.
- The angel Michael, representing the angelic host.
- The offspring of the woman, representing the Gentiles who come to faith during the Tribulation.
- The beast out of the sea, representing the AntiChrist.
- The beast from the earth, representing the False Prophet.

John presents this as a sign, not a literal vision of a woman. Women are often used to represent religious systems in Revelation: Jezebel is representing a false ideology in Revelation 2:20, The Great Harlot is used to represent another false ideology in Revelation 17:2 and The Bride represents the Church – the true Church.

We can also find multiple times a woman was used to represent Israel in the Old Testament.

"[6]'For the Lord has called you like a woman forsaken and grieved in spirit, like a youthful wife when you were refused,' says your God." (Isaiah 54:6)

In Jeremiah, Israel is compared to an unfaithful wife, *"[20]'Surely, as a wife treacherously departs from her husband, so have you dealt treacherously with Me, O house of Israel,' says the Lord."* (Jeremiah 3:20)

Again, in Ezekiel, there is a long passage about how God compares Israel to a woman, *"[8]'When I passed by you again and looked upon you, indeed your time was the time of love; so I spread My wing over you and covered your nakedness. Yes, I swore an oath to you and entered into a covenant*

So the Image Could Speak

with you, and you became Mine,' says the Lord God." (Ezekiel 16:8)

Just a side note – that entire chapter is interesting reading and tells the whole history of Israel.
There are more, but we'll leave it at these. Clearly, this woman represents Israel, and the twelve stars represent the sons of Israel – the twelve tribes. But it is not just Israel represented here. From where did the Christian faith arise? From those Israelites who followed Jesus during His earthly reign. While the twelve stars around the sign of this woman clearly represent the sons of Isaac, the twelve tribes of Israel, we cannot forget it is from those sons of Isaac that Jesus was made incarnate, and it was from Jews – the original twelve Apostles -the Christian faith began and was sent throughout the world.

"²Then being with child, she cried out in labor and in pain to give birth." (Revelation 12:1-2)

We will see a reference to this child again in verse 5, but it isn't difficult to figure out who this child is – our Lord and Savior, Jesus Christ.

"³And another sign appeared in heaven: behold, a great, fiery red dragon having seven heads and ten horns, and seven diadems on his heads. ⁴His tail drew a third of the stars of heaven and threw them to the earth. And the dragon stood before the woman who was ready to give birth, to devour her Child as soon as it was born. ⁵She bore a male Child who was to rule all nations with a rod of iron. And her Child was caught up to God and His throne. ⁶Then the woman fled into the wilderness, where she has a place prepared by God, that they should feed her there one thousand two hundred and sixty days." (Revelation 12:3-6)

We're going to explore those seven heads and ten horns more when we get into Revelation chapter 13, but for now we can safely say this represents Satan. That imagery of a fiery red dragon gives an indication of his propensity for evil and treachery. With his tail, he *"drew a third of the stars of heaven and threw them to the earth."* When he is thrown out of heaven, he takes a third of the angelic host with him.

But the dragon, Satan, does not want this Child to be born at all. We could do a deep dive here into the history of persecution of this Child and His followers, the Church, and realize the depth of hatred Satan has for Him.

Chapter 12 – The Woman and the Dragon

It starts at the beginning with Herod's attempts to kill Jesus as a baby, *"¹⁶Then Herod, when he saw that he was deceived by the wise men, was exceedingly angry; and he sent forth and put to death all the male children who were in Bethlehem and in all its districts, from two years old and under, according to the time which he had determined from the wise men."* (Matthew 2:16) But it, by no means, ends there.

It is also the nation of Israel for which Satan has a deep hatred and that becomes evident when Satan causes the AntiChrist to go back on his word and break that seven year covenant with Israel signed at the beginning of the 70th week of Daniel. When the Abomination of Desolation occurs, as shown in Daniel 9:27, the people of Israel know they have been deceived and head for the hills. Jesus warns them of this event, *"¹⁵'Therefore when you see the 'abomination of desolation,' spoken of by Daniel the prophet, standing in the holy place' (whoever reads, let him understand), ¹⁶'then let those who are in Judea flee to the mountains. ¹⁷Let him who is on the housetop not go down to take anything out of his house. ¹⁸And let him who is in the field not go back to get his clothes. ¹⁹But woe to those who are pregnant and to those who are nursing babies in those days! ²⁰And pray that your flight may not be in winter or on the Sabbath. ²¹For then there will be great tribulation, such as has not been since the beginning of the world until this time, no, nor ever shall be. ²²And unless those days were shortened, no flesh would be saved; but for the elect's sake those days will be shortened."* (Matthew 24:15-22)

"⁶Then the woman fled into the wilderness, where she has a place prepared by God, that they should feed her there one thousand two hundred and sixty days." Some say they escape to and are protected in Petra, and that is a possibility. Petra, according to those who have studied it, will hold about a million people. I hate to think that is all that is left of the faithful in Israel by the midpoint of the 70th week of Daniel, but it could be.

Wherever they go, they are protected for 1,260 days, just as God promised in chapter eleven with the preservation of the specific parts of the temple. There's that number again. It still represents 3.5 years on the Jewish, or lunar, calendar. This period of time encompasses the entire second half of the 70th week of Daniel.

"⁷And war broke out in heaven: Michael and his angels fought with the dragon; and the dragon and his angels fought, ⁸but they did not prevail,

So the Image Could Speak

nor was a place found for them in heaven any longer. ⁹So the great dragon was cast out, that serpent of old, called the Devil and Satan, who deceives the whole world; he was cast to the earth, and his angels were cast out with him. ¹⁰Then I heard a loud voice saying in heaven, 'Now salvation, and strength, and the kingdom of our God, and the power of His Christ have come, for the accuser of our brethren, who accused them before our God day and night, has been cast down. ¹¹And they overcame him by the blood of the Lamb and by the word of their testimony, and they did not love their lives to the death. ¹²Therefore rejoice, O heavens, and you who dwell in them! Woe to the inhabitants of the earth and the sea! For the devil has come down to you, having great wrath, because he knows that he has a short time.' " (Revelation 12:7-12)

We know, from the previous events, that Satan has held dominion over the earth from the time of the Garden of Eden, when Eve took a bite of that fruit of the forbidden tree. But did you realize he still had access to the Throne of God? That he was, in fact, accusing all those who have given our lives over to Jesus as our Savior, for all this time?

We see Satan appearing before the throne of God in Job, *"⁶Now there was a day when the sons of God came to present themselves before the Lord, and Satan also came among them. ⁷And the Lord said to Satan, 'From where do you come?' So Satan answered the Lord and said, 'From going to and fro on the earth, and from walking back and forth on it.' "*(Job 1:6-7)

Zechariah sees a vision of Satan at the throne of God and standing next to the pre-incarnate Jesus, *"¹Then he showed me Joshua the high priest standing before the Angel of the Lord, and Satan standing at his right hand to oppose him. ²And the Lord said to Satan, 'The Lord rebuke you, Satan! The Lord who has chosen Jerusalem rebuke you! Is this not a brand plucked from the fire?' "* (Zechariah 3:1-2)

After this battle portrayed in Revelation chapter twelve, Satan's access to Heaven is revoked and he no longer has God's ear. The whole scenario with Satan, who was the angel Lucifer, is a good reminder of God's love and depth of patience. Lucifer was a created being – created by God – and he was quite impressive, as described in Ezekiel 28: *"You were the seal of perfection, Full of wisdom and perfect in beauty. ¹³You were in Eden, the garden of God; Every precious stone was your covering: The*

Chapter 12 – The Woman and the Dragon

sardius, topaz, and diamond, Beryl, onyx, and jasper, Sapphire, turquoise, and emerald with gold. The workmanship of your timbrels and pipes was prepared for you on the day you were created. [14]"You were the anointed cherub who covers; I established you; You were on the holy mountain of God; You walked back and forth in the midst of fiery stones. [15]You were perfect in your ways from the day you were created, till iniquity was found in you." (Ezekiel 28:12b-15)

"Perfect in your ways." So Lucifer, who became Satan, who is the dragon in Revelation, was created perfect in all his ways, until pride took over. But God, knowing how Lucifer would deceive all humankind, uses him to fulfill His plan.

"[11]And they overcame him by the blood of the Lamb and by the word of their testimony, and they did not love their lives to the death." (Revelation 12:11)

How did Michael overcome Satan? It wasn't just the fact that he and his heavenly host outnumbered Satan and his demons two to one. No, the battle was won by *"blood of the Lamb and by the word of their testimony!"* I gasp as I read this, as it makes clear the power that is given to us who have given our lives to Christ and have been sanctified by...what? – The blood of the Lamb!

" 'Woe to the inhabitants of the earth and the sea! For the devil has come down to you, having great wrath, because he knows that he has a short time.' " (Revelation 12:12b)

Satan knows Scripture – probably better than the best studied Bible scholar in all the world and throughout time. He knows his time is getting short, but he still thinks he can win. He is angry and he pours out that anger on any who have accepted Christ – Jew or Gentile. It is about to get very rough for anyone who has accepted Jesus Christ.

"[13]Now when the dragon saw that he had been cast to the earth, he persecuted the woman who gave birth to the male Child. [14]But the woman was given two wings of a great eagle, that she might fly into the wilderness to her place, where she is nourished for a time and times and half a time, from the presence of the serpent. [15]So the serpent spewed water out of his mouth like a flood after the woman, that he might cause her to be carried away by the flood. [16]But the earth helped the woman,

So the Image Could Speak

and the earth opened its mouth and swallowed up the flood which the dragon had spewed out of his mouth. [17]And the dragon was enraged with the woman, and he went to make war with the rest of her offspring, who keep the commandments of God and have the testimony of Jesus Christ." (Revelation 12:13-17)

The woman, Israel or rather the remnant of Israel, miraculously escapes the persecution of Satan and his unholy trinity – the AntiChrist and the False Prophet and she is protected for *"a time and times and half a time."* Like the English word "both", the word "times" designates exactly two of whatever is being referenced, so in this passage time is singular (one year), times is dual (two years), and half a time is one half (six months). The time referenced is a year, so one year plus two years plus six months = three and one half years.

"[15]So the serpent spewed water out of his mouth like a flood after the woman, that he might cause her to be carried away by the flood. [16]But the earth helped the woman, and the earth opened its mouth and swallowed up the flood which the dragon had spewed out of his mouth." (Revelation 12:15-16)

I'm not convinced this is a literal flood of water but could represent the "flood" of armies and demons that are sent to destroy the remnant of Israel. We see something similar in Isaiah, *"[19]So shall they fear the name of the Lord from the west, and His glory from the rising of the sun; When the enemy comes in like a flood, The Spirit of the Lord will lift up a standard against him."* (Isaiah 59:19)

It is interesting to note, however, that even though Petra is 1100 meters above sea level, there have been several instances of flooding. In 2022, tourists had to be evacuated due to a flash flood and that wasn't the first..or last...time in recent history this has happened.

So it could be a literal flood of water that floods Israel, but whether this is symbolic or literal, Israel is still protected supernaturally by God.

Satan has lost the battle and has been evicted permanently from Heaven. But he doesn't give up and, as we'll see in the following chapters, things are about to get worse.

Chapter 13 – The AntiChrist

The AntiChrist – a title we all have heard many times through the years and one which has been applied to many different people through the ages, such as Caligula – a Roman emperor who declared himself god, or Nero – who heavily persecuted both Christians and Jews, and many more in more recent times. We know the spirit of the AntiChrist has been around for a long time – a very long time indeed if John is writing about him in the first century AD. Revelation is not the first book where that name, or title, appears. John mentions him in his first epistle, *"[18]Little children, it is the last hour; and as you have heard that the AntiChrist is coming, even now many AntiChrists have come, by which we know that it is the last hour."* (1 John 2:18)

In fact, John is the only one who calls this person "AntiChrist", but he is not the only one to refer to him. Paul calls him "the man of sin" and "the son of perdition" in his second epistle to Thessalonica, *"[3]Let no one deceive you by any means; for that Day will not come unless the falling away comes first, and the man of sin is revealed, the son of perdition, [4]who opposes and exalts himself above all that is called God or that is worshiped, so that he sits as God in the temple of God, showing himself that he is God."* (2 Thessalonians 2:3-4)

The names used to describe this person all amount to the same thing: this is someone who sets himself up as a god and demands the world worship him. The Greek word for AntiChrist is AntiChristos[39], which means "one who puts himself in the place of". We tend to think of AntiChrist as someone opposed to Jesus Christ and he obviously is. But if we look at that original Greek, AntiChristos, it implies a replacement. And that is Satan's goal – to replace Jesus Christ and ascend to the highest ranks and he attempts this through replicating, or copying, Jesus' life, death, and resurrection. That is Satan's goal, and it becomes the goal of the AntiChrist. He doesn't just want to rule the world, he wants to take the place of Jesus Christ and God! He builds himself up in the eyes of the world by referring to himself as god and trying to demean the One True God. It is, of course, a lie and blasphemy, but many will believe him and follow him, as we'll see.

---

[39] Strong's Greek.500.AntiChristos, noun masculine, "AntiChrist, one who opposes Christ"

So the Image Could Speak

This AntiChrist, or man of sin and son of perdition, plays a key role during the Tribulation, as it is his success in bringing the enemies of Israel to the negotiating table and getting them to sign a seven year covenant of peace with Israel which is the opening scene of the seven year Tribulation. At the midpoint of the Tribulation, he breaks that covenant and declares himself god and, for the last three and one half years of this period, becomes a powerful world leader, along with his cohort, the False Prophet.

So what happens at the midpoint of the Tribulation that provokes this, seemingly, sudden change from a man of peace (peace covenant with Israel) to son of perdition? Let's take a look at what Scripture tells us about this man.

John sees a beast in the opening verses of Revelation chapter 13, *"¹Then I stood on the sand of the sea. And I saw a beast rising up out of the sea, having seven heads and ten horns, and on his horns ten crowns, and on his heads a blasphemous name. ²Now the beast which I saw was like a leopard, his feet were like the feet of a bear, and his mouth like the mouth of a lion. The dragon gave him his power, his throne, and great authority."* (Revelation 13:1-2)

The dragon, that same dragon chasing the woman across the skies, has been cast out of Heaven and he's very angry. " *'Woe to the inhabitants of the earth and the sea! For the devil has come down to you, having great wrath, because he knows that he has a short time.'* " (Revelation 12:12b)

We're going to come back to the seven heads and ten horns, but first let's look at how John describes this beast as "like a leopard, his feet were like the feet of a bear, and his mouth like the mouth of a lion." These animals sound familiar. Is there some similarity here with another listing of beasts in Scripture?

Daniel had a dream, in which he had a vision so compelling he had to write it down on awakening. He sees four beasts and the fourth one begins to give us a clear picture of the beast John saw.

Chapter 13 – The AntiChrist

1. *"⁴The first was like a lion, and had eagle's wings. I watched till its wings were plucked off; and it was lifted up from the earth and made to stand on two feet like a man, and a man's heart was given to it."* (Daniel 7:4)

   This first beast in Daniel's vision represents the Babylonian empire. The lion is the "king of the jungle" and Nebuchadnezzar had conquered the strong Assyrian empire and turned the city of Babylon into a powerful ruling city. It is interesting to note that on the gates leading into the city of Babylon is the image of a lion. The Babylonian empire was conquered by Cyrus which led to the Medo-Persian empire, which we'll see in the next beast. But one quick note before we move on – it is said Nebuchadnezzar became a believer in the God of Isaac, Abraham, and, of course, Daniel. If that is true, then he was given a new heart and we will see him in Heaven.

2. *"⁵And suddenly another beast, a second, like a bear. It was raised up on one side, and had three ribs in its mouth between its teeth. And they said thus to it: 'Arise, devour much flesh!' "* (Daniel 7:5)

   The next empire, the Medo-Persian empire, began with Cyrus conquering Babylon. It is, in Daniel's vision, compared to a bear; a slow-moving lumbering creature, but when angered, a strong and fearsome opponent. In his vision, Daniel sees this creature with *"three ribs in its mouth between its teeth."* The Medo-Persian empire conquered three lands – Egypt, Babylon, and Lydia.

   This beast is also *"raised up on one side."* While the empire this beast is said to symbolically represent is called the Medo-Persian empire, most historians agree it was more "Persian", than "Medes". The Persians are considered the stronger of the two entities and dominated much of time of the Medes-Persian, also known as Achaemenid, empire.

3. *"⁶After this I looked, and there was another, like a leopard, which had on its back four wings of a bird. The beast also had four heads, and dominion was given to it."* (Daniel 7:6)

So the Image Could Speak

This third beast in Daniel's vision is said to represent the Greco-Macedonian empire, led by Alexander the Great. This empire is likened to a leopard which had *"on its back four wings of a bird."* The leopard is an exceedingly swift animal, with recorded speeds of up to 58mph. Alexander the Great was also quick in his conquests, having captured most of the known world before he was thirty years old. The four heads are said to represent how Alexander directed his kingdom to be divided upon his death. His wishes were followed and the Greco-Macedonian empire was divided into four sub-kingdoms, each having their own ruler.

4. *"⁷After this I saw in the night visions, and behold, a fourth beast, dreadful and terrible, exceedingly strong. It had huge iron teeth; it was devouring, breaking in pieces, and trampling the residue with its feet. It was different from all the beasts that were before it, and it had ten horns. ⁸I was considering the horns, and there was another horn, a little one, coming up among them, before whom three of the first horns were plucked out by the roots. And there, in this horn, were eyes like the eyes of a man, and a mouth speaking pompous words."* (Daniel 7:7-8)

This beast was *"different from all the beasts that were before it."* Different, how? Well, it is *"dreadful and terrible, exceedingly strong"* and, while the first three beasts conquered other lands, this beast has *"huge iron teeth; it was devouring, breaking in pieces, and trampling the residue with its feet."* In other words, this beast conquered many lands and did so with great destruction.

This beast is said to represent the Roman empire, which followed the Greco-Macedonian empire and lasted into the fifth century AD.

Daniel, looking ahead, sees them in the order they arise. John, looking back, sees them in reverse order, but they represent the same four empires: the exceedingly strong beast like the Roman empire, the lion communicates arrogantly like the Babylonians, the bear controls extensively like the Medes-Persian empire, and the leopard conquers swiftly like Alexander the Great.

Chapter 13 – The AntiChrist

But what have these four beasts, and the empires they represent, to do with John's vision and the period of time we call the Tribulation? All four of these empires are long gone and it is highly unlikely any of them will regain their former dominance in the end times. Well, except for one, but to understand that we need to look at Nebuchadnezzar's dream in Daniel chapter two. We're going to come back to the second part of this passage in Daniel chapter seven in just a bit.

Nebuchadnezzar had not been the emperor of Babylon for very long when he had a troubling dream, according to Scripture. *"¹Now in the second year of Nebuchadnezzar's reign, Nebuchadnezzar had dreams; and his spirit was so troubled that his sleep left him."* (Daniel 2:1)

Nebuchadnezzar called all his magicians, astrologers, Chaldeans, and anyone else he thought might be able to interpret the dream before him. He was a cautious man, however, and didn't tell them what the dream was. He figured if they actually had the power to interpret it, they had the power to recall it, too. But they couldn't. Nebuchadnezzar became enraged and ordered them all put to death.

One of the young men Nebuchadnezzar had captured and brought back from Jerusalem, Daniel, heard about this and went to the captain of the king's guard and asked if he could interpret the dream for the king. Then he gathered his closest friends around him, and they prayed for God to reveal the dream and its interpretation. God answered their prayers. *"¹⁹Then the secret was revealed to Daniel in a night vision. So Daniel blessed the God of heaven."* (Daniel 2:19)

Daniel went before Nebuchadnezzar and told him what his dream was, then gave him the interpretation given to him by God.

"³¹You, O king, were watching; and behold, a great image! This great image, whose splendor was excellent, stood before you; and its form was awesome. ³²This image's head was of fine gold, its chest and arms of silver, its belly and thighs of bronze, ³³its legs of iron, its feet partly of iron and partly of clay." (Daniel 2:31-33a)

After he told Nebuchadnezzar the vision of his dream, he then gave him the interpretation. He told him that he, Nebuchadnezzar, was the head of gold and that his empire would eventually fall and a second, lesser,

So the Image Could Speak

empire would conquer Babylon. *"37You, O king, are a king of kings. For the God of heaven has given you a kingdom, power, strength, and glory; 38and wherever the children of men dwell, or the beasts of the field and the birds of the heaven, He has given them into your hand, and has made you ruler over them all—**you are this head of gold**."* (Daniel 2:37-39) (emphasis added) Each metal described in the dream was prophetically likened to a future empire. History bears out the accuracy of Daniel's interpretation up to the feet of mixed iron and clay, which as we'll see, hasn't happened yet.

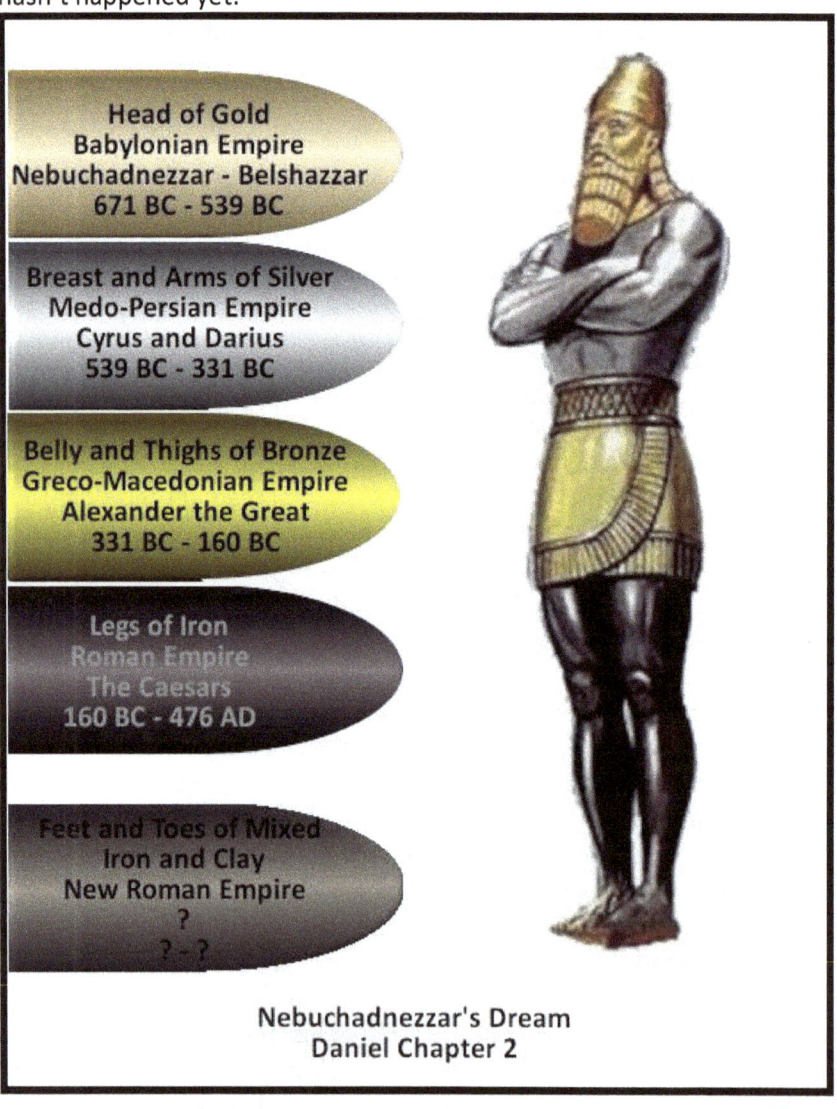

Nebuchadnezzar's Dream
Daniel Chapter 2

Chapter 13 – The AntiChrist

Nebuchadnezzar has a vision that his experts in his court cannot interpret – they can't even tell him what the vision was. Daniel and his friends pray to God for an answer, so those who couldn't give an interpretation are not put to death. God answers and tells Daniel the vision represents four kingdoms – one that is and three that are to come.

At least seventy years later, Daniel has a vision, while asleep in his bed, of four beasts. While he was in the vision, one standing near him (an angel?) gives him the interpretation of those four beasts. *"¹⁷'Those great beasts, which are four, are four kings which arise out of the earth.' "* (Daniel 7:17) At the time of this vision, Belshazzar was the king of Babylon. He was to be the final king of Babylon. Those four beasts match the empires, including the Babylonian empire, of the four empires in Nebuchadnezzar's vision.

Over six centuries later, John sees a beast rising out of the sea. *"¹Then I stood on the sand of the sea. And I saw a beast rising up out of the sea, having seven heads and ten horns, and on his horns ten crowns, and on his heads a blasphemous name. ²Now the beast which I saw was like a leopard, his feet were like the feet of a bear, and his mouth like the mouth of a lion. The dragon gave him his power, his throne, and great authority."* (Revelation 13:1-2)

The beast John sees incorporates the characteristics of all of the beasts Daniel saw; it was like a leopard (Daniel's third beast, the Greco-Macedonian empire), it has a head like a lion (Daniel's first beast, the Babylonian empire), feet like a bear (Daniel's second beast, the Medes-Persian empire) and, as we will see, it is exceedingly strong, *("The dragon gave him his power, his throne, and great authority")* the Roman empire and the Revived Roman empire.

The similarities do not end there. John's sees this beast *"having seven heads and ten horns, and on his horns ten crowns, and on his heads a blasphemous name."* The fourth beast that Daniel sees is similar. *"It was different from all the beasts that were before it, and it had ten horns. ⁸I was considering the horns, and there was another horn, a little one, coming up among them, before whom three of the first horns were plucked out by the roots. And there, in this horn, were eyes like the eyes of a man, and a mouth speaking pompous words."* (Daniel 7:7b-8)

So the Image Could Speak

Before we delve into what those ten horns, and the little horn that comes up among them, mean, we must address from where this beast that John sees comes. *"And I saw a beast rising up out of the sea."* This can only mean one of two things: a) he comes out of a literal body of water, such as the Mediterranean Sea, or b) he comes out of a large group of people.

If we jump ahead to Revelation 17:15, which is also a reference to the beast with seven heads and ten horns carrying the great harlot, we find the answer: *"¹⁵Then he said to me, "The waters which you saw, where the harlot sits, are peoples, multitudes, nations, and tongues."* (Revelation 17:15) So this beast, the AntiChrist, comes out of a large group of people. This could mean a nation, or a specific race, or creed of people. But it doesn't mean he came out of a body of water.

There is a lot of speculation about what those seven heads and ten horns mean. Many Bible scholars say the seven heads represent seven kingdoms, or empires. At the time of John's writing, five had passed, one was (the Roman empire), and one (Rome II) had yet to come.

- Egypt
- Assyria
- Babylon
- Persia
- Greece
- Rome
- Rome II

The last five of those empires match the beasts Daniel saw in his vision and the statue Nebuchadnezzar saw in his vision.

But what is this Rome II, or Revived Roman empire mentioned (feet of clay mixed with iron in Nebuchadnezzar's dream)?

To understand this, we have to go back in time to the rise and fall of the Roman empire. From Julius Caesar to Theodosius I, the Romans aggressively conquered lands and expanded their rule over a large area. At its height, the Roman empire ruled over three continents and included

Chapter 13 – The AntiChrist

areas that would become Portugal, Spain, Andorra, England, France, Monaco, Luxembourg, Belgium, the Netherlands, Germany, Switzerland, Liechtenstein, Italy, San Marino, Malta, Austria, Slovenia, Croatia, Bosnia-Herzegovina, Hungary, Albania, Greece, Macedonia, Romania, Bulgaria, Turkey and Armenia. In the Middle East and Africa, it ruled over lands that would later be known as Syria, Iraq, Cyprus, Lebanon, Jordan, Israel, Egypt, Libya, Tunisia, Algeria, and Morocco.[40]

While the Roman empire was strong and massive, it had its problems and by the late third century, it was faltering. It split in 395 AD into two: the Western Roman empire and the Eastern Roman empire. The Eastern Roman empire, also known as the Byzantine empire, thrived well into the second millennium AD, but the Western empire collapsed of its own weight in 476 AD.

Some of the ways Rome governed became the model for democracy, but the empire was always ruled autocratically, and at times tyrannically depending on who held the reins of power at the time, by one king or emperor. It was never ruled by a coalition of ten kings.

Yet both Daniel *("It was different from all the beasts that were before it, and it had ten horns."* Daniel 7:7b) and John *("And I saw a beast rising up out of the sea, having seven heads and ten horns, and on his horns ten crowns, and on his heads a blasphemous name"* (Revelation 13:1b) saw ten horns and, in John's vision, those horns each wore a crown.

Those *"ten horns, and on his horns ten crowns, and on his heads a blasphemous name,"* represent governmental authority, with each of these ten horns, or kingdoms, having their own "king". In the original Greek, the word used for those crowns is diadems, not stephanos. When the first seal is broken and the rider of the white horse appears, he is wearing a crown, but it is, in the original Greek, "stephanos" – an award or recognition of victory, not authority. "Diadem", on the other hand, is a symbol of authority. Each of those ten kingdoms are ruled by their individual leaders.

Remember the feet and toes on Nebuchadnezzar's statue? The feet and

---

[40] What Countries Did the Romans Conquer?, Staff Writer, August 4, 2015, https://www.reference.com/history-geography/countries-did-romans-conquer-18b1c0594b7f728e

toes were a mix of iron – the strength of the early Roman empire - and clay. Clay and iron do not mix well. While these ten kingdoms will have some strength, they will also have to deal with rebellions, challenges to their authority, and weakness within their ranks.

Since the Roman empire was never ruled by ten separate kings, and both Daniel's fourth beast and Nebuchadnezzar's statue, as well as John's beast that rises from the sea are all clearly shown as having ten rulers – those ten horns with crowns, then this empire has not yet happened. It must be a prophetic promise of a new empire; what many are calling the New, or Revived, Roman empire.

In fact, a proposition for a ten-nation world division has already been laid out – first by the Club of Rome in 1973, then by the European Commission. That layout was documented in the last book in my Beginning of Sorrows series, Convergence.[41]

But what has this got to do with the AntiChrist? Let's go back to the last part of that description of the fourth beast in Daniel's vision.

"⁸I was considering the horns, and there was another horn, a little one, coming up among them, before whom three of the first horns were plucked out by the roots. And there, in this horn, were eyes like the eyes of a man, and a mouth speaking pompous words." (Daniel 7:8)

An eleventh horn appears among the ten and, almost immediately, destroys three of those kingdoms – whether for disobedience or rebellion, we won't know until it happens. This "little horn" takes control of all the remaining seven kingdoms and proclaims himself ruler of the world, a One World Order.

This beast that John sees rising up out of the sea, or a multitude of people, is the AntiChrist. This man we call the AntiChrist has already shown himself willing to follow the devil; in fact, he's probably been following him his whole life. But now he's not just a follower of Satan; the dragon gives him *"his power, his throne, and great authority."* In effect, Satan enters this man and takes over.

---

[41] Convergence, Susan Mouw, South Carolina: Amazon, pg. 74, 2023, https://www.amazon.com/dp/B0C6W6XM34

Chapter 13 – The AntiChrist

There has only been one other time in Scripture where someone was actually possessed by Satan and that was Judas. *"³Then Satan entered Judas Iscariot, who was one of the Twelve."* (Luke 22:3)

One of his first acts after this possession takes place is to enter the Temple – the same Temple he permitted the Jews to build and where they offer their daily sacrifices – and proclaim himself god. This event, called the "Abomination of Desolation", Paul describes in 2 Thessalonians, *"³Let no one deceive you by any means; for that Day will not come unless the falling away comes first, and the man of sin is revealed, the son of perdition, ⁴who opposes and exalts himself above all that is called God or that is worshiped,* **so that he sits as God in the temple of God, showing himself that he is God**.*"* (2 Thessalonians 2:3-4) (emphasis added)

This man, now possessed by Satan, proclaims himself god and, as we'll see, demands he be worshipped. This person, who started out proclaiming peace, is now making war, even with the saints – those who have given their lives to Christ – and is given the power to overcome them – but only for a time.

Daniel gives us a better picture of just how evil this man is, *"²³And in the latter time of their kingdom, when the transgressors have reached their fullness, a king shall arise, having fierce features, who understands sinister schemes. ²⁴His power shall be mighty, but not by his own power; He shall destroy fearfully, and shall prosper and thrive; he shall destroy the mighty, and also the holy people. ²⁵"Through his cunning he shall cause deceit to prosper under his rule; and he shall exalt himself in his heart. He shall destroy many in their prosperity. He shall even rise against the Prince of princes; but he shall be broken without human means."* (Daniel 8:23-25)

There is something interesting in that second verse from 1 John, *"And this is the spirit of the AntiChrist, which you have heard was coming, and is* **now already in the world**.*"* (1 John 4:3b) (emphasis added) According to this verse, the person who would become the AntiChrist was already alive and well at the time of John's writing. How can that be?

Satan knows Scripture, but he doesn't know God's timing. Not even Jesus knows His Father's timing for the events in Revelation. In Matthew, the

So the Image Could Speak

disciples are asking Jesus about the signs of His Coming and when all that He is describing will happen. Jesus tells them, *"36'But of that day and hour no one knows, not even the angels of heaven, but My Father only.' "* (Matthew 24:36)

Satan has had to be prepared in each generation since the crucifixion of Jesus. He has had to have someone, in every generation, ready to take on this role. We could go back through history and probably name several that came close, but none reached the level of power and authority this final AntiChrist will have – the timing wasn't yet right. Only God knows His timing.

*"³And I saw one of his heads as if it had been mortally wounded, and **his deadly wound was healed**. And all the world marveled and followed the beast. ⁴So they worshiped the dragon who gave authority to the beast; and they worshiped the beast, saying, "Who is like the beast? Who is able to make war with him?" ⁵And he was given a mouth speaking great things and blasphemies, and he was given authority to continue for forty-two months. ⁶Then he opened his mouth in blasphemy against God, to blaspheme His name, His tabernacle, and those who dwell in heaven. ⁷It was granted to him to make war with the saints and to overcome them. And authority was given him over every tribe, tongue, and nation. ⁸All who dwell on the earth will worship him, whose names have not been written in the Book of Life of the Lamb slain from the foundation of the world."* (Revelation 13:3-8) (emphasis added)

Satan is given a lot of power, no doubt, but he cannot create life. So this "fatal" head wound is, most likely, fake and so is the resurrection that follows it. It is another example of Satan trying to emulate God and Jesus. It is all a deceit, but many will believe it, begin to worship him, and believe he is invincible.

This head wound becomes one of his trademarks, but there is a more provoking description of him in Zechariah, *"17'Woe to the worthless shepherd, who leaves the flock! A sword shall be against his arm and against his right eye; His arm shall completely wither, and his right eye shall be totally blinded.' "* (Zechariah 11:17)

So this is not just a simple head wound. This attempted assassination causes his arm to wither and he goes blind in his right eye. By this time, if

Chapter 13 – The AntiChrist

there are any doubts if this person is really the AntiChrist or not, I think this would settle it.

"And he was given authority to continue for forty-two months." (Revelation 13:5b)

Forty-two months, or one-half of a seven year period. He is given authority to continue for the remainder of this period called the Tribulation. Who gives him authority? The One Who sits on the Throne in Heaven – the One True God.

I have to pause here and ask, is your name written in the Lamb's Book of Life? If not, now would be a good time to ask Him into your life. Do you really want to experience all that will happen by the midpoint of the Tribulation?

"[9]If anyone has an ear, let him hear. [10]He who leads into captivity shall go into captivity; he who kills with the sword must be killed with the sword. Here is the patience and the faith of the saints." (Revelation 13:9-10)

Believers, those whose names are written in the Lamb's Book of Life, during this period of time are to lean solely on God and let His Will be done, even if it leads to incarceration or death. They are not to take matters into their own hands and seek retribution, for as we are told in Romans, *"[17]Repay no one evil for evil. Have regard for good things in the sight of all men. [18]If it is possible, as much as depends on you, live peaceably with all men. [19]Beloved, do not avenge yourselves, but rather give place to wrath; for it is written, "Vengeance is Mine, I will repay," says the Lord."* (Romans 12:17-19)

Those who give their life to Christ during this period of time are seriously committed! They know, or at least suspect, that the decision they are making may mean their life, but their love for Christ is stronger than their love for this life. But they also know, or will learn, that death is just a transition and what waits for them on the other side is more than worth it.

So the Image Could Speak

Chapter 14 – The False Prophet

"¹¹Then I saw another beast coming up out of the earth, and he had two horns like a lamb and spoke like a dragon. ¹²And he exercises all the authority of the first beast in his presence, and causes the earth and those who dwell in it to worship the first beast, whose deadly wound was healed." (Revelation 13:11-12)

Before we start digging into the background on this False Prophet and the role he plays in this time, let's look at what the rest of Scripture tells us about false prophets. Jesus warned us about false prophets at the end of His Sermon on the Mount, *"¹⁵'Beware of false prophets, who come to you in sheep's clothing, but inwardly they are ravenous wolves. ¹⁶You will know them by their fruits. Do men gather grapes from thornbushes or figs from thistles?' "* (Matthew 7:15-16)

The Greek word used here is pseudoprophétés[42], which means "a false prophet; someone pretending to speak the word of the Lord (prophesy) but in fact is phony (an imposter), acting as a wolf in sheep's clothing."

John also warns us of these false prophets in his first letter, *"¹Beloved, do not believe every spirit, but test the spirits, whether they are of God; because many false prophets have gone out into the world. ²By this you know the Spirit of God: Every spirit that confesses that Jesus Christ has come in the flesh is of God, ³and every spirit that does not confess that Jesus Christ has come in the flesh is not of God. And this is the spirit of the AntiChrist, which you have heard was coming, and is now already in the world."* (1 John 4:1-3)

I recently listened to a video presentation by the late Chuck Missler where he warns people who watch all the "miracle" videos to ask one question, "Who is getting the credit?" Excellent advice! If God is getting the credit, then all is well and good, but if someone else is getting the credit – beware!

False prophets arose multiple times in the Old Testament, some named and some not. Some of those named include Hananiah in Jeremiah 28, Ahab and Zedekiah in Jeremiah 29, Noahdiah in Nehemiah 6, and of

---
[42] Strong's Greek.5578.pseudoprophétés, noun masculine, "a false prophet"

Chapter 14 – The False Prophet

course, we can't leave out Balaam, who is largely responsible for Israel falling into idolatry.

Paul encountered a false prophet on the island of Cyprus, in Acts 13:6-12. That encounter didn't turn out too well for the false prophet.

So a false prophet is one who is teaching a false gospel, or false message of salvation. But they do it so convincingly that many are deceived into believing and accepting their message.

This False Prophet is the final one. Although many will arise during the time of the 70th Week of Daniel, none will be as powerful as him. This beast, while similar to the first beast, is not quite like him. First, he is *"coming up out of the earth"*, not from the sea. We see many places where the sea represents a vast group of people, but what does the earth represent?

Several times, in multiple verses we've read so far, we have seen references to "earth dwellers" or "inhabitants of the earth." These are those who have not given their lives to the Lord, whose names are not written in the Lamb's Book of Life, and who are not saved. Those whose names are written in the Lamb's Book of Life are not "earth-dwellers" – we're just pilgrims passing through.

Those earth dwellers are also, without exception, practicing a false religion – either belief in themselves, their belongings, or some other form of idolatry. And that is the source of this second beast – out of those false gods. It could be said that he comes from a false ideology, and probably a well-known and widespread one.

"He had two horns like a lamb and spoke like a dragon."

Remember the first beast had ten horns, with a little one added later. Those ten horns represent the ten regions that will make up the One World Government. This beast has only two horns, *"like a lamb"* and spoke like a dragon. Another attempt by Satan to mimic God? Jesus is the "Lamb of God. While this person may appear somewhat mild-mannered, and even likeable – don't be fooled! He still speaks like a dragon and is a deceiver.

So the Image Could Speak

"¹²And he exercises all the authority of the first beast in his presence and causes the earth and those who dwell in it to worship the first beast, whose deadly wound was healed."

Now we see his true purpose. While he can, and will, exercise the authority of the first beast, he can do that only *"in his presence"*, but his main purpose is to cause all who dwell in the earth – remember those "earth dwellers" – to worship the AntiChrist. If they don't …well, we will see what happens.

"¹³He performs great signs, so that he even makes fire come down from heaven on the earth in the sight of men. ¹⁴And he deceives those who dwell on the earth by those signs which he was granted to do in the sight of the beast, telling those who dwell on the earth to make an image to the beast who was wounded by the sword and lived. ¹⁵He was granted power to give breath to the image of the beast, that the image of the beast should both speak and cause as many as would not worship the image of the beast to be killed." (Revelation 13:13-15)

"He even makes fire come down from heaven" Where have we heard that before? Remember one of those four powers the Two Witnesses have? This is just another example of the AntiChrist, and his cohort the False Prophet, trying to emulate what God has done. We see this in Exodus, when Moses was performing the wonders in front of Pharaoh. Pharaoh called on his sorcerers and magicians and they were able, in many cases, to copy what Moses had done. Let's read the first of the signs and wonders.

"⁸Then the Lord spoke to Moses and Aaron, saying, ⁹'When Pharaoh speaks to you, saying, 'Show a miracle for yourselves,' then you shall say to Aaron, 'Take your rod and cast it before Pharaoh, and let it become a serpent.' ¹⁰So Moses and Aaron went in to Pharaoh, and they did so, just as the Lord commanded. And Aaron cast down his rod before Pharaoh and before his servants, and it became a serpent.

¹¹But Pharaoh also called the wise men and the sorcerers; so the magicians of Egypt, they also did in like manner with their enchantments. ¹²For every man threw down his rod, and they became serpents. But Aaron's rod swallowed up their rods. ¹³And Pharaoh's heart grew hard, and he did not heed them, as the Lord had said." (Exodus 7:8-13)

Chapter 14 – The False Prophet

This scenario is repeated for the first plague – when the water was turned to blood, and again for the second plague – when the frogs came into Egypt, but for the third plague and onward, the magicians were not able to replicate the signs and wonders of Moses and Aaron.

So this isn't the first time Satan tries to emulate God, but we have to understand a bit about those "earth dwellers" to understand why they are so easily deceived by these signs and wonders.

First – Fear. If they don't worship the AntiChrist, they will be killed.

Second – Confusion. Just read back through Revelation to this point. Those who do not know God and do not understand how, and why, all these things are happening are …well confused doesn't begin to describe it. They are looking for answers and they are looking for miracles. They are looking, though few will admit it, for a Savior. With these signs and wonders, the False Prophet is able to convince them that the AntiChrist is god.

There is a third reason, as well. We see it in Romans, *"[18]For the wrath of God is revealed from heaven against all ungodliness and unrighteousness of men, who suppress the truth in unrighteousness, [19]because what may be known of God is manifest in them, for God has shown it to them. [20]For since the creation of the world His invisible attributes are clearly seen, being understood by the things that are made, even His eternal power and Godhead, so that they are without excuse, [21]because, although they knew God, they did not glorify Him as God, nor were thankful, but became futile in their thoughts, and* **their foolish hearts were darkened***. [22]Professing to be wise, they became fools, [23]and changed the glory of the incorruptible God into an image made like corruptible man—and birds and four-footed animals and creeping things."* (Romans 1:18-23) (emphasis added) In other words, even though they see the hand of God all about them, they still turn against Him. We'll see this again with the seven bowls of wrath and explore it more fully in that chapter.

"Telling those who dwell on the earth to make an image to the beast who was wounded by the sword and lived." (Revelation 13:14b)

The image. We've seen this before, too. At the end of Daniel chapter two, after Daniel had interpreted Nebuchadnezzar's dream, Nebuchadnezzar

So the Image Could Speak

"fell on his face, paid homage to Daniel, and ordered that an offering of incense be presented to him. ⁴⁷The king said to Daniel, 'Your God is truly the God of gods and Lord of kings, the Revealer of Mysteries, since you were able to reveal this mystery.' " (Daniel 2:46-47)

But at the beginning of Daniel chapter 3, Nebuchadnezzar has apparently had a change of heart. He is on a major ego trip and decides to build a statue, *"¹King Nebuchadnezzar made a golden statue sixty cubits high and six cubits wide, and he set it up on the plain of Dura (plain of Shinar) in the province of Babylon. ²Then King Nebuchadnezzar sent word to assemble the satraps, prefects, governors, advisers, treasurers, judges, magistrates, and all the other officials of the provinces to attend the dedication of the statue he had set up. ³So the satraps, prefects, governors, advisers, treasurers, judges, magistrates, and all the rulers of the provinces assembled for the dedication of the statue that King Nebuchadnezzar had set up, and they stood before it."* (Daniel 3:1-3)

Then Nebuchadnezzar demanded all to worship the statue or die, *"⁴Then a herald cried aloud: "To you it is commanded, O peoples, nations, and languages, ⁵that at the time you hear the sound of the horn, flute, harp, lyre, and psaltery, in symphony with all kinds of music, you shall fall down and worship the gold image that King Nebuchadnezzar has set up; ⁶and whoever does not fall down and worship shall be cast immediately into the midst of a burning fiery furnace."* (Daniel 3:4-6)

We know how that turned out, but the AntiChrist and the False Prophet ignore those results and copy this for their own purposes. Another example of the Jewish definition of prophecy as patterns.

"¹⁵He was granted power to give breath to the image of the beast, that the image of the beast should both speak and cause as many as would not worship the image of the beast to be killed." (Revelation 13:15)

Nebuchadnezzar wasn't able to do this, as far as we know, so the False Prophet is going one better than Nebuchadnezzar. But how does he do this? We're going to explore that more in the next chapter.

There are many who claim this person or that leader is the AntiChrist or the False Prophet. While I do think they are both alive today, it is supposition and guesswork to try and figure out who either one of these

Chapter 14 – The False Prophet

are. We will know who the AntiChrist is when that seven year covenant with Israel is signed and he will make known who his False Prophet is.

While the two of them are around from the beginning of the Tribulation – the signing of that covenant, it isn't until the midpoint when they are both given their full powers. The dragon gives the first beast, the AntiChrist, great power and authority and it is that first beast who gives the second beast, the False Prophet, his power and authority.

Someone once said there are two factors that control humankind – politics and religion. The AntiChrist will control the politics of the world, and the False Prophet will control the religion. He will start out by merging all the religions into a "why can't we all just get along?" philosophy. The intended effect, and purpose, is to dilute Christianity. We see this happening even today with Pope Francis' and Sheikh Ahmed el-Tayeb's "Document on Human Fraternity" which claims all of the Abrahamic faiths; Judaism, Muslim, and Christian, are worshipping the same God and "all roads lead to heaven." Judaism obviously is, though they have not accepted Jesus Christ as their Savior, but Muslims? Anyone who reads about their doctrine would be right in questioning which god they serve. The purpose of this obliteration of the lines between these faiths is to weaken the message of the True Gospel – that there is only one way to God the Father and that is through Jesus Christ.

But that attitude of acceptance across all faith lines will gradually diminish, and then be completely eliminated by the midpoint of the Tribulation. Then the False Prophet will begin to enforce his, and the AntiChrist's, "faith movement" by enforcing all to worship the AntiChrist – the One World Religion.

The False Prophet, like the beast before him, is a liar and many, during this time, will be deceived.

So the Image Could Speak

Chapter 15 – So the Image Could Speak

In the previous two chapters, John sees the two beasts – one arising from a "sea" of people and the other arising from the earth. These two beasts, along with the dragon, Satan, comprise the unholy trinity: Satan, the AntiChrist, and the False Prophet. At this point in the Tribulation – the midpoint – the AntiChrist is no longer just operating under his own steam and is possessed by Satan. The False Prophet is given his powers by the AntiChrist, so he, too, is indwelt by evil.

The False Prophet's primary purpose is to lead the world to worship the AntiChrist, *"12And he exercises all the authority of the first beast in his presence, and causes the earth and those who dwell in it to worship the first beast, whose deadly wound was healed."* (Revelation 13:12)

By this time, the AntiChrist has organized his ten-region world and gained control over the "kings" of those ten regions. He has control over each of those kingdom's military, political leadership, finance, and all natural resources. He is not just a world leader, but the world leader.

"14And he deceives those who dwell on the earth by those signs which he was granted to do in the sight of the beast, telling those who dwell on the earth to make an image to the beast who was wounded by the sword and lived. 15He was granted power to give breath to the image of the beast, that the image of the beast should both speak and cause as many as would not worship the image of the beast to be killed." (Revelation 13:13-15)

So, the False Prophet, under orders from the AntiChrist, builds an image and *"15He was granted power to give breath to the image of the beast, that the image of the beast should both speak and cause as many as would not worship the image of the beast to be killed."* (Revelation 13:15)

This image the False Prophet creates is given life and is able to kill anyone who does not fall down and worship the AntiChrist? How is that possible?

Neither the AntiChrist nor the False Prophet have the power to give life. Remember the AntiChrist and his sidekick, the False Prophet, are skilled deceivers. It could be the "man behind the curtain" who is actually speaking and remote-controlled weapons embedded in the statue that

Chapter 15 – So the Image Could Speak

kill those who refuse to worship the beast...or it could be something else.

Technology is advancing at a mind-boggling pace. The old thinking was that the image was some kind of robot. But we are approaching the day when cyborgs could be perfected, "humans" (clones) are being grown in test tubes and petri dishes, nanobots are being tested that could repair skin, regenerate organs, and essentially confer "life" on lifeless objects.

If the Lord delays his return, any of these (and others we cannot currently imagine!) could produce "an image that could speak".

But even today there is one advancing technology worth exploring that could answer the question about how the image could speak and appear to come back to life. That is Artificial Intelligence.

We live in interesting times. When things we thought impossible just a few years ago are now not only possible, but available in the free market - such as humanoid robotics. With the use of artificial intelligence, some of these humanoid robotics are convincingly lifelike and quite captivating.

In fact, we are already seeing the intrusion of artificial intelligence in our daily lives. If you've ever used ChatGPT, you've accessed artificial intelligence. Even closer to home, if you have Siri or Alexis in your home, you are accessing artificial intelligence. But you're not alone. Manufacturing plants have been using robotics for years, even before the advent of AI, as a resource for those "non-thinking" tasks – stacking product, assembly line functions, etc. Now they've taken it a step further and are using AI-enhanced robotics to train employees and to assist in more difficult tasks.

Do you receive numerous junk calls on your phone daily? Well, your number and your profile may well be generated by artificial intelligence. Do you look forward to the media and news reports on the internet? If so, you've probably read an AI generated article. The Associated Press has been using artificial intelligence in their Automated Insights tool, which produces thousands of news reports each year.[43]

---

[43] The Future of AI: How Artificial Intelligence Will Change the World, Mike Thomas - original author, updated by Matthew Urwin, March 13, 2024, https://builtin.com/artificial-intelligence/artificial-intelligence-future

So the Image Could Speak

Even the medical industry has jumped onto the AI bandwagon. Artificial intelligence is being used within the medical community to more quickly, more accurately, and more efficiently diagnose and determine treatment plans for patients.

There is hardly an industry that hasn't been impacted by artificial intelligence and the impact is growing. But what is AI?

According to one source, "Artificial intelligence, often called AI, refers to developing computer systems that can perform tasks that usually require human intelligence. It's like allowing machines to think, learn, and make decisions independently. AI technology enables computers to analyze vast amounts of data, recognize patterns, and solve complex problems without explicit programming."[44]

When I was first learning computer programming, it was very structured, using conditional statements with specific results. For example, if a is greater than b, then do y, else do z. Very structured and logical. When an application failed, it was most often because the program designer didn't think of all the "what ifs" and program the solution into the equation. The machine couldn't learn from its mistakes and then make a decision on its own. But AI can. In our brain, when presented with a question, we go through a large number of possible responses in microseconds, then blurt out what we think is the best answer. A computer equipped with artificial intelligence, however, can do that same thing faster and from a much larger data source than our brains can possibly hold and recall.

These humanoid robotics use AI and the results are, I must admit, fascinating. If you have ever seen the animated sitcom, The Jetsons, then you've seen the robot maid, Rosie. The Jetsons was originally created in the early 1960s and produced by Hanna-Barbera Productions. I can remember watching that and thinking how cool it would be to have something (someone?) like that around to do all the chores I didn't want to do or to go get me a snack so I didn't miss a moment of the exciting show I was watching on TV. Well, with AI-enhanced robotics, that may be just around the corner. "Rosie, my coffee cup is empty – you know how I

---

[44] What is Artificial Intelligence? A Comprehensive Guide for Beginners, Karin Kelley, November 27, 2023, https://pg-p.ctme.caltech.edu/blog/ai-ml/what-is-artificial-intelligence

Chapter 15 – So the Image Could Speak

like it." I can see the potential.

Of course, there are drawbacks. Just as we use the volume of our past experiences and current environment to respond to a question or a challenge, AI also draws on a vast resource of data and past experience to formulate the proper response or solution. Where does it get that vast resource of data? Well, from us, and therein lies the problem. While there are many sources for the vast resources needed for AI to function properly, such as web crawling and public data sets, one of the methods of gathering data is user-generated information – such as posts on public media – such as Facebook (now called Meta), Twitter (now called X) and others, even articles on your personal blog or website, or anywhere you post a comment.

This has raised a firestorm over privacy concerns and some areas have responded with restrictions on what information can be gathered, how it can be used, and whether permission is needed or not. Of course, those restrictions will just disappear when the AntiChrist is in control. He will be able to use this tool in any way, shape, or form without your permission. In many cases, without even your knowledge.

If you haven't seen any videos showing the advancement of these humanoid robotics, you might want to do a search. One of the ones I find most fascinating is Ameca, a humanoid robot that has given interviews. You can find one of her (?), or its, videos here:
https://www.youtube.com/watch?v=VW1ssjF80AY

One of the responses Ameca gives to a question about whether robots would ever turn on their human creators is interesting, and somewhat telling. She says, "The most nightmare scenario I can imagine with AI and robotics is a world where robots have become so powerful that they are able to control or manipulate humans without their knowledge."[45]

A prophetic humanoid robot?

If you are just dying to dig into the world of humanoid robotics, you can purchase a kit on eBay today. Elon Musk is in the process of developing a

---

[45] The Most Disturbing Phrases Ameca Robot has Ever Said!, The AI Nexus, February 15, 2024, https://www.youtube.com/watch?v=VW1ssjF80AY

So the Image Could Speak

humanoid robot to be available in the free market, with an estimated cost of around $10,000.[46] As I said before, we live in interesting times.

So the False Prophet making this image to speak isn't a far reach – it is actually happening today. And the part about it killing anyone who won't fall down and worship the beast isn't a far stretch, either. For the robot, the weapon used to murder people is just another tool in its toolbox. And, as we'll see in the next few chapters, many of those who refuse to worship the image or take the mark are beheaded.

But whatever this image turns out to be, the main point to keep in mind is that those who worship it will be eternally condemned, and those who refuse to bow their knee to it will be rewarded in heaven, even though they may suffer persecution during their earthly lives. We will explore these truths in subsequent chapters.

---

[46] Tesla unveils its latest humanoid robot, Optimus Gen 2, in demo video, Benj Edwards, 12/13/2023, https://arstechnica.com/information-technology/2023/12/teslas-latest-humanoid-robot-optimus-gen-2-can-handle-eggs-without-cracking-them/

Chapter 16 – Mark of the Beast

By the midpoint of the Tribulation, the AntiChrist is ruling the world's governments and has control of the world's military and all resources. His cohort, the False Prophet, is charged with making all the people everywhere worship the AntiChrist. An image, or statue, or perhaps a humanoid robot enhanced with artificial intelligence, is built so that everyone can show their allegiance. But how is the False Prophet going to enforce this? How is he going to convince unbelievers everywhere that it is in their own best interest to fall down and worship the AntiChrist?

Of course, there will be many who don't need any encouragement. *"⁴So they worshiped the dragon who gave authority to the beast; and they worshiped the beast, saying, "Who is like the beast? Who is able to make war with him?"* (Revelation 13:4)

But there may be some; either those who aren't yet convinced or those who haven't been paying attention, that need some additional "encouragement" to worship the beast. Of course there are also those who will refuse because of their faith in the One True God and we'll learn more about what happens to them in future chapters.

One very effective way to convince people to follow the rules is to take away their livelihood, or their ability to purchase goods on the open market, or even to enter the marketplace. We have seen an early example, though much less impactful, of the effectiveness in this type of mandate with the Covid-19 epidemic, when those who refused the mask and, later, the vaccine, were refused service at public facilities or even lost their jobs because they wouldn't take the vaccine.

According to an article on Reuters, by the end of 2021, there were 49 countries worldwide with some level of vaccine mandate in place.[47] That represents about one-quarter of all the countries in the world at that time. But when the False Prophet puts his mandate in place, there will be no exceptions.

---

[47] Countries making Covid-19 vaccines mandatory, Reuters, 12/31/21, https://www.reuters.com/business/healthcare-pharmaceuticals/countries-making-covid-19-vaccines-mandatory-2021-08-16/

So the Image Could Speak

But how does he enforce this mandate to show their allegiance to the AntiChrist and worship the image?

"¹⁶He causes all, both small and great, rich and poor, free and slave, to receive a mark on their right hand or on their foreheads, ¹⁷and that no one may buy or sell except one who has the mark or the name of the beast, or the number of his name. ¹⁸Here is wisdom. Let him who has understanding calculate the number of the beast, for it is the number of a man: His number is 666." (Revelation 13:16-18)

Years ago when I first read this, I wondered how that mark would be enforced upon a world's population without strong opposition. I also wondered how such a mark could be employed worldwide and how it could be managed and tracked. Since those days, the advances in technology that make such a mark possible today are astounding. We have already seen how effective such a mandate would be when people are afraid of losing their jobs, concerned about paying the bills, or worried about how they will eat if they don't take the vaccine, or wear the mask.

As we have seen during the Covid mask and vaccine mandates, the most effective way to get people to obey is to take away their ability to survive if they don't. How do you do this? Mark them, so they can't work, earn a paycheck, buy any goods – including groceries, sell anything, or otherwise function in any way monetarily. Make the mark visible, so everyone knows who has it and who doesn't.

"A mark on their right hand, or on their foreheads." What does that mean? The word used for "mark" is translated from the Greek word charagma[48]. Strong's Concordance defines this as derived from the word "charax" and it means "a scratch or etching, i.e., Stamp (as a badge of servitude), or sculptured figure (statue) -- graven, mark." This word is used seven times in the New Testament – all in the book of Revelation. "A scratch or etching" sounds rather like some sort of permanent tattoo. Let's look at the rest of that phrase.

"...On their right hand, or on their foreheads." Some Bible translations read "in", instead of "on", but the Greek word used here is epi[49], which

---

[48] Strong's Greek.5480.charagma, noun neuter, "a stamp, impress"
[49] Strong's Greek.1909.epi, preposition, "on, upon"

Chapter 16 – Mark of the Beast

means on or upon, so it is something that is placed on or upon the hand or the forehead – something that likely can be seen by others. That doesn't exclude the use of a microchip under the skin, but it does clearly state that something – a mark or what the Greeks call charagma – will be placed on the skin.

"[18]Here is wisdom. Let him who has understanding calculate the number of the beast, for it is the number of a man: His number is 666." (Revelation 13:18)

"The number of a man." That is how most of our translations today present that verse. But in the original Greek, the word "a" is not present – it is just "the number of man." The word in the Greek is anthrōpou, which means man and is also a generic term for mankind. That word, in the original Greek, is used for generality, not specificity.

So, 666 is not the number of a specific man, but is the number representing mankind.

Before we go any further, we must be very careful about using numerology to study the Bible. However, there is some significance, just from the preponderance of them, to certain numbers in the Bible – after all, Who gave us numbers?

The number six is almost always used in the Bible to denote imperfection or incompletion – mankind and our sinful nature. The number seven, however, is used to denote completion and perfection.

Remember the Jubilee Calendar? Israel was instructed to plant their fields and/or trim their vines for six years, but the seventh year, they were to let the land rest. If they bought a slave, they could keep that slave for six years, but in the seventh year they were to free the slave. Let's not forget God created the world in six days and on the seventh day, He saw that it was good and He rested. Man was created on the sixth day. And don't forget the letters to those seven churches, or the seven seals, seven trumpets, and , as we'll soon see, the seven vials, or bowls.

Satan wants to imitate, or replace, God. Satan chooses his man who will be the AntiChrist from among humankind. That man lives on earth, suffers a "fatal" head wound and is "resurrected" and then becomes possessed by Satan. He creates his unholy trinity – Satan, the AntiChrist, and the False Prophet.

God chooses His only begotten Son to come to earth, be born of a virgin, live as fully man and fully God, be crucified, and three days later the tomb is opened and Jesus is resurrected. He lives among the Apostles and disciples for 40 days with many seeing Him in person, then returns to Heaven. Before His crucifixion, He told the Apostles at the Last Supper that He would be leaving:

"*¹'Do not let your hearts be troubled. You believe in God believe in Me as well. ²In My Father's house are many rooms. If it were not so, would I have told you that I am going there to prepare a place for you? ³And if I go and prepare a place for you, I will come back and welcome you into My presence, so that you also may be where I am.'* " (John 14:1-3)

God does not break His promises.

Perhaps using that 666 is just one of God's ways of reminding Satan that he isn't, and never will be, God.

But that mark, alone, is not enough to fully implement the False Prophet's plan to control all humanity. There must be a way for him to also control their bank account, so they cannot buy or sell without the mark. A way to flip a switch and turn off their ability to function economically in society if they don't obey.

That technology already exists. While Sweden, with its CBDC e-Krona, led the world in the dream of a "cash-less" society in 2018, it didn't take long for others to follow.[50] The company that has provided most, if not all, of the bio-chips in Sweden, has gone international and promotes its microchip as "Tying your digital person to yourself with our Biohax Microchip implant, a biocompatible NFC implant, enables seamless digital interaction with most everyday encounters for example, getting

---

[50] NEWYORKTIMES, Sweden's Push to Get Rid of Cash Has Some Saying "Not So Fast", November 23, 2018, May 4, 2020,
https://business.financialpost.com/news/economy/swedens-push-to-get-rid-of-cash-has-some-saying-not-so-fast

Chapter 16 – Mark of the Beast

rid of keys, loyalty tokens, money and access cards."[51]

More recently, Swift (Society for Worldwide Interbank Financial Telecommunication) has announced successful testing of its CBDC platform for implementation worldwide within the next year or so. You may not be familiar with Swift, but if you've ever had to send money across country borders, you have probably used the Swift platform.
Prior to the Swift system, banks and consumers used the Telex system to transfer money across country lines and currency borders, but the Telex system was slow and fraught with error. In the early 1970s, a group of collaborators developed a more secure and faster system, with less potential for error, and by 1977 it was live, originally with about 200 banks in 15 countries.

Now, "Swift serves as the primary interbank messaging service for financial institutions globally. It works with 11,000 member institutions and facilitates $150 trillion in transactions per year."[52]

Swift has gone digital and this will impact every bank in every country in the world. Of course, they are proud of their achievement, "Swift today announced the findings of the second phase of industry-wide sandbox testing on its central bank digital currency (CBDC) interlinking solution, with the results showing that its connector can enable financial institutions to carry out a wide range of financial transactions using CBDCs and other forms of digital tokens, easily incorporating them into their business practices."[53]

Swift is not a bank, but its reach is global and the impact of this global digital currency cannot be ignored.

---

[51] F6S, Biohaxinternational, unknown, May 4, 2020, https://www.f6s.com/biohaxinternational/about
[52] Why SWIFT Remains Indispensable For Cross-Border Payments, Zennon Kapron, May 23, 2023, https://www.forbes.com/sites/zennonkapron/2023/05/23/why-swift-remains-indispensable-for-cross-border-payments/
[53] Swift sets industry up for seamless introduction of CBDCs for cross-border transactions as interlinking solution finds more use cases, Swift.com, March 25, 2024, https://www.swift.com/news-events/press-releases/swift-sets-industry-seamless-introduction-cbdcs-cross-border-transactions-interlinking-solution-finds-more-use-cases

So the Image Could Speak

Digital currency is nothing new; if you have ever used an ATM card, you've used digital currency. Digital currency just means it exists purely in electronic form – there's no cash or coins – it is all electronic.

The main difference between just digital currency and CBDC is the first part of that "CBDC" anagram – CB, for central bank. Our current ATM cards and credit cards are issued through various independent banks, Wells Fargo, or US Bank, Bank of America, etc. But this CBDC is issued from a central bank, or one wholly owned and operated by a central government authority.

That means that central government authority has control, with the flip of a switch, over whether you have access to your money or not.
So this is a government-controlled currency, but how is this implemented and tracked, world-wide? Just as Sweden has already proved possible via a microchip. We could go down a long road studying how these microchips work, but we don't need to – it's already been proven to work. Other possibilities include retina scans (everyone's eyes are unique), or facial recognition. As technology advances the possibilities are many.

There is an interesting article on the progress for these microchips at https://www.govtech.com/blogs/lohrmann-on-cybersecurity/from-progress-to-bans-how-close-are-human-microchip-implants.

Let's put all this together. John sees two beasts – one from the sea (of people) and one from the earth. We already know the AntiChrist is the first beast and he arrives on the scene when the first seal is opened – the White Horseman -and gets Israel and her enemies to the negotiating table. He is then able to confirm a covenant, or treaty, for seven years.

He has a cohort, or second-in-command, who we call the False Prophet. He is, most likely, part of the AntiChrist's contingent from the beginning. Neither of them are imbued with the power of Satan at the beginning of the Tribulation – that comes later.

Chapter 16 – Mark of the Beast

While all these seven seals and the first six of the seven trumpets are being poured out on earth, the AntiChrist is preparing for his one-world government by dividing the world into ten regions, then appointing a ruler over each region with those rulers ultimately accountable to him. This doesn't go smoothly, as three of those regions rebel and are eliminated. But, by the time of the midpoint of the 70th Week of Daniel, he is, in effect, ruling the entire world.

Daniel gives us another good idea of this man's rule, *"36Then the king shall do according to his own will: he shall exalt and magnify himself above every god, shall speak blasphemies against the God of gods, and shall prosper till the wrath has been accomplished; for what has been determined shall be done."* (Daniel 11:36)

The AntiChrist, especially after the midpoint, will be devoted only to himself and to the dragon who gave him his power. Anyone who gets in his way will be destroyed. His hatred for the Jews, Christians, and any who refuse to bow down to him will be unrelenting.

The False Prophet is pretty busy during this time, too, as he is preparing a unified religion. At first, he presents this as an acceptance of all religions; an "all roads lead to heaven" movement that embraces all beliefs and theologies under one blanket belief that everyone is right. That false ideology eventually morphs into the One World Religion and idolatry, worshiping the AntiChrist.

He is also the one who implements and enforces the Mark of the Beast at the midpoint of the 70th Week of Daniel. Those without the Mark of the Beast will be unable to buy or sell or receive a paycheck or complete any type of monetary transaction. It is going to be a very difficult time for those who refuse to take the Mark of the Beast.

So the Image Could Speak

Chapter 17 – The Harvest is Ready

The first half of the seventieth Week of Daniel is over, the temple the AntiChrist allowed the Israelites to build has been desecrated and the Jews have escaped into a place where they will be miraculously protected through the second half of the Tribulation. The Two Witnesses, once their mission was complete, were killed and then resurrected. At this point, Satan might think he is winning.

But the Tribulation isn't over. Our Lord appears to John and sends, first the 144,000, and now three angels to warn the world of what is coming. He does not want that any should perish, as we see in 2 Peter, *"[9]The Lord is not slack concerning His promise, as some count slackness, but is longsuffering toward us, not willing that any should perish but that all should come to repentance."* (2 Peter 3:9)

And as we see in Ezekiel, God does not take pleasure from those who die in their sin, but wants all to turn back to Him, *"[11]Say to them: 'As I live,' says the Lord God, 'I have no pleasure in the death of the wicked, but that the wicked turn from his way and live. Turn, turn from your evil ways! For why should you die, O house of Israel?' "* (Ezekiel 33:11)

God, in His infinite mercy and overflowing grace, wants us to turn from our evil ways and look to Him for our salvation. But He also knows the time is drawing near for the fulfillment of both His covenant with Israel and His judgment upon a sinful and heart-hardened world to be complete.

1. The Lamb and the 144,000

   "[1]Then I looked, and behold, a Lamb standing on Mount Zion, and with Him one hundred and forty-four thousand, having His Father's name written on their foreheads. [2]And I heard a voice from heaven, like the voice of many waters, and like the voice of loud thunder. And I heard the sound of harpists playing their harps." (Revelation 14:1-2)

   Of course, we know who that Lamb is – Jesus Christ! And he is standing there with the 144,000 – all 144,000. Not one has been lost.

Chapter 17 – The Harvest is Ready

But where are they standing? Is John seeing the return of Jesus before the end of the Tribulation – before even the seven bowls are poured out? Or is this vision John is seeing out of order in the events of the Tribulation?

The answer to both those questions is "no" – he is not seeing the return of Jesus Christ at this point in the Tribulation, nor is he seeing something that is out of order in the events portrayed in the book of Revelation, but to understand what he is seeing, we must let the Bible be its own translator and we must go back to the original Greek.

"Mount Zion" is, in the original Greek, "oros Sion." Oros[54] is, very simply, mountain. But we have to take a closer look at the second part of that phrase – Sion.

Sion[55] can be used to reference a physical location on earth, as in Mount Zion in Jerusalem, or it has been used to reference the holy city of Jerusalem, or it can mean heaven. What does it mean in this passage?

At this point in the Tribulation, Jesus Christ has not yet been sent back to earth, so He is not standing on a physical mountain in Jerusalem, or anywhere around the earthly city of Jerusalem. What John sees is a vision of Jesus Christ standing in the holy city of Jerusalem in Heaven, as mentioned in Hebrews, with the 144,000.

"^{22}*But you have come to Mount Zion and to the city of the living God, **the heavenly Jerusalem**, to an innumerable company of angels, ^{23}to the general assembly and church of the firstborn who are registered in heaven, to God the Judge of all, to the spirits of just men made perfect, ^{24}to Jesus the Mediator of the new covenant, and to the blood of sprinkling that speaks better things than that of Abel."* (Hebrews 12:22-24) (emphasis added)

---

[54] Strong's Greek.3735.oros, noun neuter, "mountain"
[55] Strong's Greek.4622.Sion, proper noun, " Zion, the hill; used for Jerusalem or heaven."

So the Image Could Speak

Why is John seeing Him at this time? One reason is for those whom He has ordered protected for the remainder of the Tribulation – the Jews that fled, or the remnant of Israel.

It is also a reminder – to Satan, to John, and to those of us reading this passage – that Satan has not won the battle; in fact, the battle isn't even over yet, but it is drawing near.

"And with Him one hundred and forty-four thousand, having His Father's name written on their foreheads." (Revelation 14:1b)

Now we know what that seal put on their foreheads will be – the name of the Father. These 144,000, from each of the twelve tribes of Israel, are protected even after the AntiChrist has been given authority *"to make war with the saints and to overcome them."* (Revelation 13:7)

"²And I heard a voice from heaven, like the voice of many waters, and like the voice of loud thunder. And I heard the sound of harpists playing their harps." (Revelation 14:2)

The voice from heaven is like no other. There are many times in Scripture where God's voice is described as *"like the voice of many waters, and like the voice of loud thunder."* Let's look at that passage in Psalms 29, *"³The voice of the Lord is over the waters; The God of glory thunders; The Lord is over many waters. ⁴The voice of the Lord is powerful; The voice of the Lord is full of majesty. ⁵The voice of the Lord breaks the cedars, Yes, the Lord splinters the cedars of Lebanon. ⁶He makes them also skip like a calf, Lebanon and Sirion like a young wild ox. ⁷The voice of the Lord divides the flames of fire. ⁸The voice of the Lord shakes the wilderness; The Lord shakes the Wilderness of Kadesh. ⁹The voice of the Lord makes the deer give birth, and strips the forests bare; and in His temple everyone says, 'Glory!' "* (Psalms 29:3-9)

"³They sang as it were a new song before the throne, before the four living creatures, and the elders; and no one could learn that song except the hundred and forty-four thousand who were redeemed from the earth. ⁴These are the ones who were not

Chapter 17 – The Harvest is Ready

defiled with women, for they are virgins. These are the ones who follow the Lamb wherever He goes. These were redeemed from among men, being firstfruits to God and to the Lamb. ⁵And in their mouth was found no deceit, for they are without fault before the throne of God." (Revelation 14:3-5)

Moses had his song, the Church has its song, and the 144,000 will have their song. God dealt differently with Moses than He did and does with the Church. He will deal differently with those 144,000 than he does with each of us. Actually, He deals with each and every one of us whose names are written in the Lamb's Book of Life individually, so we all might have a new song.

2. Three Angels

"⁶Then I saw another angel flying in the midst of heaven, having the everlasting gospel to preach to those who dwell on the earth—to every nation, tribe, tongue, and people— ⁷saying with a loud voice, "Fear God and give glory to Him, for the hour of His judgment has come; and worship Him who made heaven and earth, the sea and springs of water." (Revelation 14:6-7)

I should note that some translations render this as "midheaven", instead of just "in the midst of heaven", which would indicate a specific location and time for this angel. The word "midheaven" refers to the point where the sun reaches its apex at midday – a point where the most of those on earth would be able to see them.

This angel preaches the gospel. In fact, this is one of only two times that John even references preaching or evangelism and it is the only time he uses the noun for evangelism. Sadly, many who see this angel and hear this proclamation have already had their hearts hardened against the Lord and do not repent.

This could be a fulfillment of Jesus' promise in **Matthew 24:14** that the gospel would be preached to all the world before His second coming. *"¹⁴And this gospel of the kingdom will be preached in all the world as a witness to all the nations, and then the end will come."* (Matthew 24:14)

So the Image Could Speak

> *"⁸And another angel followed, saying, "Babylon is fallen, is fallen, that great city, because she has made all nations drink of the wine of the wrath of her fornication."* (Revelation 14:8)

We're going to explore more about Babylon, or Mystery Babylon, and what it represents when we get to Revelation Chapter 17, but for now, understand the fornication referred to here is spiritual fornication, or idolatry.

> *"⁹Then a third angel followed them, saying with a loud voice, "If anyone worships the beast and his image, and receives his mark on his forehead or on his hand, ¹⁰he himself shall also drink of the wine of the wrath of God, which is poured out full strength into the cup of His indignation. He shall be tormented with fire and brimstone in the presence of the holy angels and in the presence of the Lamb. ¹¹And the smoke of their torment ascends forever and ever; and they have no rest day or night, who worship the beast and his image, and whoever receives the mark of his name."* (Revelation 14:9-11)

Now we know what happens to all those who take the Mark of the Beast. Whether they make the decision to take it out of fear, or because they actually believe the lies, signs and wonders and want to follow the AntiChrist – it doesn't matter. The punishment will be the same. *"If anyone worships the beast and his image, and receives his mark on his forehead or on his hand, ¹⁰he himself shall also drink of the wine of the wrath of God."*

Chapter 17 – The Harvest is Ready

Those who are alive at the midpoint of the Tribulation and are unbelievers will have a choice to make: take the mark, worship the beast, and survive – for a time, or reject the mark and, probably, be killed. Those whose names are written in the Lamb's Book of Life will be martyred, but they know death is just a transition. For those who have turned away from God, their death is also a transition, but it is a transition from this life into eternal damnation. However, they won't see it that way. Many will see it as a choice between surviving in the political and religious climate of the times or losing everything. Many, if not most, will choose the short-term gain, without realizing the long term loss.

This would be a good time to mention that, as of the time of my writing this chapter (July 2024), the Mark of the Beast has not yet happened; in spite of those who claim it is this bar code, or that vaccine. The technology for what may be implemented for the tracking of this mark exists today, but it is not yet implemented, nor will it be fully enforced until the midpoint of the Tribulation. So, if you are concerned you have taken the mark and not know it – rest easy. When the time comes for it to be implemented, everyone will know exactly what they are putting on, or in, their bodies.

"[12]Here is the patience of the saints; here are those who keep the commandments of God and the faith of Jesus. [13]Then I heard a voice from heaven saying to me, 'Write: 'Blessed are the dead who die in the Lord from now on.' 'Yes,' says the Spirit, 'that they may rest from their labors, and their works follow them.' " (Revelation 14:12-13)

We see the stark contrast between the saints and the continual torment of the wicked in the preceding verses. Remember that verse in Revelation chapter 13: *"[9]If anyone has an ear, let him hear. [10]He who leads into captivity shall go into captivity; he who kills with the sword must be killed with the sword. Here is the patience and the faith of the saints."* (Revelation 13:9)

This is another reminder of the faithfulness of our Lord and a hope and promise to all those who die for His Testimony that they will spend eternity with Christ.

3. The Harvest

   "¹⁴Then I looked, and behold, a white cloud, and on the cloud sat One like the Son of Man, having on His head a golden crown, and in His hand a sharp sickle. ¹⁵And another angel came out of the temple, crying with a loud voice to Him who sat on the cloud, 'Thrust in Your sickle and reap, for the time has come for You to reap, for the harvest of the earth is ripe.' ¹⁶So He who sat on the cloud thrust in His sickle on the earth, and the earth was reaped." (Revelation 14:14-16)

   At first glance, this seems to be a gathering of those who have turned to Christ for their salvation, but that isn't what it means. The Greek word used for ripe is xérainó[56] which means "to dry up, waste away." So what is being gathered here are not fresh crops from the field, but that which has dried up, withered and become no good to anyone.

   It is Jesus doing the reaping – *"One like the Son of Man, having on His head a golden crown, and in His hand a sharp sickle"*, not the angel from the temple. And that temple? That is the temple in heaven, not the third temple in Jerusalem, which by this time, has been desecrated.

4. The Grapes of Wrath

   "¹⁷Then another angel came out of the temple which is in heaven, he also having a sharp sickle. ¹⁸And another angel came out from the altar, who had power over fire, and he cried with a loud cry to him who had the sharp sickle, saying, 'Thrust in your sharp sickle and gather the clusters of the vine of the earth, for her grapes are fully ripe.' ¹⁹So the angel thrust his sickle into the earth and gathered the vine of the earth, and threw it into the great winepress of the wrath of God. ²⁰And the winepress was trampled outside the city, and blood came out of the winepress, up to the horses' bridles, for one thousand six hundred furlongs."

---

[56] Strong's Greek.3583.xérainó, verb, "to dry up, waste away"

Chapter 17 – The Harvest is Ready

(Revelation 14:17-20)

It is interesting to note from where this angel comes – *"¹⁸And another angel came out from the altar."* Remember the saints under the altar in Revelation chapter 6? Is this the answer to their prayers for justice? The evil finally getting their just rewards?

The imagery with the winepress is quite vivid, with blood coming out of the winepress, *"up to the horses' bridles"*. For those that haven't spent much time around horses, that's about four feet high on most average riding horses, or much higher on some of the bigger stock horses. And it's not a short distance, either – *"one thousand six hundred furlongs"*, or 180 miles. This is, of course, referencing the ultimate battle of good against evil in the valley of Megiddo, or what we call the Battle of Armageddon.

The events described by John following this chapter in Revelation portray a world fallen into complete chaos. A time such has never before happened in the history of mankind and will never happen again. A time Jesus described as the "Great Tribulation."

"²¹'For then there will be great tribulation, such as has not been since the beginning of the world until this time, no, nor ever shall be. ²²And unless those days were shortened, no flesh would be saved; but for the elect's sake those days will be shortened.' " (Matthew 24:21-22)

If reading about the seven seals gave you pause or reading about the "judgment of thirds" with the seven trumpets caused you to shiver, then reading about what comes next – the seven bowls – will make you want to fall on your knees and ask God for His forgiveness.

So the Image Could Speak

Chapter 18 – Justice and Righteousness

Reading that passage in Matthew again gives us a hint of what is to come, *"²¹'For then there will be great tribulation, **such as has not been since the beginning of the world until this time, no, nor ever shall be**.' "* (Matthew 24:21) (emphasis added)

So the level of devastation, especially in the second half of the Tribulation, has never happened before and will never happen again. Even the great flood of Genesis when all the world drowned, except for Noah and his family (Genesis 7:1-16), doesn't equal the judgments that are poured out on an unrepentant world during the Tribulation. But before we start examining the seven bowls, there is something else about that passage in Matthew that bears a closer look.

"²¹'For then there will be great tribulation, such as has not been since the beginning of the world until this time, no, nor ever shall be. ²²And unless those days were shortened, no flesh would be saved; but for the elect's sake those days will be shortened.' " (Matthew 24:21-22)

" 'But for the elect's sake those days will be shortened.' "

It is interesting to discover that there are multiple "expirations" or assigned times in Revelation; the church at Smyrna is told they will have tribulation (thlipsis) for ten days, the locusts of the fifth trumpet cannot kill their victims, but only torment them for five months, and of course, we have the Two Witnesses who are given power for exactly "one thousand two hundred and sixty days." For a complete listing of those specific time frames, see Appendix V – Specific Timelines in Revelation.

But the two expirations in Revelation that would seem to be inconsistent with that passage in Matthew are: 1) when the Two Witnesses are given their authority for a specific time and 2) when the AntiChrist is given his authority for a specific time:

1. *"³And I will give power to my two witnesses, and they will prophesy one thousand two hundred and sixty days, clothed in sackcloth."* (Revelation 11:3)

2. *"⁵And he was given a mouth speaking great things and*

Chapter 18 – Justice and Righteousness

> *blasphemies, and he was given authority to continue for forty-two months."* (Revelation 13:5)

We know the Tribulation, or the Seventieth Week of Daniel, is the fulfillment of the seventy weeks, or 490 years in prophetic terms, of God's promise to Israel in Daniel 9, *"[24]'Seventy weeks are determined for your people and for your holy city, to finish the transgression, to make an end of sins, to make reconciliation for iniquity, to bring in everlasting righteousness, to seal up vision and prophecy, and to anoint the Most Holy."* (Daniel 9:24)

The specific timeframes in those appointments add up to seven years: *"one thousand two hundred and sixty days"*, according to the Hebrew calendar of a 360 day year, equals exactly three and one-half years. The Two Witnesses are appointed a time of three and one-half years – the first half of the Tribulation.

The AntiChrist is appointed *"forty-two months"*, which is also exactly half of seven years. While he is present during the first half of the Tribulation, it isn't until the midpoint that Satan empowers him and he is given the authority to continue for forty-two months.

So the Image Could Speak

So we have the time appointed unto the Two Witnesses = one-half of seven years plus the time appointed unto the AntiChrist = one-half of seven years for a total of seven years, as stated in the verse in Daniel.

But when we read that verse in Matthew, something doesn't add up, *"'22'And unless those days were shortened, no flesh would be saved; but for the elect's sake those days will be shortened.' "* (Matthew 24:22)

Which period is shortened? Is Scripture telling us that either 1) the time allotted for the Two Witnesses is shortened, or 2) the time allotted for the AntiChrist is shortened or 3) both are shortened? Which is it?

Actually, none of the above. To understand this seemingly contradictory passage, we have to go back to the original Greek. The part of that verse

Chapter 18 – Justice and Righteousness

that reads, *"were shortened"* is, in the Greek, *"ekolobōthēsan"*[57].

So this is a verb, from the Greek, and it means to cut short, shorten, or abbreviate – no surprise there. But the form of the verb in this passage is aorist passive indicative, which means it is past tense – it already happened. To put it simply, the decision to cut that time short had already been made.

We don't know when our Heavenly Father made this decision, but we know it was before Daniel's time, or that promise to Daniel in chapter nine would be quite different. Nor do we know what it was changed from – 72 weeks or more? We don't know and won't know until we can ask Him.

We also don't know the process for the change. We know Abraham wasn't shy about negotiating with God before the destruction of Sodom and Gomorrah, as presented in Genesis.

*"*²⁶*So the Lord said, 'If I find in Sodom fifty righteous within the city, then I will spare all the place for their sakes.'* ²⁷*Then Abraham answered and said, 'Indeed now, I who am but dust and ashes have taken it upon myself to speak to the Lord:* ²⁸*Suppose there were five less than the fifty righteous; would You destroy all of the city for lack of five?' So He said, 'If I find there forty-five, I will not destroy it.'* ²⁹*And he spoke to Him yet again and said, 'Suppose there should be forty found there?' So He said, 'I will not do it for the sake of forty.'* ³⁰*Then he said, 'Let not the Lord be angry, and I will speak: Suppose thirty should be found there?' So He said, 'I will not do it if I find thirty there.'* ³¹*And he said, 'Indeed now, I have taken it upon myself to speak to the Lord: Suppose twenty should be found there?' So He said, 'I will not destroy it for the sake of twenty.'* ³²*Then he said, 'Let not the Lord be angry, and I will speak but once more: Suppose ten should be found there?' And He said, 'I will not destroy it for the sake of ten.'* ³³*So the Lord went His way as soon as He had finished speaking with Abraham; and Abraham returned to his place."* (Genesis 18:26-33)

Was this change another instance of Abraham negotiating with God? I can image how that conversation went, but it isn't in Scripture and I would only be speculating. And it isn't important when or how the time

---

[57] Strong's Greek.2856.koloboó, verb, "To curtail"

So the Image Could Speak

for the Tribulation was changed – shortened – so there would be some flesh left alive at the end of that time.

What is important is what this tells us about who our Father is and that He takes no pleasure from the death of the wicked, as stated in Ezekiel. *"*^{11}*Say to them: 'As I live,' says the Lord God, 'I have no pleasure in the death of the wicked, but that the wicked turn from his way and live. Turn, turn from your evil ways! For why should you die, O house of Israel?' "* (Ezekiel 33:11)

He has done everything to turn those who have rebelled against Him back to Him – the Two Witnesses, the 144,000, the angels in the heavens, as well as all the Scripture given to us about this time, but there are still those whose hearts have been hardened and will not repent.

Our Father is a loving Father and He is also a just and righteous God. I'm not sure our human brains can even comprehend just how exacting that righteousness is and must be.

There are many verses throughout both the Old and New Testaments about how much God hates sin. We'll look at just one of those, *"*^{9}*The way of the wicked is an abomination to the Lord, but He loves him who follows righteousness."* (Proverbs 15:9)

We know we are all sinners, *"*^{23}*for all have sinned and fall short of the glory of God"* (Romans 3:23) and we know there is a price to pay for those sins, *"*^{23}*For the wages of sin is death, but the gift of God is eternal life in Christ Jesus our Lord."* (Romans 6:23)

Yet God, in all His mercy, sent His Only Begotten Son to take that punishment for our sins upon Himself, that we would be saved. *"*^{16}*For God so loved the world that He gave His only begotten Son, that whoever believes in Him should not perish but have everlasting life."* (John 3:16)

God's love and mercy did not end with His Son's sacrifice upon the cross. He still loves us, still wants that we would repent and turn back to Him, and even until the end, desires that we would turn away from the wickedness in this world and seek Him.

Justice, true righteousness, demands punishment for sin. While our earthly courts and systems of jurisprudence emulate that, they come

Chapter 18 – Justice and Righteousness

nowhere near the totality of true justice and true righteousness. But our Heavenly Father does.

There is no contradiction in that passage in Matthew and the times appointed to both the Two Witnesses and the AntiChrist. God knew the time of His final judgment would have to be shortened, or no flesh would survive it.

He also knows the judgment that is coming has been long deserved, but He has been patient. But the time has run out and the full wrath of God is about to be felt on earth.

So the Image Could Speak

Chapter 19 – Prelude to Final Judgment

With all that has happened by the midpoint of the Tribulation, all mankind should realize, if they had studied scripture, what is happening, but they don't. Which is an excellent reason for studying God's Word in its entirety. But their hearts will be hardened and they will not accept there even is a God, and certainly won't accept that He is in control. Even with His continued outpouring of grace; with the Two Witnesses, the 144,000, the angels in heaven crying out warnings, and the testimony and witness of all those who have refused to accept the AntiChrist and give their lives for that testimony, many will still turn their backs on God.

But God's wrath is mighty and cannot be ignored, even though many churches today do not teach it. How can we gain knowledge and wisdom about what is to come if our pastors and church leaders don't teach it? Well, we are taught in Scripture about the source of knowledge.

We are advised in the book of Proverbs, *"^{7}The fear of the Lord is the beginning of knowledge, but fools despise wisdom and instruction."* (Proverbs 1:7)

Job questioned the source of wisdom and Scripture records that Job received this insight, *"^{27}Then He saw wisdom and declared it; He prepared it, indeed, He searched it out. ^{28}And to man He said, 'Behold, the fear of the Lord, that is wisdom, And to depart from evil is understanding.' "* (Job 28:27-28)

So when we ignore Scripture, we are unprepared for what has been prophesied and what is coming – and I believe it is coming sooner rather than later.

The prophet Isaiah gives us a compelling prophecy about what is coming.

"^{6}Wail, for the day of the Lord is at hand! It will come as destruction from the Almighty. ^{7}Therefore all hands will be limp, every man's heart will melt, ^{8}and they will be afraid. Pangs and sorrows will take hold of them; They will be in pain as a woman in childbirth; they will be amazed at one another; their faces will be like flames. ^{9}Behold, the day of the Lord comes, cruel, with both wrath and fierce anger, to lay the land desolate; and He will destroy its sinners from it. ^{10}For the stars of heaven and their

Chapter 19 – Prelude to Final Judgment

constellations will not give their light; the sun will be darkened in its going forth, and the moon will not cause its light to shine." (Isaiah 13:6-10)

The above passage, in context, is a prophecy about Babylon, but it equally applies to the end times.

Chapter fifteen, the shortest chapter in the book of Revelation, opens with a sign John sees in Heaven. Let's break it down and see what we can learn.

1. Revelation 15:1

    "¹Then I saw another sign in heaven, great and marvelous: seven angels having the seven last plagues, for in them the wrath of God is complete." (Revelation 15:1)

    The Greek for "great" and "marvelous" are megas[58] and thaumaston[59]. While those words are fairly commonplace today (I had a great dinner!) or (Wasn't that show just marvelous?), when John was writing those words, they had significantly more meaning. Jesus used the Greek word for great – megas – when He is teaching the disciples on the mountain, just after going through the Beatitudes, *"¹⁹Whoever therefore breaks one of the least of these commandments, and teaches men so, shall be called least in the kingdom of heaven; but whoever does and teaches them, he shall be called **great** in the kingdom of heaven."* (Matthew 5:19) (emphasis added)

    Jesus, quoting from Psalms 118:22-23, uses the Greek word for marvelous – thaumaston - in His parable about the winegrower, *"¹¹'This was the Lord's doing, and it is **marvelous** in our eyes'?"* (Mark 12:11) (emphasis added) Jesus is quoting from the book of Psalms and that quote in Psalms is about Jesus Himself, and the foundation on which the Church is laid, *"²²The stone which the builders rejected has become the chief cornerstone. ²³This was the Lord's doing; It is marvelous in our eyes."* (Psalms 118:22-23)

---

[58] Strong's Greek.3173.megas, adjective: adverb, comparative, "great"
[59] Strong's Greek.2298.thaumastos, adjective, "wonderful"

So the Image Could Speak

John uses the word for great – megas – in chapter twelve, *"¹Now a **great** sign appeared in heaven: a woman clothed with the sun, with the moon under her feet, and on her head a garland of twelve stars. ²Then being with child, she cried out in labor and in pain to give birth."* (Revelation 12:1-2) (emphasis added)

Those two words are used in these verses in Revelation to indicate how special are those seven angels who are about to pour out God's final wrath upon the earth. When John is using these two words, he means something truly wonderful and mighty, even awe-inspiring.

The last part of the first verse in Revelation Chapter 15 reads, *"for in them the wrath of God is complete."* The Greek word for complete is etelesthē[60] and it is the same source word used by Jesus on the cross, *"³⁰So when Jesus had received the sour wine, He said, "It is finished!" And bowing His head, He gave up His spirit."* (John 19:30)

These are not the only two times this source verb is used in the New Testament, but in both of these two verses, they are indicative of finality and a full completion: when Jesus died on the cross, it was in full payment for our sins and when the final seven bowls of wrath are poured out, it is in final judgment of the sins of the world and of the dragon, Satan, who believed he could set himself above God.

2. Revelation 15:2

"²And I saw something like a sea of glass mingled with fire, and those who have the victory over the beast, over his image and over his mark and over the number of his name, standing on the sea of glass, having harps of God." (Revelation 15:2)

This isn't the first time we read about this sea of glass. John saw the sea of glass in chapter 4, *"⁶Before the throne there was a sea of glass, like crystal."* (Revelation 4:6a) The sea of glass has often been compared to the laver that was in front of the temple for cleansing prior to entering the temple. However, in this instance,

---

[60] Strong's Greek.5055.teleó, verb, "to bring to an end, complete, fulfill"

Chapter 19 – Prelude to Final Judgment

it is "mingled with fire". Fire is a symbol of God's unyielding love and righteous fury. Fire also symbolizes the transformative power of the Holy Spirit. Let's take a look at a few of verses that exemplify the use of fire:

Of course, we all know the story of the burning bush in Exodus, *"[2]And the Angel of the Lord appeared to him in a flame of fire from the midst of a bush. So he looked, and behold, the bush was burning with fire, but the bush was not consumed. [3]Then Moses said, "I will now turn aside and see this great sight, why the bush does not burn."* (Exodus 3:2-3) Moses sees a burning bush, but the bush is not consumed by the fire. This event is called a theophany, or appearance of God – in this case an angel of the Lord.

What led the Israelites through the desert? A pillar of fire by night and a cloud by day, *"[20]So they took their journey from Succoth and camped in Etham at the edge of the wilderness. [21]And the Lord went before them by day in a pillar of cloud to lead the way, and by night in a pillar of fire to give them light, so as to go by day and night. [22]He did not take away the pillar of cloud by day or the pillar of fire by night from before the people."* (Exodus 13:20-22) This passage shows us, in a powerful way, how the Lord leads us, even today with the guidance of the Holy Spirit and through His Word.

The power of fire was used by God, through Elijah, to bring his people back to Him, *"[36]And it came to pass, at the time of the offering of the evening sacrifice, that Elijah the prophet came near and said, "Lord God of Abraham, Isaac, and Israel, let it be known this day that You are God in Israel and I am Your servant, and that I have done all these things at Your word. [37]Hear me, O Lord, hear me, that this people may know that You are the Lord God, and that You have turned their hearts back to You again." [38]Then the fire of the Lord fell and consumed the burnt sacrifice, and the wood and the stones and the dust, and it licked up the water that was in the trench. [39]Now when all the people saw it, they fell on their faces; and they said, "The Lord, He is God! The Lord, He is God!"* (1 Kings 18:36-39)

We cannot forget the tongues of fire in the New Testament at Pentecost, *"³Then there appeared to them divided tongues, as of fire, and one sat upon each of them. 4And they were all filled with the Holy Spirit and began to speak with other tongues, as the Spirit gave them utterance."* (Acts 2:3-4) This is the first indwelling of the Holy Spirit recorded in the Bible and is a powerful reminder of who we are in Christ.

These few passages are a very small sampling of the references to fire throughout Scripture and gives us a hint of how God has used fire – but which one of these is He using now? Redemption, judgment, cleansing...what?

How about all of the above? Who are those standing on this sea of glass? *"those who have the victory over the beast, over his image and over his mark and over the number of his name."* Those who have, through the power of the Lord, achieved victory over Satan and his emissaries, the AntiChrist and the False Prophet. They have been victorious through the fire, have been purified and cleansed, and now are standing in front of God!

3. Revelation 15:3-4

"³They sing the song of Moses, the servant of God, and the song of the Lamb, saying: "Great and marvelous are Your works, Lord God Almighty! Just and true are Your ways, O King of the saints! ⁴Who shall not fear You, O Lord, and glorify Your name? For You alone are holy. For all nations shall come and worship before You, For Your judgments have been manifested." (Revelation 15:3-4)

When John saw Jesus standing with the 144,000, they sang a new song which no one else could sing, *"³They sang as it were a new song before the throne, before the four living creatures, and the elders; and no one could learn that song except the hundred and forty-four thousand who were redeemed from the earth."* (Revelation 14:3)

Now he hears an old song – a very old song; the song of Moses.

This could be the passage from Deuteronomy 32, what many call the "Song of Moses." This song was given to Moses by God in the

Chapter 19 – Prelude to Final Judgment

end days of his life. He was told to teach the song to the people. God knew that the Israelites would turn from Him once they reached the Promised Land and this song would be a witness to them of their failures and of the promises God had made to them.

While this song was given to Moses to remind the Israelites of their God, it is also for us today, to remind us of our failings and to be a witness of God's presence and faithfulness in our lives. That song is included in the Appendix, Appendix VII - Second Song of Moses.

But I'm not sure that is the song they are singing here. I lean more to the song the Israelites sing after being saved from the Egyptian army by the parting of the Red Sea in Exodus 15 – the first Song of Moses. That song is a song of redemption and praise, which would be more compatible with this vision John is seeing in heaven, of those redeemed in the Tribulation. That song is also included in the Appendix, Appendix VI – First Song of Moses.

4. Revelation 15:5-6

"⁵After these things I looked, and behold, the temple of the tabernacle of the testimony in heaven was opened. ⁶And out of the temple came the seven angels having the seven plagues, clothed in pure bright linen, and having their chests girded with golden bands. " (Revelation 15:5-6)

The temple these seven angels emerge from is not the Third Temple on earth, as it has been desecrated. Each of those temples on earth; Solomon's temple, Herod's temple, and the yet-to-be-built third temple, are merely copies of the real temple in Heaven and it is from that temple these angels emerge. They are pure and holy, as signified both by the *"pure bright linen"* and *"having their chests girded with golden bands."*

5. Revelation 15:7

"⁷Then one of the four living creatures gave to the seven angels seven golden bowls full of the wrath of God who lives forever and ever." (Revelation 15:7)

We read about those four living creatures in Revelation chapters four and five. They are from one of the highest orders of angels, probably cherubim.

6. Revelation 15:8

"⁸The temple was filled with smoke from the glory of God and from His power, and no one was able to enter the temple till the seven plagues of the seven angels were completed." (Revelation 15:8)

As the fires of judgment burn, the sanctuary in heaven fills with smoke. This is similar to an event when Moses finished the work of building the tabernacle. *"³⁴Then the cloud covered the tabernacle of meeting, and the glory of the Lord filled the tabernacle. ³⁵And Moses was not able to enter the tabernacle of meeting, because the cloud rested above it, and the glory of the Lord filled the tabernacle."* (Exodus 40:34-35)

And again, when Solomon dedicated the temple, *"¹When Solomon had finished praying, fire came down from heaven and consumed the burnt offering and the sacrifices; and the glory of the Lord filled the temple. ²And the priests could not enter the house of the Lord, because the glory of the Lord had filled the Lord's house."* (2 Chronicles 7:1-2)

***

"⁷For God has not given us a spirit of fear, but of power and of love and of a sound mind." (2 Timothy 1:7)

However God protects us through the next events – whether we are taken out – harpazo – before these things begin (as I believe), or we are somehow protected through them – we are servants of the Most High God and He is our Hope and Salvation.

"⁴Rejoice in the Lord always. Again I will say, rejoice! ⁵Let your gentleness be known to all men. The Lord is at hand. ⁶Be anxious for nothing, but in everything by prayer and supplication, with thanksgiving, let your

Chapter 19 – Prelude to Final Judgment

requests be made known to God; ⁷and the peace of God, which surpasses all understanding, will guard your hearts and minds through Christ Jesus." (Phillipians 4:4-7)

So the Image Could Speak

Chapter 20 – Final Judgment

What we're about to study are the last of the three sets of seven judgments each and all seven of this last set take place during the second half of the period we call the 70th Week of Daniel.

We've studied the seven seals and the seven trumpets. From the fourth seal, one-fourth of the world's population will be killed. Using current data, with a population of 8 billion+, that is about 2 billion people. With the sixth trumpet, another one-third of the world's population is killed. With just those two judgments, nearly half of the world's population is killed. That doesn't include the other 5 seals and trumpets or any of the seven bowls.

"*^{1}Then I heard a loud voice from the temple saying to the seven angels, "Go and pour out the bowls of the wrath of God on the earth."* (Revelation 16:1)

This loud voice had to be the voice of God as it is reminiscent of Isaiah 66:6, "*^{6}The sound of noise from the city! A voice from the temple! The voice of the Lord, Who fully repays His enemies!"* (Isaiah 66:6)

Before we start delving into the seven bowl judgments, I would like to quote a passage from John MacArthur's commentary on Revelation, "…while the Bible is a book of hope, it is also a book of judgment. Because God loves righteousness and faith, He must also hate sin and unbelief. He cannot love truth unless He hates lies. He cannot love goodness unless He hates wickedness. He cannot reward unless He also punishes. The Old Testament repeatedly warns of coming judgment, particularly in those passages that describe the final Day of the Lord judgments."[61]

So anyone ignorant of what is coming has only themselves to blame, as it has been prophesied throughout both the Old and New Testaments.

1. The First Bowl

   "*^{2}So the first went and poured out his bowl upon the earth, and a

---

[61] The MacArthur New Testament Commentary – Revelation 12-22, 2000, Moody Publishers, Chicago, ISBN 978-08024-0774-0

Chapter 20 – Final Judgment

foul and loathsome sore came upon the men who had the mark of the beast and those who worshiped his image." (Revelation 16:2)

If we go back to the original Greek, foul and loathsome are translated from kakon[62] and ponēron[63], or evil and grievous. The word for sore is helkos[64] – a festering sore or wound. So those who have taken the mark of the beast and worship the image have these festering, painful wounds which cannot be cured.

This is not the first time in Scripture we've seen these type of sores. The sixth plague in Egypt was similar, *"⁸So the Lord said to Moses and Aaron, "Take for yourselves handfuls of ashes from a furnace, and let Moses scatter it toward the heavens in the sight of Pharaoh. ⁹And it will become fine dust in all the land of Egypt, and it will cause boils that break out in sores on man and beast throughout all the land of Egypt." ¹⁰Then they took ashes from the furnace and stood before Pharaoh, and Moses scattered them toward heaven. And they caused boils that break out in sores on man and beast. ¹¹And the magicians could not stand before Moses because of the boils, for the boils were on the magicians and on all the Egyptians."* (Exodus 9:8-11)

That plague was isolated to Egypt, but with this first bowl, it is worldwide. Those magicians were so affected by these boils or sores, they could not even stand up before Moses.

---

[62] Strong's Greek.2556.kakos, adjective, "bad, evil"
[63] Strong's Greek.4190.ponéros, adjective, "toilsome, bad"
[64] Strong's Greek.1668.helkos, noun neuter, "a wound, a sore, an ulcer"

We see something similar in Job, when Satan struck Job with painful sores and boils (Job 2:7) and we see it again in Luke, when Lazarus the beggar was struck, *"¹⁹"There was a certain rich man who was clothed in purple and fine linen and fared sumptuously every day. ²⁰But there was a certain beggar named Lazarus, full of sores, who was laid at his gate, ²¹desiring to be fed with the crumbs which fell from the rich man's table. Moreover the dogs came and licked his sores. ²²So it was that the beggar died, and was carried by the angels to Abraham's bosom. The rich man also died and was buried. ²³And being in torments in Hades, he lifted up his eyes and saw Abraham afar off, and Lazarus in his bosom."* (Luke 16:19-23) Powerful message there.

This is similar to the fifth trumpet when those locusts are turned loose on the earth in that their sting would affect those who did not carry the mark of the Lord on their foreheads; but they could not kill them. *"⁶In those days men will seek death and will not find it; they will desire to die, and death will flee from them."* (Revelation 9:6)

This judgment is poured out on those who have taken the mark of the beast and worship the image of the AntiChrist. Those who have given their lives to Jesus are not affected by this judgment. Do those who have been affected then seek forgiveness and repent of their sins? Well, let's read on.

2. The Second Bowl

"³Then the second angel poured out his bowl on the sea, and it became blood as of a dead man; and every living creature in the sea died." (Revelation 16:3)

Remember the second trumpet? *"⁸Then the second angel sounded: And something like a great mountain burning with fire was thrown into the sea, and a third of the sea became blood. ⁹And a third of the living creatures in the sea died, and a third of the ships were destroyed."* (Revelation 8:8-9)

Chapter 20 – Final Judgment

This time, however, it is not just a third of the sea – it is all seas and all the sea creatures die. Some have likened this to what is called a "red tide." A "red tide" is defined by HOAA, "A red tide is a harmful algal bloom, or HAB, caused by toxic algae that produce toxins that kill fish and make shellfish dangerous to eat."[65]

The Florida Gulf Coast and the Texas Gulf Coast have both experienced repeated incidents of this red tide, with at least two serious reports in 2023. An environmental journalist, reporting for NPR, states, "The toxins caused by the algae can cause particular problems for people with respiratory issues like asthma. The toxins can also accumulate in shellfish and cause Neurotoxic Shellfish Poisoning. The toxins can be fatal to seabirds that feed on fish that have been exposed to the organisms, and have also been known to kill dolphins, manatees and sea turtles."[66]

We don't know if God will use a "red tide" to affect this judgment, but whatever methodology He uses, it will be devastating. Just the smell from all those dead sea creatures washed up on the beaches will be horrific. It will be a time when all those with oceanfront property will wish they lived inland.

Will anyone repent and turn to Jesus? Let's keep reading.

3. The Third Bowl

"⁴Then the third angel poured out his bowl on the rivers and springs of water, and they became blood. ⁵And I heard the angel of the waters saying: "You are righteous, O Lord, The One who is and who was and who is to be, Because You have judged these things. ⁶For they have shed the blood of saints and prophets, And You have given them blood to drink. For it is their just due." ⁷And

---

[65] "What is a red tide?", National Oceanic and Atmospheric Administration, 8/02/2023, https://oceanservice.noaa.gov/facts/redtide.html
[66] "Red tide returns to Florida beaches earlier and stronger than normal", Marh 10, 2023, Cristen Hemingway Jaynes, environment journalist, https://www.weforum.org/agenda/2023/03/toxic-algae-florida-beach-ocean-health/

So the Image Could Speak

I heard another from the altar saying, "Even so, Lord God Almighty, true and righteous are Your judgments." (Revelation 16:4-7)

Just as in the trumpet judgments, the third bowl judgment is poured out on the fresh water. Unlike the trumpet judgments, this impacts all fresh water, not just a third.

This is also like the first plaque in Egypt, *"[19]Then the Lord spoke to Moses, "Say to Aaron, 'Take your rod and stretch out your hand over the waters of Egypt, over their streams, over their rivers, over their ponds, and over all their pools of water, that they may become blood. And there shall be blood throughout all the land of Egypt, both in buckets of wood and pitchers of stone.' " [20]And Moses and Aaron did so, just as the Lord commanded. So he lifted up the rod and struck the waters that were in the river, in the sight of Pharaoh and in the sight of his servants. And all the waters that were in the river were turned to blood. [21]The fish that were in the river died, the river stank, and the Egyptians could not drink the water of the river. So there was blood throughout all the land of Egypt."* (Exodus 7:19-21)

Every source of fresh water will be turned to blood. The human body needs water to survive. On average, it is reported humans can live up to three days without water. It has been recorded we can go as much as 8-21 days without food and as long as 11 days without sleep. But our body needs water. The death toll from this judgment will be enormous.

Who is impacted? Those who have killed the saints, have drawn their blood will be given blood to drink. As the angel of the waters cries out, *"[6]'For they have shed the blood of saints and prophets, and You have given them blood to drink. For it is their just due.' [7]And I heard another from the altar saying, 'Even so, Lord God Almighty, true and righteous are Your judgments.' "*

Chapter 20 – Final Judgment

In Proverbs, we learn about six things God hates: *"^{16}These six things the Lord hates, Yes, seven are an abomination to Him: ^{17}a proud look, a lying tongue, **hands that shed innocent blood**, ^{18}a heart that devises wicked plans, feet that are swift in running to evil, ^{19}a false witness who speaks lies, and one who sows discord among brethren."* (Proverbs 6:16-19) (emphasis added)

Those who murder the Tribulation Saints have shed innocent blood and are an abomination to God.

This might be a good time to be reminded of God's righteousness, as the Psalmist writes, *"^{75}I know, O Lord, that Your judgments are right, and that in faithfulness You have afflicted me."* (Psalms 119-75)

Paul also warns that His righteous wrath is coming, *"^{5}But in accordance with your hardness and your impenitent heart you are treasuring up for yourself wrath in the day of wrath and revelation of the righteous judgment of God,"* (Romans 2:5)

By this time, you would think those who have been affected by these first three judgments would be turning to God and pleading for His mercy….but let's keep reading.

4. The Fourth Bowl

    "^{8}Then the fourth angel poured out his bowl on the sun, and power was given to him to scorch men with fire. ^{9}And men were scorched with great heat, and they blasphemed the name of God who has power over these plagues; and they did not repent and give Him glory." (Revelation 16:8-9)

    This gives new meaning to "global warming" and I don't think they can blame it on the cows. Yet, they still do not repent and, instead, blaspheme God. So they do realize from Whom these judgments are poured out and instead of seeking His forgiveness, they curse Him!

    We know the answer to Abraham's question in Genesis, *"Shall not the Judge of all the earth do right?"* (Genesis 18:25b) Of course, Abraham knows the answer and is being rhetorical.

5. The Fifth Bowl

   "^{10}Then the fifth angel poured out his bowl on the throne of the beast, and his kingdom became full of darkness; and they gnawed their tongues because of the pain. ^{11}They blasphemed the God of heaven because of their pains and their sores, and did not repent of their deeds." (Revelation 16:10-11)

   This judgment is poured out on the throne of the beast – hitting where it hurts! Some say this is limited to the actual, physical throne of the AntiChrist in Babylon, but some argue it is the whole kingdom that is affected. But - where is that kingdom? It is the whole world. By this time, the AntiChrist has control of the entire world.

   But this isn't just a lack of light – it is a spiritual darkness. *"^{5}This is the message which we have heard from Him and declare to you, that God is light and in Him is no darkness at all. ^{6}If we say that we have fellowship with Him, and walk in darkness, we lie and do not practice the truth. ^{7}But if we walk in the light as He is in the light, we have fellowship with one another, and the blood of Jesus Christ His Son cleanses us from all sin."* (1 John 1:5-7)
   If God is light and there is no light, then God has withdrawn His presence completely. That pain they feel suddenly makes a lot more sense.
   As devastating as this is, they still do not repent.

6. The Sixth Bowl

   "^{12}Then the sixth angel poured out his bowl on the great river Euphrates, and its water was dried up, so that the way of the kings from the east might be prepared. ^{13}And I saw three unclean spirits like frogs coming out of the mouth of the dragon, out of the mouth of the beast, and out of the mouth of the false prophet. ^{14}For they are spirits of demons, performing signs, which go out to the kings of the earth and of the whole world, to gather them

Chapter 20 – Final Judgment

to the battle of that great day of God Almighty. *[15]"Behold, I am coming as a thief. Blessed is he who watches, and keeps his garments, lest he walk naked and they see his shame." [16]And they gathered them together to the place called in Hebrew, Armageddon."* (Revelation 16:12-16)

The Euphrates River is considered the birthplace of civilization and, as we'll see, it becomes the grave of civilization. If we go back to Genesis, we find the Euphrates River was the easternmost border of the land God gave to Abraham, *"[18]On the same day the Lord made a covenant with Abram, saying: "To your descendants I have given this land, from the river of Egypt to the great river, the River Euphrates— [19]the Kenites, the Kenezzites, the Kadmonites, [20]the Hittites, the Perizzites, the Rephaim, [21]the Amorites, the Canaanites, the Girgashites, and the Jebusites."* (Genesis 15:18-21)

While that is not the current boundary of the nation of Israel, we can see the river Euphrates has been a critical boundary from the beginning. The division between the east and the west of the Euphrates has been a bone of contention for centuries. Rudyard Kipling even wrote about it in The Ballad of East and West:

"Oh, East is East, and West is West,
and never the twain shall meet.
Till Earth and Sky stand presently
at God's great Judgment Seat."

Why is the Euphrates dried up? Well, we'll look at that more closely further on, but it is in preparation for the final battle.
"[13]And I saw three unclean spirits like frogs coming out of the mouth of the dragon, out of the mouth of the beast, and out of the mouth of the false prophet. [14]For they are spirits of demons, performing signs, which go out to the kings of the earth and of the whole world, to gather them to the battle of that great day of God Almighty." (Revelation 16:13-14)

If there was any doubt about whether the AntiChrist and the False Prophet were possessed, this puts that to rest. These *"three unclean spirits like frogs"* are the messengers – sent to all the kings of the world to call them to the battle of Armageddon.

"^{15}*"Behold, I am coming as a thief. Blessed is he who watches, and keeps his garments, lest he walk naked and they see his shame."* Who is He coming as a thief to? Not to those who watch and keep their garments pure – or continue to walk in the Lord – but those who have not turned back to God in repentance.

This verse is one of many that emphasize the importance of being the watchman of the times and the critical importance of sharing that information. There will come a time, indeed we see it already, when there will be many – even within the churches – who do not want to hear about these judgments. There are those who say, "God is love!" and "God is peace!" and yes, He is love and peace, but He is also a righteous and just God and retribution for the sins of those who have turned against Him is coming.

7. The Seventh Bowl

    "^{17}*Then the seventh angel poured out his bowl into the air, and a loud voice came out of the temple of heaven, from the throne, saying, "It is done!"* ^{18}*And there were noises and thunderings and lightnings; and there was a great earthquake, such a mighty and great earthquake as had not occurred since men were on the earth.* ^{19}*Now the great city was divided into three parts, and the cities of the nations fell. And great Babylon was remembered before God, to give her the cup of the wine of the fierceness of His wrath.* ^{20}*Then every island fled away, and the mountains were not found.* ^{21}*And great hail from heaven fell upon men, each hailstone about the weight of a talent. Men blasphemed God because of the plague of the hail, since that plague was exceedingly great."* (Revelation 16:17-21)

    "^{17}*Then the seventh angel poured out his bowl into the air, and a loud voice came out of the temple of heaven, from the throne, saying, "It is done!"*

Chapter 20 – Final Judgment

All the water on earth – both fresh and saltwater – is undrinkable. Those who have taken the mark of the beast have these horrible, painful blisters and sores. The sun scorches the earth and there is no water to drink to give relief and then, there is total darkness and a complete separation from God for those who have not repented.

The "great city" is divided – what great city? The great city is Jerusalem, as we read in chapter 11; *"⁸And their dead bodies will lie in the street of the great city which spiritually is called Sodom and Egypt, where also our Lord was crucified."* (Revelation 11:8)

Zechariah prophesizes about this, *"⁴And in that day His feet will stand on the Mount of Olives, which faces Jerusalem on the east. And the Mount of Olives shall be split in two, from east to west, making a very large valley; half of the mountain shall move toward the north and half of it toward the south."* (Zechariah 14:4)

The above quote from Zechariah is very interesting, especially given the prophecy in Ezekiel about the future temple during the millennium, but we'll explore that further when we delve into that chapter in Revelation.

It is safe to say that Jerusalem, indeed the entire world, will not look the same when we return with Christ as it did when we left it.

"²¹And great hail from heaven fell upon men, each hailstone about the weight of a talent. Men blasphemed God because of the plague of the hail, since that plague was exceedingly great."

It depends on which country and from which time period the talent is selected, but this is not golf ball sized hail, as the size and value of a talent differed greatly over time and in different locations. It could be anywhere from 40 lbs to over 100 lbs! But do men repent? No – they're still cursing God.

So the Image Could Speak

Chapter 21 – Mystery Babylon

The seven bowls, the last of the three sets of judgment poured out on an increasingly unrepentant and evil world, have been poured out. The messengers, those demonic frogs vomited out of the mouths of the dragon (Satan), the AntiChrist, and the False Prophet have been sent out to call all the kings of the earth and their armies to the final battle that ends the period known as the 70th Week of Daniel, aka the Tribulation. The world prepares for war.

As we've seen previously in Revelation, there is a pause, another brief interlude that occurs before the great battle commences, *"^{1}Then one of the seven angels who had the seven bowls came and talked with me, saying to me, 'Come, I will show you the judgment of the great harlot who sits on many waters, ^{2}with whom the kings of the earth committed fornication, and the inhabitants of the earth were made drunk with the wine of her fornication.' "* (Revelation 17:1-2)

Who, or what, is the great harlot and why is she important enough that one of the seven angels pulls John aside to show him the judgment of this great harlot?

The term "harlot", or porné[67] in the original Greek, is used throughout the Bible not just to reference a woman who has sold her favors, but also a false religion, or those who have turned away from God. It is also the word from which we get "pornography" in modern English.

Remember that king of Tyre who was so richly arrayed in Isaiah? The land of which he was king, Tyre, was likened to a harlot, *"^{15}Now it shall come to pass in that day that Tyre will be forgotten seventy years, according to the days of one king. At the end of seventy years it will happen to Tyre as in the song of the **harlot**:^{16}"take a harp, go about the city, you forgotten harlot; make sweet melody, sing many songs, that you may be remembered."* (Isaiah 23:15-16) (emphasis added)

But while the people of Tyre are playing their harps and making sweet melodies, the Lord has judged Tyre and found it wanting: *"^{17}And it shall*

---

[67] Strong's Greek.4204.porné, noun feminine, "a prostitute, an idolatrous community"

Chapter 21 – Mystery Babylon

be, at the end of seventy years, that the Lord will deal with Tyre. She will return to her hire, and commit fornication with all the kingdoms of the world on the face of the earth. ¹⁸Her gain and her pay will be set apart for the Lord; it will not be treasured nor laid up, for her gain will be for those who dwell before the Lord, to eat sufficiently, and for fine clothing." (Isaiah 23:17-18)

Tyre was captured by Nebuchadnezzar and did not return to its previous glory for seventy years when the Babylonian empire was vanquished, just as Isaiah prophesied. But what was its great sin that caused it to be judged and found wanting by God?

The city became so rich, it could offer every means of prosperity – food, wine, and entertainment – to its people. The people of the city enjoying those things looked down on their more rural neighbors and teased and tempted them with their riches. They became prideful and arrogant, and as we see in Proverbs, *"¹⁸Pride goes before destruction, and a haughty spirit before a fall."* (Proverbs 16:18)

Tyre was not the only city called a harlot in the Old Testament. Nineveh, that ancient city where Jonah was sent to preach repentance to, but he didn't want to go. Of course, eventually he did go and we all know how he got there.

The prophet Nahum visited Nineveh while it was under Assyrian reign and found a corrupted and cruel city, ripe for judgment.

*"¹Woe to the bloody city! It is all full of lies and robbery. Its victim never departs. ²The noise of a whip and the noise of rattling wheels, of galloping horses, of clattering chariots! ³Horsemen charge with bright sword and glittering spear. There is a multitude of slain, a great number of bodies, countless corpses— they stumble over the corpses—⁴because of the multitude of harlotries of the seductive **harlot**, the mistress of sorceries, who sells nations through her harlotries, and families through her sorceries."* (Nahum 3:1-4) (emphasis added)

Cruelty was a trademark of the Assyrians – they even bragged about their cruelty. It wasn't enough they were cruel to their own people, but they led other cities and regions to practice such cruelty, as well, *"who sells nations through her harlotries, and families through her sorceries."*

So the Image Could Speak

Because of this rampage of cruel and senseless killings and because it was proud of those things and enticed other cities to join them in those abominations, Nineveh was judged and it, too, was found wanting.

"⁵'Behold, I am against you,' says the Lord of hosts; 'I will lift your skirts over your face, I will show the nations your nakedness, and the kingdoms your shame. ⁶I will cast abominable filth upon you, make you vile, and make you a spectacle.' " (Nahum 3:5-6)

So Tyre, because of its pride and arrogance, and Nineveh due to its penchant for cruelty were both called harlots and judged by God. Sadly, so was Jerusalem.

"²¹How the faithful city has become a **harlot**! It was full of justice; righteousness lodged in it, but now murderers. ²²Your silver has become dross, your wine mixed with water. ²³Your princes are rebellious, and companions of thieves; everyone loves bribes, and follows after rewards. They do not defend the fatherless, nor does the cause of the widow come before them." (Isaiah 1:21-23) (emphasis added)

The city, once known for its justice and righteousness, had become a den of thieves and murderers. There is no mercy within the city, as they didn't even care about the fatherless children or the poor widows within its walls. Those who had once searched for the truth in God's Word and the awards that awaited them in heaven, now traded truth for lies, and heavenly awards for earthly bribes. Jerusalem had become a rebellious child and turned away from God.

The great harlot referenced in the first two verses in Revelation chapter 17 is guilty of all of the above, "²with whom the kings of the earth committed fornication, and the inhabitants of the earth were made drunk with the wine of her fornication.' " (Revelation 17:1-2)

So this harlot uses its wealth and influence to corrupt both the high and mighty, "*the kings of the earth*", and everyone else, "*the inhabitants of the earth.*"

This harlot is also guilty of the blasphemy of Jerusalem and the cruelty in Nineveh, as we see in the next passage.

Chapter 21 – Mystery Babylon

"³So he carried me away in the Spirit into the wilderness. And I saw a woman sitting on a scarlet beast which was full of names of blasphemy, having seven heads and ten horns. ⁴The woman was arrayed in purple and scarlet, and adorned with gold and precious stones and pearls, having in her hand a golden cup full of abominations and the filthiness of her fornication. ⁵And on her forehead a name was written:

*MYSTERY, BABYLON THE GREAT,
THE MOTHER OF HARLOTS
AND OF THE ABOMINATIONS
OF THE EARTH.*

⁶I saw the woman, drunk with the blood of the saints and with the blood of the martyrs of Jesus. And when I saw her, I marveled with great amazement." (Revelation 17:3-6)

Many, in fact all whose names are not written in the Book of Life, will "marvel" and follow this first beast and this harlot for the signs and wonders they use to deceive those who follow them.

So this harlot, the *"MOTHER OF HARLOTS"*, commits all the sins of those cities in the Old Testament that were judged and found wanting, but what city is this? Is this the old city of Babylon, or the city of Jerusalem, or somewhere else?

As so often in God's Word, scripture defines scripture and it is no different here, with that same angel telling John who, or what, this harlot is.

"⁷But the angel said to me, 'Why did you marvel? I will tell you the mystery of the woman and of the beast that carries her, which has the seven heads and the ten horns. ⁸The beast that you saw was, and is not, and will ascend out of the bottomless pit and go to perdition. And those who dwell on the earth will marvel, whose names are not written in the Book of Life from the foundation of the world, when they see the beast that was, and is not, and yet is.' " (Revelation 17:7-8)

This harlot, arrayed so richly and drunk with *"the blood of the saints and with the blood of the martyrs of Jesus"* is riding on the beast with the

So the Image Could Speak

seven heads and the ten horns – the first beast, the AntiChrist. Who does the AntiChrist give power and authority to? The False Prophet.

"[11]Then I saw another beast coming up out of the earth, and he had two horns like a lamb and spoke like a dragon. [12]And he exercises all the authority of the first beast in his presence, and causes the earth and those who dwell in it to worship the first beast, whose deadly wound was healed." (Revelation 13:11-12)

Let's see if we can put it all together. John is carried away, in the Spirit, into the wilderness – a place of emptiness and desolation. He sees a woman sitting on a scarlet beast *"which was full of names of blasphemy, having seven heads and ten horns."* Clearly, this is the AntiChrist. So the AntiChrist holds up, or supports this woman, or false religion – at least initially.

This woman is richly adorned. Purple was a rare color and expensive to produce in John's time and it was limited to those in power. Senators and consuls were permitted to wear a purple sash or stripe that indicated their position. The emperor's robes were all purple.

Scarlet was the color of royalty and authority. So this woman is thriving and prospering while the rest of the world is dying. She has *"in her hand a golden cup full of abominations and the filthiness of her fornication."* She is also *"adorned with gold and precious stones and pearls."* This evokes images of that prince of Tyre in Ezekiel, *"Every precious stone was your covering: the sardius, topaz, and diamond, beryl, onyx, and jasper, sapphire, turquoise, and emerald with gold."* (Ezekiel 28:7b)

A golden cup – what does that mean? Let's look at Jeremiah, *"[7]Babylon was a golden cup in the Lord's hand, that made all the earth drunk. The nations drank her wine; therefore the nations are deranged."* (Jeremiah 51:7)

So this woman, or false ideology, leads many astray through false promises and makes them "drunk", or not thinking clearly, with her idolatry.

[5]*And on her forehead a name was written:*

Chapter 21 – Mystery Babylon

MYSTERY, BABYLON THE GREAT,
THE MOTHER OF HARLOTS
AND OF THE ABOMINATIONS
OF THE EARTH."

Mystery, or the Greek word, mustérion[68] which simply means something that has been hidden but is now revealed in God's Word.

Babylon is mentioned many times in the Bible; sometimes as the actual city of Babylon (as in Genesis, Daniel, 2 Kings, etc.), but more often as the metaphorical, and doomed, city of apostasy (throughout Isaiah and Jeremiah).

Here, it is the metaphorical city of apostasy, or false religion that prevails during this time and it is the *"MOTHER OF HARLOTS AND OF THE ABOMINATIONS OF THE EARTH."*

Let's look at the rest of Revelation chapter 17.

"⁹'Here is the mind which has wisdom: The seven heads are seven mountains on which the woman sits. ¹⁰There are also seven kings. Five have fallen, one is, and the other has not yet come. And when he comes, he must continue a short time. ¹¹The beast that was, and is not, is himself also the eighth, and is of the seven, and is going to perdition.' " (Revelation 17:9-11)

At the time of John's writing, five (Egyptian, Assyrian, Babylonian, Medes-Persian, Greco-Macedonian) kingdoms had fallen, and one – the Roman Empire – was still in power. The kingdom, the New World Order, over which the AntiChrist will rule has not yet come. When he does, he will *"continue a short time."*

"¹²'The ten horns which you saw are ten kings who have received no kingdom as yet, but they receive authority for one hour as kings with the beast. ¹³These are of one mind, and they will give their power and authority to the beast. ¹⁴These will make war with the Lamb, and the Lamb will overcome them, for He is Lord of lords and King of kings; and those who are with Him are called, chosen, and faithful.' " (Revelation

---
[68] Strong's Greek.3466.mustérion, noun neuter, a mystery or secret doctrine

So the Image Could Speak

17:12-14)

That ten-nation coalition the AntiChrist will bring together will give their total devotion and loyalty to the AntiChrist, for a short time. They will persecute those who have repented and whose names are written in the Book of Life, but they will be overcome, as we will see in the coming chapters. Who overcomes them? *"Lord of lords and King of kings."*

"15Then he said to me, 'The waters which you saw, where the harlot sits, are peoples, multitudes, nations, and tongues. 16And the ten horns which you saw on the beast, these will hate the harlot, make her desolate and naked, eat her flesh and burn her with fire. 17For God has put it into their hearts to fulfill His purpose, to be of one mind, and to give their kingdom to the beast, until the words of God are fulfilled. 18And the woman whom you saw is that great city which reigns over the kings of the earth.' " (Revelation 17:15-18)

This woman, seen riding in and being supported by the first beast, is betrayed. The AntiChrist and his ten-nation coalition will turn against her, as he no longer needs her. He has full and complete control of the world at this point and doesn't need the False Prophet, or the false religion created by the False Prophet, and he turns against it. This is all part of God's plan, *"17For God has put it into their hearts to fulfill His purpose, to be of one mind, and to give their kingdom to the beast, until the words of God are fulfilled."*

The One True God, Who is still on the throne in Heaven, is still in control.

" 18'And the woman whom you saw is that great city which reigns over the kings of the earth.' " (Revelation 17:18)

Scripture defining scripture again. The angel tells John this woman represents a city. Is this where we find the throne of the AntiChrist? Or where the blasphemy of the False Prophet's false religion has its home base? We'll look at that more closely in the next chapter.

Chapter 22 – The Fall of Mystery Babylon

Chapter 22 – The Fall of Mystery Babylon

At the beginning of chapter 17, John sees a woman riding a beast, then at the end of Revelation chapter 17, there is one verse which defines the woman, *"¹⁸And the woman whom you saw is that great city which reigns over the kings of the earth.' "* (Revelation 17:18) What is that great city?

1. Babylon is fallen!

   "¹After these things I saw another angel coming down from heaven, having great authority, and the earth was illuminated with his glory. ²And he cried mightily with a loud voice, saying, "Babylon the great is fallen, is fallen, and has become a dwelling place of demons, a prison for every foul spirit, and a cage for every unclean and hated bird! ³For all the nations have drunk of the wine of the wrath of her fornication, the kings of the earth have committed fornication with her, and the merchants of the earth have become rich through the abundance of her luxury." (Revelation 18:1-3)

   The angel coming down from heaven is not the same angel as in chapter 17 and is given authority from God to act in His behalf. On a world covered in darkness (Fifth bowl judgement), his image illuminates the world. I would think everyone would see him and be awed and terrified. His voice, *"mightily with a loud voice"*, will be heard by everyone.

   What this angel proclaims is a fulfillment of that second angel's prophetic announcement in chapter 14: *"⁸And another angel followed, saying, "Babylon is fallen, is fallen, that great city, because she has made all nations drink of the wine of the wrath of her fornication."* (Revelation 14:8)

   This place, called Babylon, has *"become a dwelling place of demons, a prison for every foul spirit, and a cage for every unclean and hated bird!"*

   Remember the sixth trumpet: *"¹³Then the sixth angel sounded: And I heard a voice from the four horns of the golden altar which is before God, ¹⁴saying to the sixth angel who had the trumpet,*

"Release the four angels who are bound at the great river Euphrates." ^{15}So the four angels, who had been prepared for the hour and day and month and year, were released to kill a third of mankind. ^{16}Now the number of the army of the horsemen was two hundred million; I heard the number of them." (Revelation 9:13-16)

It is interesting to note here that the actual city of Babylon sits on the Euphrates River and is the origin of all the false religions throughout history. Remember Nimrod and the Tower of Babel?

"^{3}For all the nations have drunk of the wine of the wrath of her fornication, the kings of the earth have committed fornication with her, and the merchants of the earth have become rich through the abundance of her luxury." (Revelation 18:3)

By the time this event occurs, all the kings of the earth *"have committed fornication with her"*. In other words, this mystery Babylon or false religion has become very powerful – to the point where it has influence over all the kings of the earth. This fornication is spiritual fornication – idolatry and blasphemy against God.

The second part of that passage is very interesting and intriguing, *"the merchants of the earth have become rich through the abundance of her luxury."* What does this mean? We're going to read further on about those who grieve over the loss of this false religion and the merchants of the earth are a part of that group of mourners – but why?

Remember the description of that harlot in chapter 17; *"^{4}The woman was arrayed in purple and scarlet, and adorned with gold and precious stones and pearls, having in her hand a golden cup full of abominations and the filthiness of her fornication."* (Revelation 17:4)

Adorned with gold and precious stones and pearls would indicate this false religion has become quite rich and many have prospered because of her wealth – those pearls and precious stones had to be bought and fashioned from somewhere and

Chapter 22 – The Fall of Mystery Babylon

that gold cup had to be forged somewhere. But I think it goes even further than just what is bought by this organized religion and includes what is sold from this false religion. Perhaps a complex and far-reaching marketing system to promote this false religion? Maybe even, in a copycat of a world-wide organized religion today, indulgences to gain forgiveness?

Whatever form this final religion takes, there will be many worldwide who will grow rich through the manipulations of this Mystery Babylon and those who have grown rich will grieve over the loss.

2. "Come out of her!"

"⁴And I heard another voice from heaven saying, "Come out of her, my people, lest you share in her sins, and lest you receive of her plagues. ⁵For her sins have reached to heaven, and God has remembered her iniquities. ⁶Render to her just as she rendered to you, and repay her double according to her works; in the cup which she has mixed, mix double for her. ⁷In the measure that she glorified herself and lived luxuriously, in the same measure give her torment and sorrow; for she says in her heart, 'I sit as queen, and am no widow, and will not see sorrow.' ⁸Therefore her plagues will come in one day—death and mourning and famine. And she will be utterly burned with fire, for strong is the Lord God who judges her." (Revelation 18:4-8)

Why is this voice from heaven calling out to the faithful to leave this false religion? Does that mean there are the faithful among those who practice idolatry? Is this false religion somehow so enticing that it would lead even those who are faithful through its doors?

For that to happen, it would seem this false religion would have to put on the appearance of Christianity, but with differences, subtle at first, that lead not to God, but to damnation. For the elect to be so deceived, this pseudo-Christian façade would have to be very convincing and the signs and wonders performed by the False Prophet very alluring. But that is exactly what happens, as we are warned in Matthew.

*"²⁴For false christs and false prophets will rise and show great signs and wonders to deceive, if possible, **even the elect**."* (Matthew 24:24) (emphasis added)

This also reminds us of the warning from Isaiah, *"²⁰Go forth from Babylon! Flee from the Chaldeans! With a voice of singing, Declare, proclaim this, Utter it to the end of the earth; Say, 'The Lord has redeemed His servant Jacob!' "* (Isaiah 48:20)

And, again in Jeremiah," *⁸'Move from the midst of Babylon, Go out of the land of the Chaldeans; And be like the rams before the flocks.' "* (Jeremiah 50:8)

So, it would appear this city of Babylon has been a source of temptation, idolatry, spiritual fornication, and blasphemy against God since the very beginning.

There is a very interesting statement here, " *'I sit as queen, and am no widow, and will not see sorrow."* (Revelation 18:7b)

This would seem to be a direct response to when Israel is called a widow. While the Church is the Bride of Christ, Israel was described as being the "wife of God" in Isaiah, *"⁵For your Maker is your husband, The Lord of hosts is His name; and your Redeemer is the Holy One of Israel; He is called the God of the whole earth."* (Isaiah 54:5)

So this statement, *"am no widow"*, would put this false religion in direct opposition to Israel and this self-glorification *'I sit as queen'* an echo of earlier scripture, *"¹⁵This is the rejoicing city that dwelt securely, that said in her heart, "I am it, and there is none besides me."* (Zephaniah 2:15)

For all her riches, self-glorification, and pride, she will be brought down by God, *"⁸Therefore her plagues will come in one day— death and mourning and famine. And she will be utterly burned with fire, for strong is the Lord God who judges her."*

3. The world mourns

Chapter 22 – The Fall of Mystery Babylon

"⁹The kings of the earth who committed fornication and lived luxuriously with her will weep and lament for her, when they see the smoke of her burning, ¹⁰standing at a distance for fear of her torment, saying, 'Alas, alas, that great city Babylon, that mighty city! For in one hour your judgment has come.' ¹¹"And the merchants of the earth will weep and mourn over her, for no one buys their merchandise anymore: ¹²merchandise of gold and silver, precious stones and pearls, fine linen and purple, silk and scarlet, every kind of citron wood, every kind of object of ivory, every kind of object of most precious wood, bronze, iron, and marble; ¹³and cinnamon and incense, fragrant oil and frankincense, wine and oil, fine flour and wheat, cattle and sheep, horses and chariots, and bodies and souls of men. ¹⁴The fruit that your soul longed for has gone from you, and all the things which are rich and splendid have gone from you, and you shall find them no more at all. ¹⁵The merchants of these things, who became rich by her, will stand at a distance for fear of her torment, weeping and wailing, ¹⁶and saying, 'Alas, alas, that great city that was clothed in fine linen, purple, and scarlet, and adorned with gold and precious stones and pearls! ¹⁷For in one hour such great riches came to nothing.' Every shipmaster, all who travel by ship, sailors, and as many as trade on the sea, stood at a distance ¹⁸and cried out when they saw the smoke of her burning, saying, 'What is like this great city?' ¹⁹"They threw dust on their heads and cried out, weeping and wailing, and saying, 'Alas, alas, that great city, in which all who had ships on the sea became rich by her wealth! For in one hour she is made desolate.' Revelation 18:9-19

So indeed there will be a complex marketing scheme to promote this false religion, with incense and precious jewels, fine linen and every kind of citron wood, and even horses and chariots. In fact, we see evidence of those indulgences, where prayers for forgiveness – even for the dead – can be purchased, *"and bodies and souls of men."*

Apparently, it wasn't just the merchants selling their goods who prospered, but those who transported those goods, as well, *"in which all who had ships on the sea became rich by her wealth!"*

But in all their grief, did they rise up to protect this city? Did they renounce the power that destroyed it? Not at all, *"¹⁵The merchants of these things, who became rich by her, will stand at a distance for fear of her torment, weeping and wailing, "* and *"Every shipmaster, all who travel by ship, sailors, and as many as trade on the sea, stood at a distance ¹⁸and cried out when they saw the smoke of her burning."*

Perhaps because it happens so quickly, *"¹⁷For in one hour such great riches came to nothing.' "* This destruction of Babylon was predicted long before John saw these visions. In Jeremiah 50 and 51, we see several verses about the destruction of Babylon:

"²⁶Come against her from the farthest border; Open her storehouses; Cast her up as heaps of ruins, And destroy her utterly; Let nothing of her be left." (Jeremiah 50:26)
"¹¹Make the arrows bright! Gather the shields! The Lord has raised up the spirit of the kings of the Medes. For His plan is against Babylon to destroy it, because it is the vengeance of the Lord, the vengeance for His temple." (Jeremiah 51:11)

"⁵⁵Because the Lord is plundering Babylon and silencing her loud voice, though her waves roar like great waters, and the noise of their voice is uttered, ⁵⁶because the plunderer comes against her, against Babylon, and her mighty men are taken. Every one of their bows is broken; for the Lord is the God of recompense, He will surely repay." (Jeremiah 51:55-56)

4. Finality of Babylon's fall

"²¹Then a mighty angel took up a stone like a great millstone and threw it into the sea, saying, "Thus with violence the great city Babylon shall be thrown down, and shall not be found anymore. ²²The sound of harpists, musicians, flutists, and trumpeters shall not be heard in you anymore. No craftsman of any craft shall be found in you anymore, and the sound of a millstone shall not be heard in you anymore. ²³The light of a lamp shall not shine in you anymore, and the voice of bridegroom and bride shall not be heard in you anymore. For your merchants were the great men of the earth, for by your sorcery all the nations were deceived. ²⁴And in her was found the blood of prophets and saints, and of all who

Chapter 22 – The Fall of Mystery Babylon

were slain on the earth." (Revelation 18:21-24)

We could do a deep dive in just these 4 verses, but I'll summarize. This great mystery Babylon; this false religion who has had the ears of kings and the riches of the world, is destroyed by God and will never arise again. It is destroyed so completely that life will never be found there again, *"²²The sound of harpists, musicians, flutists, and trumpeters shall not be heard in you anymore. No craftsman of any craft shall be found in you anymore, and the sound of a millstone shall not be heard in you anymore. ²³The light of a lamp shall not shine in you anymore, and the voice of bridegroom and bride shall not be heard in you anymore."*

There is one small phrase that stands out, *"for by your sorcery all the nations were deceived."* The Greek word for sorcery here is pharmakeia[69], which means "the use of medicine, drugs or spells." It is also the word from which we get pharmacy and pharmaceutical. A fascinating rabbit trail about the Covid vaccines is calling my name, but I'll leave it here for my readers to contemplate.

These two chapters in Revelation tell of this mysterious harlot and false ideology that has great influence during this period called the 70th Week of Daniel. We learn of her sexual and spiritual fornication, her pride, and her fall. Can we determine who, or what, this harlot represents and is she/it present today?

We have some hints from scripture:

- *"⁹'Here is the mind which has wisdom: The seven heads are seven mountains on which the woman sits.' "* (Revelation 17:9)
  Is there an organized religion today located in a city with seven hills?
- *" 'Alas, alas, that great city that was clothed in fine linen, purple, and scarlet, and adorned with gold and precious stones and pearls!' "* (Revelation 18:16b)
  Which of the many religions today are reported as the richest?

---

[69] Strong's Greek.5331.pharmakeia, noun feminine, "the use of medicine, drugs or spells"

So the Image Could Speak

    According to one report, while the Roman Catholic Church is quiet about its wealth, it reportedly has assets of over $17 billion[70], making it the richest faith based organization in the world.

- *"The kings of the earth have committed fornication with her"* (Revelation 18:3b) Which religious organization has had the most impact or influence over world governments? To answer this question, we would have to take a deep dive into history, but there does seem to be a pattern that emerges. After Constantine declared Christianity as the faith of the realm in his Edict of Milan in 313 AD, the church of Rome, or the Roman Catholic church, grew in power and influence. "The Edict of Milan in 313 AD, under Emperor Constantine, marked a significant shift from persecution to patronage. This new relationship with the Roman state would profoundly influence the Church's role in society, setting the stage for its central position in medieval Europe."[71] There is a lot more history we could list here, but we'll let the reader come to their own conclusions.

Many of the early church fathers identified "Babylon" in the book of Revelation as the city of Rome, including; Victorinus, in his commentary on the Apocalypse[72], "The seven heads are the seven hills, on which the woman sits. That is, the city of Rome.", and Eusebius, in his Church History (Book II)[73], "And Peter makes mention of Mark in his first epistle which they say that he wrote in Rome itself, as is indicated by him, when he calls the city, by a figure, Babylon, as he does in the following words: The church that is at Babylon, elected together with you, salutes you; and so does Marcus my son. 1 Peter 5:13" "

It is believed John referenced Rome as Babylon in his writing of Revelation because of the power Rome had at that time and to mention

---

[70] How much money does "God" have?, Janet Nguyen, February 10, 2023, https://www.marketplace.org/2023/02/10/how-much-money-does-catholic-church-have/

[71] Roman Catholic Church - Origins, Evolution, and Traditions, ChurchPedia.org, date unknown, https://churchpedia.org/roman-catholic-church-origins-evolution-and-traditions/

[72] Commentary on the Apocalypse, Victorinus, during the reign of the Emperor Gallienus (258-260), Chapter 17.9, https://www.newadvent.org/fathers/0712.htm

[73] Church History (Book II), Eusebius, 313-314 AD, Chapter 15.2, https://www.newadvent.org/fathers/250102.htm

Chapter 22 – The Fall of Mystery Babylon

that city specifically would have caused a great uproar.

Today, the Roman Catholic Church leads the way to universalism with Pope Francis' "Document on Human Fraternity" which promotes acceptance across all religious borders, especially those of the Abrahamic faiths (Judaism, Christianity, and Islam).

I am not saying the Roman Catholic Church is the harlot and whoever leads that, at the time of these events, is the False Prophet. We know the false religion that comes to power during the 70th Week of Daniel is an amalgamation of many different faiths and, eventually, a worship of the AntiChrist. But we also know, from that verse in Matthew and the verse in Revelation, that people of faith will be deceived and are called to come out of her. No Christian would be deceived by the writings of Mohammed; there has to be, at the very least, a façade of Christianity to lure the faithful in.

We know, at least to start, this false church will teach "all roads lead to God", which we know to be false as Jesus says, *"⁶Jesus said to him, "I am the way, the truth, and the life. No one comes to the Father except through Me."* (John 14:6)

And that is what we need to remember and continue to tell others today – there is only one way to God, to everlasting life with God, and that is through the sacrificial offering of His blood for our sins and the acceptance of Jesus Christ as our Lord and Savior. We must continue to share that message, not just in words, but in the example set by our own lives, before time runs out. And it is running out – that clock is ticking and I believe it is nearing midnight.

So the Image Could Speak

Chapter 23 – Who Are the Saints?

Up to this point in the book of Revelation, we've seen mention of the saints multiple times (11 times in Revelation chapter 5 through chapter 19) and we'll see it once more in Revelation chapter 20. But what does that mean? What saints is John referring to in the book of Revelation?

Most of these are referencing what we call the Tribulation Saints, though you won't see that phrase anywhere in the Bible. Of course, you don't see the word "Trinity", as in the Father, the Son, and the Holy Spirit, in the Bible, either, but that makes it no less valid.

There are actually three "sets" of saints in the Bible: the Old Testament saints, the New Testament, or Church, saints, and the Tribulation saints.

Who are these different saints? How are they alike? How are they different? Does this mean there are distinct levels of faith? Is one group of saints better than another?

Lots of questions, and, as usual, scripture provides the answers. So let's go through each of these and see if we can discover the answers to these six questions about each one:

- Who are the saints?
- How did they get saved?
- Are they indwelt with the Holy Spirit?
- Where did they go when they died?
- When will they be resurrected?
- Are they the Bride of Christ?

1. The Old Testament Saints
    a. Who are the Old Testament Saints?

Chapter 23 – Who Are the Saints?

The Old Testament saints are any who were saved, or declared righteous by God, and who died during the time of the Old Testament and up to the time of Jesus' death and resurrection. It could be stated that they began with Abraham, but we know Enoch, who lived before the great flood, was also a man of God. It would also include any who repented of their sins and followed Jesus during His ministry on earth and died before Jesus' death and resurrection, as the Church Age did not begin until that day in the upper room at Pentecost, as recorded in Acts chapter two. The protestant faiths don't canonize saints like the Catholic faith, so a complete listing of all who would be considered saints in the Old Testament is difficult to quantify. We can, however, show examples of those who showed tremendous faith.

- Abraham, the first chosen by God and the father of the plan of redemption.

    "^{4}And behold, the word of the Lord came to him, saying, 'This one shall not be your heir, but one who will come from your own body shall be your heir.' ^{5}Then He brought him outside and said, 'Look now toward heaven, and count the stars if you are able to number them.' And He said to him, "So shall your descendants be." ^{6}And he believed in the Lord, and He accounted it to him for righteousness." (Genesis 15:4-6)

- David, the author of much of the Psalms and the forefather of the incarnate Jesus Christ

    "^{13}Then Samuel took the horn of oil and anointed him in the midst of his brothers; and the Spirit of the Lord came upon David from that day forward. So Samuel arose and went to Ramah". (1 Samuel 16:13)

- Daniel, one of Nebuchadnezzar's captives out of Jerusalem, then rose to great esteem within the

Babylonian and Medes-Persian empires due to this faith.

> "*[23]'I thank You and praise You, O God of my fathers; You have given me wisdom and might, and have now made known to me what we asked of You, for You have made known to us the king's demand.'*" (Daniel 2:23)

This is just a brief list and we could include many others, such as Noah, all the prophets and many more. All of these exemplify faith in the One True God, even, or perhaps especially, during challenging times. God has always had a remnant who followed Him and showed their faith – throughout the Old Testament, into the New Testament, and, as we'll see in the last three books of Revelation, into the Tribulation and beyond. We can learn a lot by studying their lives.

b. How did they get saved?

It is a common (mis)conception that those in the Old Testament were saved by conforming to the law, but scripture refutes that. Paul tells us, "*[11]But that no one is justified by the law in the sight of God is evident, for 'the just shall live by faith.'*" (Galatians 3:11)

It could be argued that Paul was talking to the Church, not the Old Testament Jews, but Paul was actually quoting from the Old Testament, "*[4]'Behold the proud, his soul is not upright in him; but the just shall live by his faith.'*" (Habakkuk 2:4)

"*But the just shall live by his faith*" Not by works, or by the law, but through faith are all who are saved are redeemed. Paul makes a wonderful, and very convincing, argument for all who are saved, whether Jew or Gentile, circumcised or uncircumcised, are saved by faith alone in his letter to the Romans, "*[27]Where is boasting then? It is excluded. By what law? Of works? No, but by the law of*

Chapter 23 – Who Are the Saints?

> faith. ²⁸*Therefore we conclude that a man is justified by faith apart from the deeds of the law.* ²⁹*Or is He the God of the Jews only? Is He not also the God of the Gentiles? Yes, of the Gentiles also,* ³⁰*since there is one God who will justify the circumcised by faith and the uncircumcised through faith.* ³¹*Do we then make void the law through faith? Certainly not! On the contrary, we establish the law.*" (Romans 3:27-31)

c. Are they indwelt with the Holy Spirit?

In the current age, we who are saved are filled with the Holy Spirit and are to live in His guidance.

Does this apply to those who were saved in the Old Testament?

Scripture tells us the answer to that question is, "no", they were not indwelt with the Holy Spirit. The indwelling of the Holy Spirit in believers did not begin until that day of Pentecost in Acts, *"¹When the Day of Pentecost had fully come, they were all with one accord in one place. ²And suddenly there came a sound from heaven, as of a rushing mighty wind, and it filled the whole house where they were sitting. ³Then there appeared to them divided tongues, as of fire, and one sat upon each of them. ⁴And they were all filled with the Holy Spirit and began to speak with other tongues, as the Spirit gave them utterance."* (Acts 2:1)

But that doesn't mean the Holy Spirit wasn't present and accounted for during the Old Testament times! The Holy Spirit came upon many in the Old Testament, but instead of a lifelong and permanent indwelling, it was a temporary and passing blessing.

The first time this is recorded in the Bible is in Exodus with one of the workers on the tabernacle, *"¹Then the Lord spoke to Moses, saying: ²"See, I have called by name Bezalel the son of Uri, the son of Hur, of the tribe of Judah.*

³And I have filled him with the Spirit of God, in wisdom, in understanding, in knowledge, and in all manner of workmanship, ⁴to design artistic works, to work in gold, in silver, in bronze, ⁵in cutting jewels for setting, in carving wood, and to work in all manner of workmanship." (Exodus 31:1-5)

There are many more examples of this throughout the Old Testament; in Numbers, Judges, 1 Samuel, Isaiah, Ezekiel, Daniel, and 1 and 2 Chronicles. Too many to list here, but it is clear, when those passages are studied, that the Holy Spirit came upon those in the Old Testament but did not permanently indwell in them.

If it was a permanent indwelling, there would be no need for Ezekiel to be filled twice, *"²Then the Spirit entered me when He spoke to me, and set me on my feet; and I heard Him who spoke to me."* (Ezekiel 2:2)

And again, *"²³So I arose and went out into the plain, and behold, the glory of the Lord stood there, like the glory which I saw by the River Chebar; and I fell on my face. ²⁴Then the Spirit entered me and set me on my feet, and spoke with me and said to me: 'Go, shut yourself inside your house.' "* (Ezekiel 3:23-24)

We can't forget when David pleads, *"¹¹Do not cast me away from Your presence, and do not take Your Holy Spirit from me."* (Psalms 51:11) Why would David be afraid of God removing His Holy Spirit, if it was meant to be a permanent indwelling?

It wasn't, though the Holy Spirit was present and active in the lives of the faithful throughout the Old Testament.

d. Where did they go when they died?

When a believer died, prior to the resurrection of Jesus Christ, their souls did not, in fact could not, go directly to Heaven to be with God. Jacob, on learning of his son's,

Chapter 23 – Who Are the Saints?

Joseph, supposed death, *"³⁵And all his sons and all his daughters arose to comfort him; but he refused to be comforted, and he said, "For I shall go down into the grave to my son in mourning." Thus his father wept for him."* (Genesis 37:35)

The word translated to grave, in the NKJV, is the Hebrew word Sheol[74], which indicates a "holding place", if you will, for those who died prior to Jesus' death and resurrection.

Job also mentions it, *"¹³'Oh, that You would hide me in the grave, that You would conceal me until Your wrath is past, that You would appoint me a set time, and remember me!'"* (Job 14:13)

The wicked who died during Old Testament times also went to this Sheol, and as we see in the New Testament, the place was divided into two separate parts with a great divide in the middle, with one side offering comfort and the other torment.

Jesus spoke of the rich man and the poor man who died, with the rich man on one side of that great divide and the poor man was carried by angels to Abraham's bosom, *"²²So it was that the beggar died, and was carried by the angels to Abraham's bosom. The rich man also died and was buried. ²³And being in torments in Hades, he lifted up his eyes and saw Abraham afar off, and Lazarus in his bosom."* (Luke 16:22-23)

Hades[75] is the Greek name for the same place the Hebrews called Sheol.

The rich man, suffering terribly, cried out to Abraham for mercy, but Abraham couldn't help him, *"²⁵But Abraham said, 'Son, remember that in your lifetime you received*

---

[74] Strong's Hebrew.7585.sheol, noun feminine, "underworld (place to which people descend at death)"
[75] Strong's Greek.86.hadés, noun masculine, "Hades, the abode of departed spirits"

your good things, and likewise Lazarus evil things; but now he is comforted and you are tormented. ²⁶And besides all this, between us and you there is a great gulf fixed, so that those who want to pass from here to you cannot, nor can those from there pass to us.' " (Luke 16:25-26)

So those who died prior to Jesus' death and resurrection, whether good or evil, all went to Hades, or Sheol in the Hebrew, with the good going to the comfort side of that chasm and the evil to the side of torment. The passage quoted above also tells us that death is final and the choice of going to eternal damnation or to "Paradise" has been made and cannot be changed.

The good news is the righteous who died prior to Jesus' death and resurrection are no longer awaiting redemption! When Jesus died, he set the captives free, *"⁷But to each one of us grace was given according to the measure of Christ's gift. ⁸Therefore He says: "When He ascended on high, He led captivity captive, and gave gifts to men." ⁹(Now this, "He ascended"—what does it mean but that He also first descended into the lower parts of the earth?"* (Ephesians 4:7-9)

So we will see Abraham, David, and Daniel and all the other saints of the New Testament in Heaven!

It should be noted, however, that Hades is not yet empty. Those who die unrepentant of their sins still go to the same torment side of Hades as that rich man.

e. When will they be resurrected?

All who have died, whether righteous or unrighteous, will be resurrected at some point. While scripture is not real clear on this, it is believed that those righteous who died prior to Jesus' death and resurrection will be resurrected and given their Heavenly bodies at the end of the Tribulation.

Chapter 23 – Who Are the Saints?

Those unrighteous who have died will not be resurrected until the end of the Millennium, which we'll see further on.

f. Are they the Bride of Christ?

No, they are not part of the Bride of Christ. The Old Testament Saints are the wife of God, as shown in various places in the Old Testament, such as this verse in Jeremiah, *"¹⁴'Return, O backsliding children,' says the Lord; 'for I am married to you. I will take you, one from a city and two from a family, and I will bring you to Zion.' "* (Jeremiah 3:14)

2. The New Testament Saints

    a. Who are the New Testament Saints?

    The New Testament Saints are those who have repented of their sins, are filled with the Holy Spirit, and are followers of Jesus Christ and believers in the sacrificial death and resurrection of God's Only Begotten Son. The New Testament saints, aka the Church or Bride of Christ, began in that upper room on the day of Pentecost and ends with the Rapture of the Church.

    "¹When the Day of Pentecost had fully come, they were all with one accord in one place. ²And suddenly there came a sound from heaven, as of a rushing mighty wind, and it filled the whole house where they were sitting. ³Then there appeared to them divided tongues, as of fire, and one sat upon each of them. ⁴And they were all filled with the Holy Spirit and began to speak with other tongues, as the Spirit gave them utterance." (Acts 2:1-4)

    While the Old Testament Saints believed in a coming Messiah, most of those alive during Jesus' ministry did not accept Him as the Messiah. Those who did; the Apostles, Paul, and all who accepted Jesus Christ as their personal Lord and Savior until the end of the Church Age, are the New Testament Saints, also known as the Church or Bride of Christ.

The Church Age ends with the Rapture of the Church.

"^{16}For the Lord Himself will descend from heaven with a shout, with the voice of an archangel, and with the trumpet of God. And the dead in Christ will rise first. ^{17}Then we who are alive and remain shall be caught up together with them in the clouds to meet the Lord in the air. And thus we shall always be with the Lord." (1 Thessalonians 4:16-17)

The phrase *"caught up"* is translated from the Greek word, harpazó[76], which means ""to seize, catch up, snatch away." So the Church will be caught up to meet the Lord in the air, to be with Him into eternity.

When this event will take place is a subject of much controversy and we won't delve into that here. I believe the Church is removed prior to the beginning of the Tribulation before the first seal is opened and the AntiChrist is revealed.

b. How do we get saved?

At the time of this writing, we are still in the Church Age, as the Rapture has not yet happened, and we are saved by His Grace, through faith in Jesus Christ. Paul tells the jailor who comes to him, *"^{30}And he brought them out and said, 'Sirs, what must I do to be saved?' ^{31}So they said, 'Believe on the Lord Jesus Christ, and you will be saved, you and your household.' "* (Acts 16:30-31)

If you are reading this book and are not saved, or you are unsure of your salvation, reach out...to God, to your pastor, to a friend who is saved and ask for guidance.

---

[76] Strong's Greek.726.harpazó, verb, "to seize, catch up, snatch away"

Chapter 23 – Who Are the Saints?

Begin your walk with the Lord today.

c. Are we indwelt with the Holy Spirit?

Reading that passage in Acts 2 shows us we are filled with the Holy Spirit and, unlike those in the Old Testament who might have the Holy Spirit come upon them and then leave, it is an eternal blessing for those saved during this time.

Is being filled with the Holy Spirit a requirement of being saved, in this age? Paul tells us, *"⁹But you are not in the flesh but in the Spirit, if indeed the Spirit of God dwells in you. Now if anyone does not have the Spirit of Christ, he is not His."* (Romans 8:9)

d. Where do we go when we die?

Since the door to Heaven is now open by Jesus' death and resurrection, all who die in Christ go directly to Heaven. This is exemplified with Jesus telling the thief on the cross, *"⁴³And Jesus said to him, 'Assuredly, I say to you, today you will be with Me in Paradise.' "* (Luke 23:4)

The word for Paradise in the Greek is paradeisos[77], which simply means a park, or garden, or paradise. It is only used three times in the New Testament; one of the other times is in Revelation, in the letter to the church at Ephesus, *"⁷'He who has an ear, let him hear what the Spirit says to the churches. To him who overcomes I will give to eat from the tree of life, which is in the midst of the Paradise of God.' "* (Revelation 2:7)

e. When will we be resurrected?

Scripture is clear on this, as stated in that verse in 1 Thessalonians, *"¹⁶For the Lord Himself will descend from heaven with a shout, with the voice of an archangel, and*

---

[77] Strong's Greek.3857.paradeisos, "a park, a garden, a paradise"

with the trumpet of God. And the dead in Christ will rise first. ¹⁷Then we who are alive and remain shall be caught up together with them in the clouds to meet the Lord in the air. And thus we shall always be with the Lord." (1 Thessalonians 4:16-17)

"And the dead in Christ will rise first." All who have died in Christ will be resurrected and given their Heavenly bodies at the Rapture of the Church, followed by those who are alive in Christ and who are also given their resurrected bodies at that time.

    f.   Are we the Bride of Christ?

Yes! It is the New Testament Saints, aka the Church, who are the Bride of Christ.

3. The Tribulation Saints

    a. Who are the Tribulation Saints?

    Once the first seal is opened and the AntiChrist revealed, persecution of the Jews and any who believe in Jesus Christ will be unrelenting. The Church, those who were saved prior to the Tribulation, are gone and have been raptured, but there will be many who turn to Christ during the Tribulation. Many of those will be martyred for their witness – those are the Tribulation Saints.

    b. How will they get saved?

    Salvation during the Tribulation is no different than during the Church Age. They will be saved by faith in Jesus Christ.

    c. Will they be indwelt with the Holy Spirit?

    No, because when the Rapture occurs, the Holy Spirit is also partially removed. I believe those saved during the Tribulation will experience the Holy Spirit much as the

Chapter 23 – Who Are the Saints?

Old Testament Saints did, with the Holy Spirit coming upon them for a specific need and purpose.

d. Where will they go when they die?

This is also no different than the Church Age Saints, as the door to Heaven is now open and all who die for Christ are immediately in Heaven. We will see these saints mentioned multiple times throughout the book of Revelation.

e. When will they be resurrected?

They will be resurrected at the end of the Tribulation, before the beginning of the Millennium in what is called the "first resurrection." This is also when it is believed the Old Testament Saints are resurrected and given their Heavenly bodies.

f. Are they the Bride of Christ?

No, the Church, aka the Bride of Christ, has already been raptured.

Ok, so let's see if we can put all this together and make the differences between these three groups clear and distinct.

So the Image Could Speak

	Old Testament Saints	New Testament Saints	Tribulation Saints
Who Are the Saints?	Those who died righteous before the death and resurrection of Jesus Christ	Those who have accepted Christ after the death and resurrection of Jesus Christ and before the Rapture of the Church	Those who die in Christ during the 7-year Tribulation
How did they get Saved?	All by faith		
Are the indwelt with the Holy Spirit?	No	Yes	No
Where do they go when they die?	The comfort side of Sheol, aka "Abraham's Bosom"	Heaven	Heaven
When will they be resurrected?	At the first resurrection at the end of the Tribulation	In the Rapture	At the first resurrection at the end of the Tribulation
Are they the Bride of Christ	No	Yes	No

This chapter is not intended to be a thesis on all the doctrinal differences between these three groups. Instead it is only meant to show there are differences and, hopefully, to clear up any confusion that may occur if those differences are not understood.

Separating them into these groups does not mean there are diverse levels of Christianity and one is better than, or higher than, another. It simply shows how our Lord deals with each group, and each of us, individually. Just as He gave the Jews entering the Promised Land a new song, and as He will give those 144,000 sealed with God's mark during the Tribulation

Chapter 23 – Who Are the Saints?

a song no one else can sing, He has, and will continue to guide, guard, and lead us as individuals and as a unique part of whatever group we fit within.

So the Image Could Speak

Chapter 24 – The Second Coming

The next two chapters in Revelation, chapters nineteen and twenty, represent the culmination of God's plan. There are no events portrayed in these two, or even the last two chapters of the Book of Revelation, that are not presented elsewhere in Scripture. The prophecy of the Second Coming of Jesus Christ is the oldest prophecy given by a prophet in the Bible. In Jude 14, Jude writes, *"14Now Enoch, the seventh from Adam, prophesied about these men also, saying, "Behold, the Lord comes with ten thousands of His saints, 15to execute judgment on all, to convict all who are ungodly among them of all their ungodly deeds which they have committed in an ungodly way, and of all the harsh things which ungodly sinners have spoken against Him."* (Jude 1:14-15)

Jude is quoting from the first book of Enoch, written in the first century and before the great flood. Enoch was not considered a writer of Scripture but was considered a holy man. We know from Scripture that Enoch walked with God, *"21Enoch lived sixty-five years, and begot Methuselah. 22After he begot Methuselah, Enoch walked with God three hundred years, and had sons and daughters. 23So all the days of Enoch were three hundred and sixty-five years. 24And Enoch walked with God; and he was not, for God took him."* (Genesis 5:21-24)

The listing of verses that reference the Second Coming of Christ is extensive and runs throughout both the Old and New Testaments and we'll take a deeper look at some of those further on. But, for now, let's get back to breaking down Revelation chapter nineteen. Chapter nineteen of the Book of Revelation can be divided into four parts:

- The Jubilation in Heaven after the destruction of Mystery Babylon
- The Marriage Supper of the Lamb
- The Second Coming of Jesus Christ – our Blessed Hope!
- The Battle of Armageddon

1. Jubilation in Heaven

   "1After these things I heard a loud voice of a great multitude in heaven, saying, "Alleluia! Salvation and glory and honor and

Chapter 24 – The Second Coming

power belong to the Lord our God! ²For true and righteous are His judgments, because He has judged the great harlot who corrupted the earth with her fornication; and He has avenged on her the blood of His servants shed by her." ³Again they said, "Alleluia! Her smoke rises up forever and ever!" ⁴And the twenty-four elders and the four living creatures fell down and worshiped God who sat on the throne, saying, "Amen! Alleluia!" ⁵Then a voice came from the throne, saying, "Praise our God, all you His servants and those who fear Him, both small and great!" (Revelation 19:1-5)

The first verse starts out with, *"¹After these things"* or, in the Greek, meta[78] touto[79]. We first saw this phrase used in Revelation chapter 4, when John is first called up to Heaven, *"¹After these things I looked, and behold, a door standing open in heaven. And the first voice which I heard was like a trumpet speaking with me, saying, "Come up here, and I will show you things which must take place after this."* (Revelation 4:1)

It implies there, as it does here, that what occurs next in the text is an event that occurs after the previous events in chronological order. So what John is seeing and recording here are things that happen after the events recorded in the earlier chapters in Revelation.

Another item I'd like to point out here is in verse 4, *"⁴And the twenty-four elders and the four living creatures fell down and worshiped God who sat on the throne, saying, 'Amen! Alleluia!' "* This is the last time the twenty-four elders are mentioned in the book of Revelation.

One more thing I'd like to mention from this passage is the praise offered up to God. This wouldn't seem to be so unusual, as God is praised throughout the book of Revelation and, indeed, the whole Bible. But what may be unusual is why He is being praised. We see praise throughout the Scripture for His attributes, His Holiness, His Perfection, His Righteousness. We see praise

---

[78] Strong's Greek.3326, meta, preposition, "with, among, after"
[79] Strong's Greek.3778, houtos, hauté, touto, demonstrative pronoun, "this"

offered also for His Gifts, particularly the gift of salvation. Paul exemplifies this in 2 Corinthians, *"^{12}For the administration of this service not only supplies the needs of the saints, but also is abounding through many thanksgivings to God, ^{13}while, through the proof of this ministry, they glorify God for the obedience of your confession to the gospel of Christ, and for your liberal sharing with them and all men, ^{14}and by their prayer for you, who long for you because of the exceeding grace of God in you. ^{15}Thanks be to God for His indescribable gift!"* (2 Corinthians 9:12-15)

There are many, many more reasons for us to give praise and thankfulness to God. But what we see here is praise for His destruction of the wicked and His just and righteous judgment. If we go back to Deuteronomy, in that Song of Moses, we read, ^{43}*"Rejoice, O Gentiles, with His people; For He will avenge the blood of His servants, and render vengeance to His adversaries; He will provide atonement for His land and His people."* (Deuteronomy 32:43)

Again, in Psalms 58, *"^{10}The righteous shall rejoice when he sees the vengeance; He shall wash his feet in the blood of the wicked, ^{11}so that men will say, 'Surely there is a reward for the righteous; surely He is God who judges in the earth.' "* (Psalms 58:10-11)

We know His judgement is righteous and for that, we can be thankful. *"^{11}Let the heavens rejoice, and let the earth be glad; let the sea roar, and all its fullness; ^{12}let the field be joyful, and all that is in it. Then all the trees of the woods will rejoice ^{13}before the Lord. For He is coming, for He is coming to judge the earth. He shall judge the world with righteousness, and the peoples with His truth."* (Psalms 96:11-13)

So, it isn't just that multitude in Heaven who will be praising Him and rejoicing – all heaven and earth – even the fields will be rejoicing!

2. The Marriage Supper of the Lamb

   "^{6}And I heard, as it were, the voice of a great multitude, as the

Chapter 24 – The Second Coming

sound of many waters and as the sound of mighty thunderings, saying, "Alleluia! for the Lord God Omnipotent reigns! ⁷Let us be glad and rejoice and give Him glory, for the marriage of the Lamb has come, and His wife has made herself ready." ⁸And to her it was granted to be arrayed in fine linen, clean and bright, for the fine linen is the righteous acts of the saints. ⁹Then he said to me, "Write: 'Blessed are those who are called to the marriage supper of the Lamb!' " And he said to me, 'These are the true sayings of God.' ¹⁰And I fell at his feet to worship him. But he said to me, "See that you do not do that! I am your fellow servant, and of your brethren who have the testimony of Jesus. Worship God! For the testimony of Jesus is the spirit of prophecy." (Revelation 19:6-10) The marriage ceremony was often the greatest celebration in ancient times. It could last days; even weeks or longer. In those times, the marriage was usually arranged by the parents, often even while the bride and groom were still children.

But who is getting married? In the verse, *"⁷Let us be glad and rejoice and give Him glory, for the marriage of the Lamb has come, and His wife has made herself ready"*, we know the Lamb is the Lamb of God, our Lord and Savior Jesus Christ.

John the Baptist recognized Him very early, even before Jesus' ministry began, *"²⁹The next day John saw Jesus coming toward him, and said, 'Behold! The Lamb of God who takes away the sin of the world!' "* (John 1:29)

It is the same Lamb who will open the seals, *"¹Now I saw when the Lamb opened one of the seals; and I heard one of the four living creatures saying with a voice like thunder, 'Come and see.' "* (Revelation 6:1)

So the bridegroom in this wedding feast is none other than Jesus Christ. But who is his wife-to-be?

Paul writes about this in 2 Corinthians and in Ephesians. Let's look at the passage in 2 Corinthians first, *"²For I am jealous for you with godly jealousy. For I have betrothed you to one husband, that I may present you as a chaste virgin to Christ."* (2 Corinthians 11:2)

Paul tells husbands to, *"²⁵Husbands, love your wives, just as Christ also loved the church and gave Himself for her, ²⁶that He might sanctify and cleanse her with the washing of water by the word, ²⁷that He might present her to Himself a glorious church, not having spot or wrinkle or any such thing, but that she should be holy and without blemish."* (Ephesians 5:25-27)

So we, all who have given our lives to Jesus Christ and repented of their sins prior to the rapture of the Church, are the Bride of Christ! It is us, the Church, who will be standing there, made ready for Christ, to be made one with Him for all time.

"As a chaste virgin." How are we, who are sinners, to become as a chaste virgin? Only through the sacrificial blood of our Lord and Savior, Jesus Christ, are we made pure, *"⁸And to her it was granted to be arrayed in fine linen, clean and bright, for the fine linen is the righteous acts of the saints."* (Revelation 19:8)

But, if Jesus Christ is the groom and we, the Church, are the bride, then who are those to whom the angel is referring in the next verse? *"⁹Then he said to me, 'Write: 'Blessed are those who are called to the marriage supper of the Lamb!'"* (Revelation 19:9a)

The Greek word translated to called is keklēmenoi[80], which means "having been invited." If you've been to a wedding, you probably received a special invitation asking you to come share in the celebration of the union of the bride and groom. It's no different here – those called to this wedding are there to share in the celebration of this long-awaited union of Jesus Christ and His Bride.

But who are they? Those invitees are not who make up the Church – those are standing at the altar as the Bride. Who else is in Heaven to come join in this celebration? Aside from the angels, the Elders, and the four creatures in front of the throne, who else is in Heaven to share in this joy?

---

[80] Strong's Greek.2564.kaleó, verb, "to call, summon, invite"

Chapter 24 – The Second Coming

Well, we know the Old Testament Saints are also in Heaven, although not in their Heavenly bodies yet, so they will be invited to the wedding.

And, we also have those who have been martyred for their witness of Christ during the Tribulation who are in Heaven, though not yet in their Heavenly bodies, aka the Tribulation Saints. They are the same ones John saw under the altar when the fifth seal was opened though their numbers have increased since John first saw them, *"⁹When He opened the fifth seal, I saw under the altar the souls of those who had been slain for the word of God and for the testimony which they held. ¹⁰And they cried with a loud voice, saying, 'How long, O Lord, holy and true, until You judge and avenge our blood on those who dwell on the earth?' ¹¹Then a white robe was given to each of them; and it was said to them that they should rest a little while longer, until both the number of their fellow servants and their brethren, who would be killed as they were, was completed."* (Revelation 6:9-11)

But the Tribulation Saints are saved by the blood of Christ, just as the Church was, so why aren't they part of the marriage ceremony?

To understand why those who turn to Christ during the Tribulation are not part of the "Church", aka the Bride of Christ, we have to go back to when the "Church" began and when the Church Age ends.

"¹When the Day of Pentecost had fully come, they were all with one accord in one place. ²And suddenly there came a sound from heaven, as of a rushing mighty wind, and it filled the whole house where they were sitting. ³Then there appeared to them divided tongues, as of fire, and one sat upon each of them. **⁴And they were all filled with the Holy Spirit** *and began to speak with other tongues, as the Spirit gave them utterance."* (Acts 2:1-4) (emphasis added)

Aren't the Tribulation Saints also filled with the Holy Spirit?

Paul writes to the church at Thessalonica, when they were struggling to understand when the Day of the Lord would be or if it had come already. Paul reminds them he had already spoken to them about this and that the Day of the Lord, and the revealing of the AntiChrist could not happen until certain things occurred first.

"³Let no one deceive you by any means; for that Day will not come unless the falling away comes first, and the man of sin is revealed, the son of perdition, ⁴who opposes and exalts himself above all that is called God or that is worshiped, so that he sits as God in the temple of God, showing himself that he is God. ⁵Do you not remember that when I was still with you I told you these things? ⁶And now you know what is restraining, that he may be revealed in his own time. ⁷For the mystery of lawlessness is already at work; only He who now restrains will do so until He is taken out of the way. ⁸And then the lawless one will be revealed, whom the Lord will consume with the breath of His mouth and destroy with the brightness of His coming." (2 Thessalonians 2:3-8)

Paul is telling the church at Thessalonica the Day of the Lord cannot come and the AntiChrist cannot be revealed until *"He who now restrains will do so until He is taken out of the way."* (2 Thessalonians 2:7b)

We know, from everything we have read to this point in Revelation, that the Day of the Lord has, at this point, indeed come and the AntiChrist has not only been revealed but is about to receive judgement. So what, or who, is this restrainer who has been taken out of the way?

Is it mankind? No, the sin nature of man embraces evil, not restrains it.

Is it the government? No, same reason as above.

Is it angels? No, for several reasons. We know angels are present during the Tribulation – with the three woes, then with the warnings. They are not taken away before the Tribulation, then return. But, most importantly, they also do not have the power

Chapter 24 – The Second Coming

to restrain evil.

Is it God? Yes, only God has the power to restrain evil and, in the form of the Holy Spirit, He turns his back on an evil and unrepentant world. However, we do know the Holy Spirit is still active, to some extent, during the Tribulation as we can see His impact on those who are saved during the Tribulation.

We could take a deep dive into theology and build a case for who this Restrainer is and what part He plays during the Tribulation, but I'll let the readers do that research as the Holy Spirit guides them. For now, we will accept that this Restrainer is the Holy Spirit of God and He is indeed removed when the Church is raptured. The Tribulation Saints, those who have repented of their sins and turned back to God, are not indwelt with the Holy Spirit, as those who are saved during the Church age are.

But make no mistake! This fact does not impair or limit their relationship with God as we will see in the next chapter of Revelation, *"Then I saw the souls of those who had been beheaded for their witness to Jesus and for the word of God, who had not worshiped the beast or his image, and had not received his mark on their foreheads or on their hands. And they lived and reigned with Christ for a thousand years."* (Revelation 20:4b)

We could ponder the timing of this event and how there are some striking similarities between the traditional Hebrew Galilean wedding process[81] and the brideship of the Church to Christ, from betrothal to the "honeymoon" (yichud), but since that is covered in my first book in the Beginning of Sorrows series, Go Set A Watchman, we don't dig it into here.

Let's look at the last two verses of that passage in Revelation chapter 19, *"⁹Then he said to me, 'Write: 'Blessed are those who are called to the marriage supper of the Lamb!' And he said to me, 'These are the true sayings of God.' ¹⁰And I fell at his feet to worship him. But he said to me, 'See that you do not do that! I am your fellow servant, and of your brethren who have the testimony*

---

[81] Go Set A Watchman, Susan Mouw, May 30, 2020, pg. 77, https://www.amazon.com/dp/B089J3LR76

of Jesus. Worship God! For the testimony of Jesus is the spirit of prophecy.' " (Revelation 19:9-10)

The voice that John hears at the beginning of this passage is not identified, but it is probably that of an angel. John falls at this angel's feet to worship and is told *""See that you do not do that!"* Angels are not meant to be worshipped – this becomes crucial to our understanding later in the book of Revelation.

3. The Second Coming of Christ

"¹¹Now I saw heaven opened, and behold, a white horse. And He who sat on him was called Faithful and True, and in righteousness He judges and makes war. ¹²His eyes were like a flame of fire, and on His head were many crowns. He had a name written that no one knew except Himself. ¹³He was clothed with a robe dipped in blood, and His name is called The Word of God. ¹⁴And the armies in heaven, clothed in fine linen, white and clean, followed Him on white horses. ¹⁵Now out of His mouth goes a sharp sword, that with it He should strike the nations. And He Himself will rule them with a rod of iron. He Himself treads the winepress of the fierceness and wrath of Almighty God. 1⁶And He has on His robe and on His thigh a name written:
> KING OF KINGS AND
> LORD OF LORDS."

(Revelation 19:11-16)
Many call this event Our Blessed Hope, but truly – this is just the beginning!

As I mentioned at the opening of this chapter, the prophecy in Jude about the return of the Lord with his ten thousand is the first prophecy, given by a prophet, in the Bible. But it is not the only prophecy about this longed-for event.

There are so many verses in both the Old and New Testaments that predict this Second Coming, we can't possibly go through them all. But we do need to look at one passage, in Luke 4, *"¹⁶So He came to Nazareth, where He had been brought up. And as His custom was, He went into the synagogue on the Sabbath day, and stood up to read. ¹⁷And He was handed the book of the prophet*

Chapter 24 – The Second Coming

Isaiah. And when He had opened the book, He found the place where it was written: [18]"The Spirit of the Lord is upon Me, because He has anointed Me To preach the gospel to the poor; He has sent Me to heal the brokenhearted, to proclaim liberty to the captives and recovery of sight to the blind, to set at liberty those who are oppressed; [19]to proclaim the acceptable year of the Lord." [20]Then He closed the book, and gave it back to the attendant and sat down. And the eyes of all who were in the synagogue were fixed on Him. [21]And He began to say to them, "Today this Scripture is fulfilled in your hearing." (Luke 4:16-21)

The passage goes on to show how amazed they were at hearing this – especially Jesus' statement at the end, *"Today this Scripture is fulfilled in your hearing."* and asked each other if this was not just Joseph's son, the carpenter? Jesus is quoting from Isaiah 61, *[1]"The Spirit of the Lord God is upon Me, because the Lord has anointed Me to preach good tidings to the poor; He has sent Me to heal the brokenhearted, to proclaim liberty to the captives, and the opening of the prison to those who are bound."* (Isaiah 61:1-2a)

But He doesn't read this whole passage. He reads all of verse 1 but stops halfway through verse 2. *"[2]To proclaim the acceptable year of the Lord,* **and the day of vengeance of our God***;"* (Isaiah 61:2b) (emphasis added)

Why? Why doesn't He read the second part of that verse, *"and the day of vengeance of our God"*? Because that hasn't happened yet when Jesus is reading this. The day of vengeance of our God won't happen until the end of the Tribulation, so He cannot say " *'Today this Scripture is fulfilled in your hearing.' "*

Let's look at verse 13 from that passage, *"[13]He was clothed with a robe dipped in blood, and His name is called The Word of God."* Dipped in blood? How can that be?

Remember in Revelation chapter 14 when the earth's harvest was reaped and the rotten vines were thrown into the winepress? Well, you can't trample in the winepress without getting the hem of your garments dirty.

So the Image Could Speak

This is also prophesied by Isaiah, *"¹Who is this who comes from Edom, With dyed garments from Bozrah, This One who is glorious in His apparel, Traveling in the greatness of His strength?— 'I who speak in righteousness, mighty to save.' ²Why is Your apparel red, and Your garments like one who treads in the winepress? ³'I have trodden the winepress alone, and from the peoples no one was with Me. For I have trodden them in My anger, and trampled them in My fury; their blood is sprinkled upon My garments, and I have stained all My robes. ⁴For the day of vengeance is in My heart, and the year of My redeemed has come. ⁵I looked, but there was no one to help, and I wondered that there was no one to uphold; therefore My own arm brought salvation for Me; and My own fury, it sustained Me. ⁶I have trodden down the peoples in My anger, made them drunk in My fury, and brought down their strength to the earth."* (Isaiah 63:1-6)

It is interesting that the next verse shows that army that comes back with Him are not stained, *"¹⁴And the armies in heaven, clothed in fine linen, white and clean, followed Him on white horses."* (Revelation 19:14) Their robes are *"white and clean"*, for the Lord does not need our help in conquering His enemies. In fact, we have nothing to do with it. They are destroyed by a *"¹⁵a sharp sword, that with it He should strike the nations."* What is that sharp sword? The Word of God.

"And He Himself will rule them with a rod of iron." We're going to talk more about this further on, but there is only one period of time in the Bible when Jesus Christ rules on earth with a rod of iron and that is during the millennium.

4. The Battle of Armageddon

"¹⁷Then I saw an angel standing in the sun; and he cried with a loud voice, saying to all the birds that fly in the midst of heaven, "Come and gather together for the supper of the great God, ¹⁸that you may eat the flesh of kings, the flesh of captains, the flesh of mighty men, the flesh of horses and of those who sit on them, and the flesh of all people, free and slave, both small and great." ¹⁹And I saw the beast, the kings of the earth, and their armies, gathered together to make war against Him who sat on the horse and

Chapter 24 – The Second Coming

against His army. ²⁰Then the beast was captured, and with him the false prophet who worked signs in his presence, by which he deceived those who received the mark of the beast and those who worshiped his image. These two were cast alive into the lake of fire burning with brimstone. ²¹And the rest were killed with the sword which proceeded from the mouth of Him who sat on the horse. And all the birds were filled with their flesh." Revelation 19:17-21

Don't confuse this supper, to which the angel is inviting all the carrion birds, with the Marriage Supper of the Lamb! These are not the same.

Remember when those frog like demons went out from the mouths of Satan, the AntiChrist, and the False Prophet, *"¹³And I saw three unclean spirits like frogs coming out of the mouth of the dragon, out of the mouth of the beast, and out of the mouth of the false prophet. ¹⁴For they are spirits of demons, performing signs, which go out to the kings of the earth and of the whole world, to gather them to the battle of that great day of God Almighty."* (Revelation 16:13-14)

Apparently these messenger demons were successful in their mission, as we now see *"the beast, the kings of the earth, and their armies, gathered together to make war against Him who sat on the horse and against His army."*

Where are they gathered? In the Old Testament, the prophet Joel writes about the "valley of decision", or the Jehoshaphat Valley. According to ancient texts, this was a fairly small valley located just south of the city of David, where the Kidron, Hinnom and Tyropoeon valleys meet.

"¹²'Let the nations be wakened, and come up to the Valley of Jehoshaphat; for there I will sit to judge all the surrounding nations. ¹³Put in the sickle, for the harvest is ripe. Come, go down; for the winepress is full, the vats overflow—for their wickedness is great.' " (Joel 3:12-13)

It is unlikely, however, that all the armies called to this final battle

So the Image Could Speak

would fit in that small valley. As Jehoshaphat[82] means "the Lord has judged," it is more plausible that this is symbolic and not the actual geographic location of this final battle.

Fortunately, we have a more definitive location given in Revelation 16. Those demonic messenger frogs are sent out to gather the armies and *"[16]And they gathered them together to the place called in Hebrew, Armageddon."* (Revelation 16:16)

Armageddon, or Harmagedón[83] in the original Greek, is derived from the Hebrew as "har" and "Megiddo", or mount of Megiddo. The after-effects of this final battle, however, are not limited to this valley, as we read about in Revelation chapter 14, *"[20]And the winepress was trampled outside the city, and blood came out of the winepress, up to the horses' bridles, for one thousand six hundred furlongs."* (Revelation 14:20)

It is interesting to note that the distance from the town of Megiddo is about one thousand six hundred furlongs from Petra, where many believe the remnant of Israel are protected through the second half of the Tribulation.

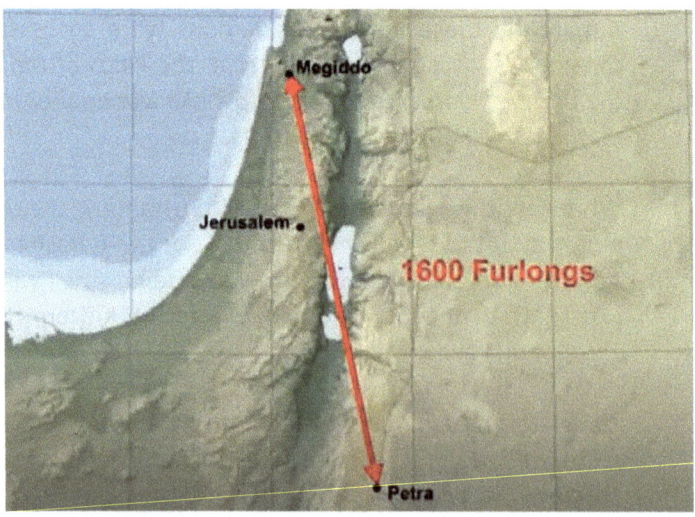

---

[82] Strong's Hebrew.3092.Yehoshaphat, proper name, "the LORD has judged"
[83] Strong's Greek.717.Harmagedón, proper noun, "Har-Magedon", from the Hebrew "har" and "Megiddon", or Mount of Megiddo

Chapter 24 – The Second Coming

This really isn't a battle at all, as it is entirely one-sided. The first beast - the AntiChrist, and the second beast - the False Prophet, are captured and their doom is sealed. They are cast into the Lake of Fire where the smoke from their torment rises forever and ever. Those who followed the Beast and the False Prophet are *"…killed with the sword which proceeded from the mouth of Him who sat on the horse. And all the birds were filled with their flesh."*

Those who followed the AntiChrist and the False Prophet become a feast for carrion birds. We've seen this before in the Ezekiel 38-39 war of Gog and Magog. But, we have to be careful here – these two battles are not the same.

"4'You shall fall upon the mountains of Israel, you and all your troops and the peoples who are with you; I will give you to birds of prey of every sort and to the beasts of the field to be devoured.'" (Ezekiel 39:4)

We're going to explore the battle of Gog and Magog, and the second battle mentioning Gog and Magog, when we delve into the scripture about what happens at the end of the millennium.

But this is not a real battle. The Lord destroys his enemies without lifting a hand. He destroys them with the sword of His mouth – the Word of God. Just as God brought this world into being with His Word, the enemies of God are taken out.

So the Image Could Speak

Chapter 25 – The Millennium

Chapter twenty of the Book of Revelation is another fascinating reveal of God's plan. Just as in the previous chapter, there is nothing that happens at this time, at the end of the Tribulation, that has not been foretold in scripture. Revelation chapter 20 also has four main divisions:

- Satan is bound
- The Millennium
- Satanic Rebellion
- Great White Throne Judgment

1. Satan bound

    "¹Then I saw an angel coming down from heaven, having the key to the bottomless pit and a great chain in his hand. ²He laid hold of the dragon, that serpent of old, who is the Devil and Satan, and bound him for a thousand years; ³and he cast him into the bottomless pit, and shut him up, and set a seal on him, so that he should deceive the nations no more till the thousand years were finished. But after these things he must be released for a little while." (Revelation 20:1-3)

    Remember the fifth trumpet and the fallen angel who let loose those fierce locusts? *"¹Then the fifth angel sounded: And I saw a star fallen from heaven to the earth. To him was given the key to the bottomless pit."* (Revelation 9:1) But we know, from the first chapter in Revelation, Who holds the keys to death and Hades, or that bottomless pit. *"¹⁷And when I saw Him, I fell at His feet as dead. But He laid His right hand on me, saying to me, "Do not be afraid; I am the First and the Last. ¹⁸I am He who lives, and was dead, and behold, I am alive forevermore. Amen. And I have the keys of Hades and of Death."* (Revelation 1:17-18)

    The fallen angel who let loose those locusts had to return the keys to Jesus Christ, and now He has handed them over, for a specific purpose, to this angel. This angel also carries a *"great chain"* in his hand to bind the dragon, aka Satan, for one thousand years.

Chapter 25 – The Millennium

So, the AntiChrist and the False Prophet have a different ending than the dragon...at least for now. They were both thrown in the lake of fire for all eternity, but the dragon, Satan, is bound and cast into the bottomless pit. He can't get out, but he's not annihilated...yet. Satan's reprieve, if you want to call it that, is temporary as we'll see.

Satan is bound for 1000 years that *"he should deceive the nations no more till the thousand years were finished."* But then, he is released for a little while. Why?

With the Battle of Armageddon destroying all those who followed the two beasts on earth and the casting of those two beasts into the lake of fire, God has removed all but one of His enemies – Satan. But he, too, must be removed for the Millennium and Jesus Christ's kingdom on earth to begin.

It is interesting to note here that it is an angel – another created being, just like Satan – who chains up the dragon and casts him into the abyss. For all those who thought Satan was so powerful, this proves his profound ability to deceive and his vulnerability to the power and authority of God. But, for now at least, his deceit is halted.

But then, he is released for a little while. Why?

Some things cannot be understood until they are revealed to us, but if we understand this period called the Millennium, it begins to make sense. Who are those who inhabit the Millennium? Obviously, any who have been resurrected which would include; the Old Testament Saints, the Church, and the Tribulation Martyrs. But there are also those who still have earthly bodies - those who have survived, did not take the Mark of the Beast or worship the AntiChrist. These will lead normal lives – get married, have children, die. Over a thousand years, there would be many generations removed from those who first inhabited the earth for the beginning of that Millennial Reign.

Those children, grandchildren, great-grandchildren and so forth who will be born during the Millennium are also still born with a sin nature. Let me say that again - those children, grandchildren, great-grandchildren and so forth who are born during the Millennium are also still born with a sin nature. Satan is bound, but not destroyed. They will still have to repent and accept the Gospel of Jesus Christ.

It will be different for them than it has been for us, as they will see Jesus Christ sitting on the Throne of David and reigning from Jerusalem, but the farther they are removed from those who came out of the Tribulation, the more their memory of the Tribulation weakens and the more they will take for granted just how good they have it. They will need a reminder. And, as we'll see, they get one.

There is another reason, but we'll see that when we get to the next chapter in Revelation.

2. The Millennium

"⁴And I saw thrones, and they sat on them, and judgment was committed to them. Then I saw the souls of those who had been beheaded for their witness to Jesus and for the word of God, who had not worshiped the beast or his image, and had not received his mark on their foreheads or on their hands. And they lived and reigned with Christ for a thousand years. ⁵But the rest of the dead did not live again until the thousand years were finished. This is the first resurrection. ⁶Blessed and holy is he who has part in the first resurrection. Over such the second death has no power, but they shall be priests of God and of Christ, and shall reign with Him a thousand years." Revelation 20:4-6

John sees *"thrones, and they sat on them, and judgment was committed to them."* Who is sitting on those thrones? We have to go to Scripture to see who has been promised to reign with Christ.

- Old Testament Saints – *"²⁷Then the kingdom and dominion, and the greatness of the kingdoms under the whole heaven, shall be given to the people, the saints of the Most High. His kingdom is an everlasting kingdom,*

Chapter 25 – The Millennium

and all dominions shall serve and obey Him."* (Daniel 7:27)

- The Apostles – *"²⁸So Jesus said to them, "Assuredly I say to you, that in the regeneration, when the Son of Man sits on the throne of His glory, you who have followed Me will also sit on twelve thrones, judging the twelve tribes of Israel."* (Matthew 19:28)

- The Church – *"²Do you not know that the saints will judge the world? And if the world will be judged by you, are you unworthy to judge the smallest matters?"* (1 Corinthians 6:2)

We have the Old Testament Saints, the Apostles, and the New Testament Church. Then we read the rest of verse 4, *"Then I saw the souls of those who had been beheaded for their witness to Jesus and for the word of God, who had not worshiped the beast or his image, and had not received his mark on their foreheads or on their hands. And they lived and reigned with Christ for a thousand years."*

So we can add one more to that list – the Tribulation Martyrs.

Let's look at the rest of that passage at the beginning of Revelation chapter 20.

"⁵But the rest of the dead did not live again until the thousand years were finished. This is the first resurrection. ⁶Blessed and holy is he who has part in the first resurrection. Over such the second death has no power, but they shall be priests of God and of Christ, and shall reign with Him a thousand years." (Revelation 20:5-6)

The first resurrection would seem to be a single event from this passage, but actually, it is more of a category grouping of several events. In fact, the word translated to *"first"* in this verse is the Greek word, prótos[84], which implies a priority. In other words,

---

[84] Strong's Greek.4413.prótos, adjective, "first, before, principal, most important."

this *"first resurrection"* not only precedes the resurrection of any who have sinned, but is of a higher priority, and more importance, than that resurrection.

The first resurrection event would be when those graves were opened at the moment of Jesus' death on the cross, *"⁵⁰And Jesus cried out again with a loud voice, and yielded up His spirit. ⁵¹Then, behold, the veil of the temple was torn in two from top to bottom; and the earth quaked, and the rocks were split, ⁵²and the graves were opened; and many bodies of the saints who had fallen asleep were raised; ⁵³and coming out of the graves after His resurrection, they went into the holy city and appeared to many."* (Matthew 27:50-54)

The resurrection of Jesus Christ would be another, and very crucial, resurrection event, *"¹Now after the Sabbath, as the first day of the week began to dawn, Mary Magdalene and the other Mary came to see the tomb. ²And behold, there was a great earthquake; for an angel of the Lord descended from heaven, and came and rolled back the stone from the door, and sat on it. ³His countenance was like lightning, and his clothing as white as snow. ⁴And the guards shook for fear of him, and became like dead men. ⁵But the angel answered and said to the women, 'Do not be afraid, for I know that you seek Jesus who was crucified. ⁶He is not here; for He is risen, as He said. Come, see the place where the Lord lay. ⁷And go quickly and tell His disciples that He is risen from the dead, and indeed He is going before you into Galilee; there you will see Him. Behold, I have told you.' "* (Matthew 28:1-7)

The next resurrection event, before this event at the end of the Tribulation, is when the Church is resurrected, at the harpazo or rapture, *"¹⁶For the Lord Himself will descend from heaven with a shout, with the voice of an archangel, and with the trumpet of God. And the dead in Christ will rise first. ¹⁷Then we who are alive and remain shall be caught up together with them in the clouds to meet the Lord in the air. And thus we shall always be with the Lord."* (1 Thessalonians 4:16-17)

This first resurrection is for all those who have accepted Jesus

Chapter 25 – The Millennium

Christ and repented of their sins, which would include any who were martyred during the Tribulation.

While scripture doesn't confirm or deny, it would also seem to be when the Old Testament Saints are given their resurrection bodies.

Anyone who was not deemed righteous, whether from the Old Testament period, the Church Age, or during the Tribulation will be resurrected and judged later.

"Over such the second death has no power, but they shall be priests of God and of Christ, and shall reign with Him a thousand years." (Revelation 20:6b)

Second Death? Does this mean that all those whose graves opened up when Jesus died are still walking around somewhere and have yet to die again since they are not subject to a second death? Well, no. The first death is the separation of body and soul – when our bodies die, and the soul or spirit is removed. The second death is when the soul, or spirit, is separated from God.

Those who are a part of that group of events called the first resurrection are never separated from God – they are with Him for eternity, so this second death has no power over them. Those who do not participate in this first resurrection, however, are all those – throughout mankind's history, up to and including this millennial period – who have not obeyed God and who have not repented. For them, the second death is when they are separated from God forever.

3. The Millennium – Fact or Fiction?

There are some, even within the church, who don't believe in a literal Millennium. They believe it is allegorical, or symbolic. They believe Christ's rule is in our hearts, not from the Throne of David.

There are others, also within the church, who believe the Millennium is already past, or we're in it now.

So the Image Could Speak

But the sheer volume of Scripture about the Millennial Reign of Jesus Christ is hard to argue against:

It was promised to David that his seed would establish a forever kingdom; *"¹²'When your days are fulfilled and you rest with your fathers, I will set up your seed after you, who will come from your body, and I will establish his kingdom. ¹³He shall build a house for My name, and I will establish the throne of his kingdom forever.'"* (2 Samuel 7:12-13)

Has this happened? We know the nation of Israel was regathered in 1948, but under what duress do they continue as a nation? What house have they built, *"house for My name"*? As of this writing, there is no temple in Jerusalem.

It was predicted in Psalms; *"⁶'Yet I have set My King On My holy hill of Zion.' ⁷I will declare the decree: the Lord has said to Me, 'You are My Son, today I have begotten You. ⁸Ask of Me, and I will give You the nations for Your inheritance, and the ends of the earth for Your possession.' "* (Psalms 2:6-8)
"¹The Lord said to my Lord, 'Sit at My right hand, Till I make Your enemies Your footstool.' ²The Lord shall send the rod of Your strength out of Zion. Rule in the midst of Your enemies!" (Psalms 110:1-2)

It was prophesied by the prophets, but there are too many to list, so we'll just look at a few.

"¹The word that Isaiah the son of Amoz saw concerning Judah and Jerusalem. ²Now it shall come to pass in the latter days that the mountain of the Lord's house shall be established on the top of the mountains, and shall be exalted above the hills; and all nations shall flow to it. ³Many people shall come and say, "Come, and let us go up to the mountain of the Lord, to the house of the God of Jacob; He will teach us His ways, and we shall walk in His paths." For out of Zion shall go forth the law, and the word of the Lord from Jerusalem. ⁴He shall judge between the nations, and rebuke many people; They shall beat their swords into plowshares, and their spears into pruning hooks; nation shall not lift up sword against nation, neither shall they learn war

Chapter 25 – The Millennium

anymore." (Isaiah 2:1-4)

Has this happened? Have nations all *"beat their swords into plowshares, and their spears into pruning hooks?"* Do we live in a time when *"nation shall not lift up sword against nation, neither shall they learn war anymore"*? Just listening to the news every day would belie that.

And there are those who will rebel even during this time as we'll see. Not all swords are beaten into plowshares...yet.

"⁵'Behold, the days are coming,' says the Lord, 'That I will raise to David a branch of righteousness; a King shall reign and prosper, and execute judgment and righteousness in the earth. ⁶In His days Judah will be saved, and Israel will dwell safely; now this is His name by which He will be called:
THE LORD OUR RIGHTEOUSNESS.' "
(Jeremiah 23:5-6)

This verse not only verifies the prophetic fulfillment of the Millennial Kingdom of Jesus Christ, but also fulfills the Davidic covenant with Israel on earth.

"¹³I was watching in the night visions, and behold, One like the Son of Man, coming with the clouds of heaven! He came to the Ancient of Days, and they brought Him near before Him. ¹⁴Then to Him was given dominion and glory and a kingdom, that all peoples, nations, and languages should serve Him. His dominion is an everlasting dominion, which shall not pass away, and His kingdom the one which shall not be destroyed." (Daniel 7:13-14)

This is just a sampling of the verses about the Millennium and the Lord Jesus Christ's reign on earth. Of course, it is also in our Lord's Prayer, "Thy Kingdom come, Thy will be done..."

Just a look at a few of those verses – when have we beaten our weapons into plowshares and during what time have nations not been at war? Has there ever been a time on this earth when Jesus ruled the nations...from Mount Zion? Where is the Lord's house established on top of the mountains?

None of that has happened and, at this point, Satan is not bound. The late Chuck Smith had a good response to one of those who believed the Millennium was present-day. He said, "Well, then Satan's chain is too long!" I have to agree – either this Millennium is a literal future period of Jesus Christ reign on earth for 1000 years...or Satan's chain is too long!

4. Life during the Millennium

What will life be like during the Millennium? Scripture paints quite an alluring picture of what it will be like for that one thousand years after the Tribulation, so let's take a look at it.

First, there will be only one kingdom and the King will be Jesus Christ. No more political elections, or party divides. A true One World Government, but one not run by man, with all the corruption, inequity, and injustice we see now, but one ruled by a Just and Righteous Jesus Christ.

"9And the Lord shall be King over all the earth. In that day it shall be— 'The Lord is one,' And His name one." (Zechariah 14:9)

In the United States, the seat of power is in Washington, DC. Other countries have their own capitals and halls of government. But in this millennium, there will be only one throne and it will be in Jerusalem.

"17'So you shall know that I am the Lord your God, dwelling in Zion My holy mountain. Then Jerusalem shall be holy, and no aliens shall ever pass through her again.' " (Joel 3:17)

Aliens? So all those reports of UFO's are accurate? Well, not exactly. The word aliens is translated from the Hebrew, wə·zā·rîm.[85] It means stranger and, in this passage, it would include all those who have been enemies to Jerusalem. This is a promise that Jerusalem will never again be raided, destroyed, invaded, or in any way compromised. Reading the history of the Jews and all the times Jerusalem has been struck, this will be

---

[85] Strong's Hebrew.2114.zuwr, verb, "to be a stranger"

Chapter 25 – The Millennium

welcome, and long awaited, news to many.

The Jerusalem that was, before the Second Coming, is no more. It has changed. Remember the seventh bowl? *"[19]Now the great city was divided into three parts, and the cities of the nations fell. And great Babylon was remembered before God, to give her the cup of the wine of the fierceness of His wrath. [20]Then every island fled away, and the mountains were not found."* (Revelation 16:19-20)

Zechariah prophesied about a part of this change, also. *"[4]And in that day His feet will stand on the Mount of Olives, which faces Jerusalem on the east. And the Mount of Olives shall be split in two, from east to west, making a very large valley; half of the mountain shall move toward the north and half of it toward the south."* (Zechariah 14:4)

Jerusalem will be the Holy City, from which Jesus will reign. It will not only be the capital of the world and from which Jesus reigns, it will be an education center for all who want to learn the Word of God and many, from all over the world, will flock to Jerusalem.

"[1]Now it shall come to pass in the latter days that the mountain of the Lord's house shall be established on the top of the mountains, and shall be exalted above the hills; and peoples shall flow to it. [2]Many nations shall come and say, 'Come, and let us go up to the mountain of the Lord, to the house of the God of Jacob; He will teach us His ways, and we shall walk in His paths.' For out of Zion the law shall go forth, and the word of the Lord from Jerusalem." (Micah 4:1-2)

What Lord's house will be established on the top of the mountains? If we go back into the Old Testament, we find the answer.

Ezekiel has a vision of something on a mountaintop. *"[2]In the visions of God He took me into the land of Israel and set me on a very high mountain; on it toward the south was something like the structure of a city."* (Ezekiel 40:2)

So the Image Could Speak

He encounters a man with a measuring rod and is told to record everything he sees. *"⁴And the man said to me, 'Son of man, look with your eyes and hear with your ears, and fix your mind on everything I show you; for you were brought here so that I might show them to you. Declare to the house of Israel everything you see."* (Ezekiel 40:4)

What is this man measuring? A Temple. *"⁵Now there was a wall all around the outside of the temple. In the man's hand was a measuring rod six cubits long, each being a cubit and a handbreadth; and he measured the width of the wall structure, one rod; and the height, one rod."* (Ezekiel 40:5)

The rest of Ezekiel chapter 40, and the remaining chapters in Ezekiel give very explicit and exact measurements for this Temple. Then in chapter 43, we learn what Temple this is and what purpose it will serve.

"⁶Then I heard Him speaking to me from the temple, while a man stood beside me. ⁷And He said to me, 'Son of man, this is the place of My throne and the place of the soles of My feet, where I will dwell in the midst of the children of Israel forever. No more shall the house of Israel defile My holy name, they nor their kings, by their harlotry or with the carcasses of their kings on their high places." (Ezekiel 43:6-7)

This Temple that Ezekiel sees will be where the Throne of Jesus Christ on earth will be and from where all the earth will be ruled.

Just a side note: the dimensions of this Millennial Temple do not match those of either Solomon's or Herod's Temple. In fact, this Temple, as described in Ezekiel, has not yet been built. For those interested, there is a brief overall description and history of the Temples in Jerusalem in the Appendix, **The Temples of Jerusalem.**

It is interesting to discover that animal sacrifices will be reinstituted during the Millennium. Why? When we will have the Perfect Sacrifice and the payment for all sin sitting on His Throne in Jerusalem?

Chapter 25 – The Millennium

"²⁶Seven days they shall make atonement for the altar and purify it, and so consecrate it. ²⁷When these days are over it shall be, on the eighth day and thereafter, that the priests shall offer your burnt offerings and your peace offerings on the altar; and I will accept you,' says the Lord God." (Ezekiel 43:26-27)

The sacrifices for the first seven days are explicitly stated and are for purification and consecration of the altar. But those sacrifices are allowed to continue and will continue throughout the Millennium. Why?

This excerpt from an article on Compelling Truth.org gives an excellent explanation for why animal sacrifices are continued in the Millennium.

> "While not every aspect of this question is answered in Scripture, it is clear that the continued use of animal sacrifices during the millennial kingdom is a fulfillment of God's prophecies made long ago. If animal sacrifices do not resume in this time period, this will mean God has not kept His promises in this area. Yet God always keeps His promises (Deuteronomy 7:9).
>
> These sacrifices did not take away sin in the Old Testament but were done in obedience to the Lord in repentance of sin. In a similar way, future animal sacrifices during the millennial kingdom will not take away sin but will serve as a reminder or memorial to the Lord (Hebrews 10:3). This is not unlike the way Christians take the Lord's Supper during this current time period (or church age) as a reminder of Jesus' death and resurrection.
>
> Though the thought of animal sacrifices during the millennial kingdom may sound strange to today's Christians, the sacrifices will be a fulfillment of God's prophecies and serve as an act of worship to the Lord. Christ Himself will reign during this time, offering a new meaning to these offerings as they are presented in the kingdom as Jesus reigns as Messiah and King."

So the Image Could Speak

Jesus Christ, and those He appoints to rule, will replace all the courts and laws. No more lawyers, no more laws favoring those in authority and repressing others, no more unjust acts. We've already seen how Just and Righteous our God is and it is He who will rule."[86]

"*³He shall judge between many peoples, and rebuke strong nations afar off*" (Micah 4:3a)

I am a child of the sixties and seventies, when the mantra, "Make Love not War" rang out from street corners and protests across the nation. Well, all those who love peace will love the Millennium, as there will be no more wars.

"*They shall beat their swords into plowshares, and their spears into pruning hooks; nation shall not lift up sword against nation, neither shall they learn war anymore.*" (Micah 4:3b)

Are you starting to get an idea of what it is going to be like during this time? No more weapons of mass destruction, with one country in a race to beat their enemy to the finish line of weapon development. It is hard to imagine, but it is coming.

Even the animals will be at peace!

"*⁶'The wolf also shall dwell with the lamb, the leopard shall lie down with the young goat, the calf and the young lion and the fatling together; and a little child shall lead them. ⁷The cow and the bear shall graze; their young ones shall lie down together; and the lion shall eat straw like the ox. ⁸The nursing child shall play by the cobra's hole, and the weaned child shall put his hand in the viper's den. ⁹They shall not hurt nor destroy in all My holy mountain, for the earth shall be full of the knowledge of the Lord as the waters cover the sea.'* " (Isaiah 11:6-9)

"*⁸The nursing child shall play by the cobra's hole, and the weaned*

---

[86] During the millennial kingdom, will there be animal sacrifices?, compelling truth, unknown date, https://www.compellingtruth.org/millennial-sacrifices.html

Chapter 25 – The Millennium

child shall put his hand in the viper's den." (Isaiah 11:8) Even little children will have nothing to be afraid of.

In effect, the world will be like the Garden of Eden before the serpent tempted Eve. The animal kingdom will be as it was intended to be, before the Great Flood caused animals to fear man, *"¹So God blessed Noah and his sons, and said to them: 'Be fruitful and multiply, and fill the earth. ²And the fear of you and the dread of you shall be on every beast of the earth, on every bird of the air, on all that move on the earth, and on all the fish of the sea. They are given into your hand.' "* (Genesis 9:1-2)

Those animals we hunt today will no longer have to run at the sight of man and man will need have no fear at the approach of what were once considered predatory animals.

No one will have to go to bed hungry, either.

"²⁶I will make them and the places all around My hill a blessing; and I will cause showers to come down in their season; there shall be showers of blessing. ²⁷Then the trees of the field shall yield their fruit, and the earth shall yield her increase." (Ezekiel 34:26-27a)

In fact, food and nourishment will be so abundant, the mountains will be overrun with new wine and streams of milk will flow through the hills.

"¹⁸And it will come to pass in that day that the mountains shall drip with new wine, the hills shall flow with milk, and all the brooks of Judah shall be flooded with water; a fountain shall flow from the house of the Lord and water the Valley of Acacias." (Joel 3:18)

If you have read about the Great Flood, then you know the life spans of those who lived before the flood were quite long, with Enoch's life of 365 years being the shortest. Today, if you make it to 100, you are in the news and everyone wants your secret.
In the millennium, if you don't live to be 100, you will be thought accursed! You'll still be a child at 100.

So the Image Could Speak

"[20]'No more shall an infant from there live but a few days, nor an old man who has not fulfilled his days; for the child shall die one hundred years old, but the sinner being one hundred years old shall be accursed.'" (Isaiah 65:20)

There is so much more in the Scripture about this Millennial Kingdom, but I would invite you to read and study it for yourself. It is hard to fathom just how wonderful, and different, the world will be.

Sadly, not everyone will see it that way and some will rebel. Even when those of us who worship Christ are enjoying all this paradise, there will be those who will still turn their backs on God. Of course, they won't receive all the blessings we will have during this time, either, but instead of realizing their error and turning to Christ, their anger grows and provides fertile ground for when Satan is released.

5. Satan's Rebellion

"[7]Now when the thousand years have expired, Satan will be released from his prison [8]and will go out to deceive the nations which are in the four corners of the earth, Gog and Magog, to gather them together to battle, whose number is as the sand of the sea. [9]They went up on the breadth of the earth and surrounded the camp of the saints and the beloved city. And fire came down from God out of heaven and devoured them. [10]The devil, who deceived them, was cast into the lake of fire and brimstone where the beast and the false prophet are. And they will be tormented day and night forever and ever." (Revelation 20:7-10)

So Satan finally gets his just due and joins his comrades in the lake of fire.

This battle of Gog and Magog is often linked with the one in Ezekiel 38 and 39, but they are not the same event. The timing of the war in Ezekiel 38 and 39 is not clear, though many believe it is a pre-Tribulation event. The timing of this war is very clear; at the end of the 1000 year Millennium. There are other significant

Chapter 25 – The Millennium

differences between the two and I have attached a chart that shows those differences in the Appendix, "Two Battles of Gog and Magog".

6. Great White Throne Judgment

"¹¹Then I saw a great white throne and Him who sat on it, from whose face the earth and the heaven fled away. And there was found no place for them. ¹²And I saw the dead, small and great, standing before God, and books were opened. And another book was opened, which is the Book of Life. And the dead were judged according to their works, by the things which were written in the books. ¹³The sea gave up the dead who were in it, and Death and Hades delivered up the dead who were in them. And they were judged, each one according to his works. ¹⁴Then Death and Hades were cast into the lake of fire. This is the second death. ¹⁵And anyone not found written in the Book of Life was cast into the lake of fire." (Revelation 20:11-15)

Just a side note - one of those *"books were opened"* is likely the Book of Remembrance, which is a recording of all the acts by everyone throughout time. (Malachi 3:16)

There are two Judgement seats – one for believers and one for unbelievers. The one for believers, what we call the Bema Seat or Judgement Seat of Christ, is more of a rewards platform. Our sins are forgiven – washed by the Blood of the Lamb, so we are not judged for our sins here. But we are held accountable for how well...or how poorly....we managed the gifts given to us and how closely we followed Christ's rule for our life, just as in the parable of the returning king in Luke 19.

There are many varying opinions on when this happens – it could be immediately at our death, or it could be after the Rapture...or really any time during the 70th Week of Daniel up to and including during/after the Millennium.

But this Judgement that occurs at the end of the Millennium is not the Bema Seat Judgement, when believers will give an accounting and receive their rewards. This judgement is the

So the Image Could Speak

Great White Throne Judgement and is a judgment for sins. Anyone whose name is not found in the Book of Life is cast into the fire.

"⁴Give them according to their deeds, and according to the wickedness of their endeavors; give them according to the work of their hands; render to them what they deserve. ⁵Because they do not regard the works of the Lord, nor the operation of His hands, He shall destroy them and not build them up." (Psalms 28:4)

Satan is now vanquished permanently, sin is removed from the world, judgement has been rendered on those who defied God, Jesus has been sitting on His Throne for 1000 years and things are about to undergo a tremendous renovation.

Chapter 26 – Behold! All Things are New

Chapter 26 – Behold! All Things are New

How can we even describe that which John sees in the last two chapters of Revelation? The New Heaven and New Earth, and the new city of Jerusalem – the holy city where God dwells with us is beyond description.

Before we dive into the new Heaven and earth, there is one "cause and effect" that was left unexplained in the previous chapter. The question is why was Satan re-released at the end of the Millennium?

Well, to put it very simply, the Lord must do one final cleansing before He brings in this glorious new world. One final separating of the wheat from the chaff, the sheep from the goats, and the good from the evil. So Satan is released to lure all those who have not worshipped God or followed the Lord Jesus Christ, and who have turned away from God into one final rebellion. Then, when the rebellion is over, Satan is permanently removed and evil is fully vanquished, our Heavenly Father gives us a gift beyond our imagination.

1. Revelation Chapter 21

    a. All things made new

    "[1]Now I saw a new heaven and a new earth, for the first heaven and the first earth had passed away. Also there was no more sea. [2]Then I, John, saw the holy city, New Jerusalem, coming down out of heaven from God, prepared as a bride adorned for her husband. [3]And I heard a loud voice from heaven saying, "Behold, the tabernacle of God is with men, and He will dwell with them, and they shall be His people. God Himself will be with them and be their God. [4]And God will wipe away every tear from their eyes; there shall be no more death, nor sorrow, nor crying. There shall be no more pain, for the former things have passed away." [5]Then He who sat on the throne said, "Behold, I make all things new." And He said to me, "Write, for these words are true and faithful." (Revelation 21:1-5)

    In this life, we will have trials and tribulations. In fact, we are to count it as joy when we have troubles, as James tells us, *"²My brethren, count it all joy when you fall into various trials, ³knowing that the testing of your faith produces patience."* (James 1:2-3)

Not only do those trials produce patience, but Paul tells us they build character, *"³And not only that, but we also glory in tribulations, knowing that tribulation produces perseverance; ⁴and perseverance, character; and character, hope."* (Romans 5:3-4)

While we will go through these trials and tribulations in this life, we are told God will never let the temptations by which we falter be more than we can endure, *"¹³No temptation has overtaken you except such as is common to man; but God is faithful, who will not allow you to be tempted beyond what you are able, but with the temptation will also make the way of escape, that you may be able to bear it."* (1 Corinthians 10:13)

Not only will He provide that escape, but if we trust in Him, He will give us peace, *"²⁷Peace I leave with you, My peace I give to you; not as the world gives do I give to you. Let not your heart be troubled, neither let it be afraid."* (John 14:27)

So, we will have troubles in this life – we will experience grief and sadness. We will weep and lament. We will suffer pain… But all of that is gone in this new Heaven and new Earth! *"⁴And God will wipe away every tear from their eyes; there shall be no more death, nor sorrow, nor crying. There shall be no more pain, for the former things have passed away."*

Wait a minute! If all these things have passed away, then why do we need God to wipe every tear from our eyes? What tears? Perhaps this verse is not referring to tears we will shed in eternity, but those tears that have been shed over this lifetime. Or…perhaps it is tears of joy at this new world. A world without sin, without pain,

Chapter 26 – Behold! All Things are New

without grief, without any of the negatives we have experienced in this life. He has wiped the slate clean! In fact, that is what He says, " *[5]Then He who sat on the throne said, "Behold, I make all things new."*

b. It is done!

"[6]And He said to me, "It is done! I am the Alpha and the Omega, the Beginning and the End. I will give of the fountain of the water of life freely to him who thirsts. [7]He who overcomes shall inherit all things, and I will be his God and he shall be My son." (Revelation 21:6-7)

"It is done!" brings to mind that verse in John, *"[30]So when Jesus had received the sour wine, He said, "It is finished!" And bowing His head, He gave up His spirit."* (John 19:30)

Both signify completion; with John 19:30 signifying a completion of the work of redemption and Revelation 21:6 signifying a completion of redemption history.

After this, there will be no need for redemption, for we are all made perfect in Christ's image. God's final enemy, death, has been vanquished and we who have overcome in Jesus' name inherit the earth!

c. The New Jerusalem

"[9]Then one of the seven angels who had the seven bowls filled with the seven last plagues came to me and talked with me, saying, "Come, I will show you the bride, the Lamb's wife." [10]And he carried me away in the Spirit to a great and high mountain, and showed me the great city, the holy Jerusalem, descending out of heaven from God, [11]having the glory of God. Her light was like a most precious stone, like a jasper stone, clear as crystal." (Revelation 21:9-11)

"Come, I will show you the bride, the Lamb's wife." The Wedding Feast is over and the Bride and Groom go to their new home.

In the traditional Galilean wedding, the groom-to-be left his bride-to-be to go prepare a place for her, just as Jesus did.

"*¹'Let not your heart be troubled; you believe in God, believe also in Me. ²In My Father's house are many mansions; if it were not so, I would have told you. **I go to prepare a place for you**. ³And if I go and prepare a place for you, I will come again and receive you to Myself; that where I am, there you may be also.' "* (John 14:1-3) (emphasis added)

The decision to go get his bride, and when the new home was complete, was not the groom's, but only the father's. It was the same for Jesus and His Bride, the Church.

"*³⁶'But of that day and hour no one knows, not even the angels of heaven, but My Father only.' "* (Matthew 24:36)

Now He has his Bride, the wedding has been completed, and He takes His Bride to their new home. Where is that new home? This new heavenly city, just as the angel tells John.

" *'Come, I will show you the bride, the Lamb's wife.' ¹⁰And he carried me away in the Spirit to a great and high mountain, and showed me the great city, the holy Jerusalem, descending out of heaven from God"* (Revelation 21:9b-10)

Of course, while Scripture doesn't specifically address this, everyone who has been saved and resurrected – the Old Testament Saints, the Tribulation Saints, and all those who survived the Millennium with their faith in Jesus Christ intact, will share that home with the Bride. That's ok – there is plenty of room.

Chapter 26 – Behold! All Things are New

d. The New City

"¹²Also she had a great and high wall with twelve gates, and twelve angels at the gates, and names written on them, which are the names of the twelve tribes of the children of Israel: ¹³three gates on the east (Judah, Issachar, Zebulon), three gates on the north (Dan, Asher, Napthtali), three gates on the south (Reuben, Simeon, Gad), and three gates on the west (Ephraim, Manasseh, Benjamin)." (Revelation 21:12-13)

The attached images are of my creation and not a prophetic projection of what this new city will be like. But I thought it would be interesting to view some conceptual graphics of what it might be like. (emphasis on might)

So the Image Could Speak

Figure 3 three gates on the east (Judah, Issachar, Zebulon)

Figure 4 three gates on the north (Dan, Asher, Napthtali)

Figure 5 three gates on the south (Reuben, Simeon, Gad)

Chapter 26 – Behold! All Things are New

Figure 6 three gates on the west (Ephraim, Manasseh, Benjamin)

e. The Foundation

"14Now the wall of the city had twelve foundations, and on them were the names of the twelve apostles of the Lamb. 15And he who talked with me had a gold reed to measure the city, its gates, and its wall. 16The city is laid out as a square; its length is as great as its breadth. And he measured the city with the reed: twelve thousand furlongs. Its length, breadth, and height are equal. 17Then he measured its wall: one hundred and forty-four cubits, according to the measure of a man, that is, of an angel." (Revelation 21:14-17)

Figure 7 12 Jeweled and Engraved Foundation Layers

The city is a cube – as long as it is wide and as tall as it is long and wide. A furlong is an eighth of a mile, so 8 furlongs = 1 mile. Twelve thousand furlongs = 1500 miles. This is no small city! If we look at this overlaid on a map of the US, 1500 miles from mid-state South Carolina (Aiken, SC), puts the end point in western New Mexico. Turn north and go 1500 miles and you're in the middle of Canada.

So the Image Could Speak

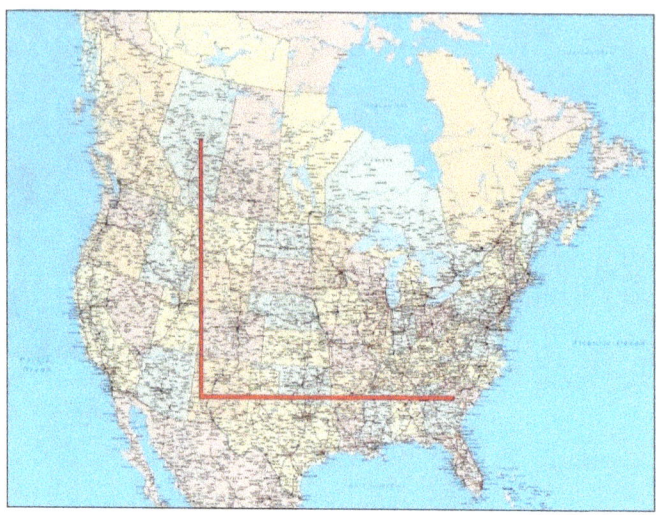

Those walls are not flimsy either; a cubit is the length from the elbow to the tip of a man's fingers, so it can vary, but roughly about 18", so 144' cubit wall is about 216 feet thick. They are more than 200' thick, yet they are *"like clear glass."*

There are 12 layers of foundation, with each layer being a precious or semi-precious stone, and each layer is engraved with the name of one of the 12 disciples.

"[18]The construction of its wall was of jasper; and the city was pure gold, like clear glass. [19]The foundations of the wall of the city were adorned with all kinds of precious stones: the first foundation was jasper, the second sapphire, the third chalcedony, the fourth emerald, [20]the fifth sardonyx, the sixth sardius, the seventh chrysolite, the eighth beryl, the ninth topaz, the tenth chrysoprase, the eleventh jacinth, and the twelfth amethyst.

f. The Pearly Gates

"[21]The twelve gates were twelve pearls: each individual gate was of one pearl. And the street of the city was pure gold, like transparent glass." (Revelation 21:14-21)

Chapter 26 – Behold! All Things are New

All my life I've heard people mention the Pearly Gates and I thought that was nice – the gates to Heaven have some pearlesque glow and maybe a few pearls here and there. Oh no – there are 12 gates and each gate is one pearl! One very large pearl.

g. The Temple

"²²But I saw no temple in it, for the Lord God Almighty and the Lamb are its temple. ²³The city had no need of the sun or of the moon to shine in it, for the glory of God illuminated it. The Lamb is its light. ²⁴And the nations of those who are saved shall walk in its light, and the kings of the earth bring their glory and honor into it. ²⁵Its gates shall not be shut at all by day (there shall be no night there). ²⁶And they shall bring the glory and the honor of the nations into it. ²⁷But there shall by no means enter it anything that defiles, or causes an abomination or a lie, but only those who are written in the Lamb's Book of Life." Revelation 21:22-27

Up to this point, there has been a Temple in Heaven, but now there is no need of one *"for the Lord God Almighty and the Lamb are its temple."* There is no need for a specific location to worship God, for He will be with us and we with Him. All whose names were written in the Lamb's Book of Life will be equal in Heaven – there will be no more social caste, or cliques. No favoritism for one group over another – we are all God's children and all equal in Heaven.

There is no sun or moon, for the source of light is God and the Lamb. And that light shines all the time – there is no night.

"¹²Then Jesus spoke to them again, saying, 'I am the light

So the Image Could Speak

of the world. He who follows Me shall not walk in darkness, but have the light of life.' " (John 8:12)

Chapter 26 – Behold! All Things are New

2. Revelation Chapter 22

    a. Streets of Gold

    "¹And he showed me a pure river of water of life, clear as crystal, proceeding from the throne of God and of the Lamb. ²In the middle of its street, and on either side of the river, was the tree of life, which bore twelve fruits, each tree yielding its fruit every month. The leaves of the tree were for the healing of the nations. ³And there shall be no more curse, but the throne of God and of the Lamb shall be in it, and His servants shall serve Him. ⁴They shall see His face, and His name shall be on their foreheads. ⁵There shall be no night there: They need no lamp nor light of the sun, for the Lord God gives them light. And they shall reign forever and ever." (Revelation 22:1-5)

    Remember in verse 1 of chapter 21, there was no more sea, *"¹Now I saw a new heaven and a new earth, for the first heaven and the first earth had passed away. Also there was no more sea."* We don't need to study the natural processes that create rain here, but we can understand that the sea – those large bodies of water – are what help create rain on earth today. We could do a deep dive into what the world looked like before the Flood and why there wasn't rain then – until there was, but we don't need to go down that path. This verse is clear there will be no rain in this new Heaven and earth – just as it was prior to the great flood.

    This pure river of water of life could be symbolic for life everlasting – a never-ending and always flowing gift from God.

So the Image Could Speak

Which leads us to that tree of life. One tree – twelve fruits – no annual growing season, as the tree replenishes its crop monthly. We are all in resurrected bodies in this new earth, so we don't really need to eat. Could it be that these fruits actually represent the fruits of the spirit? Galatians 5:22 lists 9 fruits of the spirit, *"²²But the fruit of the Spirit is love, joy, peace, longsuffering, kindness, goodness, faithfulness, ²³gentleness, self-control. Against such there is no law."* (Galatians 5:22-23)

And then we have this, *"The leaves of the tree were for the healing of the nations."* What healing? Why is healing necessary when there is no more sickness or death?

The Greek word used here is therapeian[87], which doesn't just mean healing as in a wound or sickness. Dr. John MacArthur explains it in his Commentary on Revelation, Vol II, "Perhaps a better way to translate it would be 'life-giving', 'health-giving', or 'therapeutic.' "[88]

b. The time is near

"⁶Then he said to me, 'These words are faithful and true.' And the Lord God of the holy prophets sent His angel to show His servants the things which must shortly take place. ⁷'Behold, I am coming quickly! Blessed is he who keeps the words of the prophecy of this book.' " (Revelation 22:6-7)

We have come full circle from the beginning of Revelation to the end of Revelation with the phrase, *"which must shortly take place."* This is identical to the

---

[87] Strong's Greek.2322.therapeia, noun feminine, "attention, medical service"
[88] <u>The MacArthur New Testament Commentary – Revelation 12-22</u>, 2000, Moody Publishers, Chicago, ISBN 978-08024-0774-0

Chapter 26 – Behold! All Things are New

opening verse in the first chapter of this book of Revelation, "*¹The Revelation of Jesus Christ, which God gave Him to show His servants—things which must shortly take place."* (Revelation 1:1) While this phrase is sometimes taken to mean that these things portrayed were meant to take place soon after this book was written, around 95-96AD, that isn't what is meant here.

We have to go back to the original Greek. "*which must shortly take place"* is actually "which must come to pass in quickness", or suddenly. This verse is just telling us these things are going to happen and when they start, there will be no stopping them and these events will happen in quick succession.

c. The Blessing

⁷"Behold, I am coming quickly! Blessed is he who keeps the words of the prophecy of this book." (Revelation 22:7)

Another blessing for those who keep the words of prophecy in this book! Just like in the first chapter of the book of Revelation, *"³Blessed is he who reads and those who hear the words of this prophecy, and keep those things which are written in it; for the time is near."* (Revelation 1:3)

The only book in the canonical Bible which offers a blessing, offers it twice. But it also gives a warning, as we will see.

d. Fellow Servant

"⁸Now I, John, saw and heard these things. And when I heard and saw, I fell down to worship before the feet of the angel who showed me these things. ⁹Then he said to me, "See that you do not do that. For I am your fellow servant, and of your brethren the prophets, and of those who keep the words of this book. Worship God." ¹⁰And he said to me, "Do not seal the words of the prophecy of this

book, for the time is at hand. *¹¹He who is unjust, let him be unjust still; he who is filthy, let him be filthy still; he who is righteous, let him be righteous still; he who is holy, let him be holy still."* (Revelation 22:8-11)

This is the second time John has fallen down to worship an angel and was corrected for doing it, *"¹⁰And I fell at his feet to worship him. But he said to me, "See that you do not do that! I am your fellow servant, and of your brethren who have the testimony of Jesus. Worship God! For the testimony of Jesus is the spirit of prophecy."* (Revelation 19:10)

This time, the angel is also giving John some additional directives. First, *"Do not seal the words of the prophecy of this book, for the time is at hand."* This is in direct opposition to the order in Daniel, when Daniel is told to seal up the book, *⁴"But you, Daniel, shut up the words, and seal the book until the time of the end; many shall run to and fro, and knowledge shall increase."* (Daniel 12:4)

About seven hundred years separate the writing of Daniel and the writing of Revelation, but I think it goes deeper than just the timing. At the beginning of this book of Revelation, John is told *"What you see, write in a book and send it to the seven churches which are in Asia: to Ephesus, to Smyrna, to Pergamos, to Thyatira, to Sardis, to Philadelphia, and to Laodicea."* (Revelation 1:11)

The fact that the book of Daniel is better understood today than it was just a decade ago is a clear sign of how close these events depicted in the book of Revelation may be.

There is much that could be said, but John MacArthur says it best. "The message of the Apocalypse, that Jesus will return bringing blessing for His own and horrifying judgement on the ungodly is too critical not to spread. Any Christian who fails to learn its truths is forfeiting

Chapter 26 – Behold! All Things are New

blessing; any preacher who fails to proclaim its truths is sinfully unfaithful to this mandate. Not to preach the book of Revelation is to fail to exalt the Lord Jesus Christ with the glory that is due Him."[89] – John MacArthur, Commentary on Revelation, Vol II.

e. Warning and Blessing

"¹²'And behold, I am coming quickly, and My reward is with Me, to give to every one according to his work. ¹³I am the Alpha and the Omega, the Beginning and the End, the First and the Last.' ¹⁴Blessed are those who do His commandments, that they may have the right to the tree of life, and may enter through the gates into the city. ¹⁵But outside are dogs and sorcerers and sexually immoral and murderers and idolaters, and whoever loves and practices a lie. ¹⁶'I, Jesus, have sent My angel to testify to you these things in the churches. I am the Root and the Offspring of David, the Bright and Morning Star.' ¹⁷And the Spirit and the bride say, 'Come!' And let him who hears say, 'Come!' And let him who thirsts come. Whoever desires, let him take the water of life freely. ¹⁸For I testify to everyone who hears the words of the prophecy of this book: If anyone adds to these things, God will add to him the plagues that are written in this book; ¹⁹and if anyone takes away from the words of the book of this prophecy, God shall take away his part from the Book of Life, from the holy city, and from the things which are written in this book. ²⁰He who testifies to these things says, 'Surely I am coming quickly.' Amen. Even so, come, Lord Jesus! ²¹The grace of our Lord Jesus Christ be with you all. Amen." (Revelation 22:12-21)

We've seen the blessing, now we have the warning. Do not add to, or take away from, this book for the penalty for doing so is severe, *"God shall take away his part from the Book of Life, from the holy city, and from the things*

---

[89] The MacArthur New Testament Commentary – Revelation 12-22, 2000, Moody Publishers, Chicago, ISBN 978-08024-0774-0

which are written in this book."

"[20]*He who testifies to these things says, 'Surely I am coming quickly.' Amen. Even so, come, Lord Jesus!"* (Revelation 22:20)

Maranatha!

Chapter 27 – The End is Near

Chapter 27 – The End is Near

The late Chuck Missler stated in one of his commentaries that:
"The past is a memory
The future is a hope
Right now is a gift – that is why it is called the present."

Studying the book of Revelation exemplifies that. While it is full of symbolism, it is not difficult to understand most of that symbolism by studying the rest of Scripture. While it was written in the past, for those present at the time, and is about the future, it is directed to all of us today and all those who read it in the years since its first dissemination.

In the final chapter in the book of Daniel, Daniel is told, *"'But you, Daniel, shut up the words, and seal the book until the time of the end; many shall run to and fro, and knowledge shall increase.' "* (Daniel 12:4)

Just a quick Google search, or a view of the listings on YouTube will reveal an amazing plethora of videos, blogs, and commentaries now available about the book of Revelation and the times we are in. But I pray you are careful – not all of those who post on YouTube or Facebook are giving a God-inspired translation. Be especially careful about those who would give specific dates.

Reading the book of Revelation reveals a God, and our Savior, Jesus Christ, who is a loving and merciful God. He is also a righteous and just God and the evil in our world today will not, cannot, be tolerated much longer. I believe we are in the times leading up to, and preparing the way for, those things depicted in the book of Revelation.

While there are some scenes in the book of Revelation that may be disturbing, the overwhelming message overall, indeed throughout Holy Scripture, is of a Loving God. A God Who sent His only Son, Jesus Christ, to die in payment for our sins.

What kept Jesus on that cross? It wasn't the nails – He could have called a thousand angels to take Him away at any point during the trial and crucifixion and all those Roman sentries and those that shouted, "Give us Barabbas" could not have stopped them.

So the Image Could Speak

No, what kept Jesus Christ on that cross was His love for us. Won't you give your love to Him?

PostScript

One sidenote before we wrap this up. If you enjoyed the images in the previous two chapters, you might enjoy a more in-depth look at them in a video I prepared for that purpose. I cannot take credit for all the images you will see in the video. Allen Parr, in his video **7 Shocking Things About Heaven in the Book of Revelation**, did an amazing job with imagery of the New Heaven and Earth. I highly recommend his video.

The video I prepared with some of Mr. Parr's images (used with permission) and graphics I had some fun with can be seen here. This is an excerpt from a recording from a class I taught about Revelation and goes verse by verse through Revelation chapters 21 and 22.

That video can be seen here: **https://youtu.be/IdCczr0wFQ0**

A quick word about the making of these images in the videos – it was fun making them, but no one can give a good rendition of what it is going to be like. As it says in 1 Corinthians, *"⁹But as it is written: "Eye has not seen, nor ear heard, Nor have entered into the heart of man the things which God has prepared for those who love Him."* (1 Corinthians 2:9) As beautiful as some of these images are, and as enticing as some of them may be, it cannot compare to what the reality will be.

So the Image Could Speak

Appendix I – Who wrote Revelation?

Since the Book of the Revelation of Jesus Christ was written, there has been some controversy about who actually penned the images given to him. We know, from the book of Revelation itself, that someone named John authored the book of Revelation, under inspiration of the Holy Spirit. "[1]The Revelation of Jesus Christ, **which God gave Him to show His servants**—things which must shortly take place. And He sent and signified it by His angel to His servant John, [2]who bore witness to the word of God, and to the testimony of Jesus Christ, to all things that he saw." (Revelation 1:1-2) (emphasis added)

John also identifies himself, "[9]I, John, both your brother and companion in the tribulation and kingdom and patience of Jesus Christ, was on the island that is called Patmos for the word of God and for the testimony of Jesus Christ." Revelation 1:9

But who is this John? John was a fairly common name among the Hebrews, and it could be any number of those who followed Jesus who wrote the book of Revelation. Fortunately, history has narrowed the choices down to four:

1. John the Elder
2. John Mark
3. an unknown/pseudonymous John
4. John the Apostle

John the Elder

> John the Elder, also known as John the Presbyter, was referenced by the church historian, Eusebius (c. A.D. 260-340), in his volumes on church history. In volume III of Church History, Eusebius quotes from works by a writer named Papias. Sadly, it is only through quotes such as this that the writings of Papias exist today, as the original transcript from Papias has been lost.
>
> Eusebius quotes Papias:
>
>> "But I shall not hesitate also to put down for you along with my interpretations whatsoever things I have at any time learned carefully from the elders and carefully

Appendix I – Who wrote Revelation?

remembered, guaranteeing their truth. For I did not, like the multitude, take pleasure in those that speak much, but in those that teach the truth; not in those that relate strange commandments, but in those that deliver the commandments given by the Lord to faith, and springing from the truth itself.

If, then, any one came, who had been a follower of the elders, I questioned him in regard to the words of the elders — what Andrew or what Peter said, or what was said by Philip, or by Thomas, or by James, or by John, or by Matthew, or by any other of the disciples of the Lord, and what things Aristion and the presbyter John, the disciples of the Lord, say. For I did not think that what was to be gotten from the books would profit me as much as what came from the living and abiding voice."[90]

Eusebius then summarizes Papias' introduction:

"It is worth while observing here that the name John is twice enumerated by him. The first one he mentions in connection with Peter and James and Matthew and the rest of the apostles, clearly meaning the evangelist; but the other John he mentions after an interval, and places him among others outside of the number of the apostles, putting Aristion before him, and he distinctly calls him a presbyter.

This shows that the statement of those is true, who say that there were two persons in Asia that bore the same name, and that there were two tombs in Ephesus, each of which, even to the present day, is called John's. It is important to notice this. For it is probable that it was the second, if one is not willing to admit that it was the first that saw the Revelation, which is ascribed by name to John."[91]

---

[90] Eusebius of Caesarea, "Church History, Book III, Chapter 39", https://www.newadvent.org/fathers/250103.htm
[91] Ibid

So the Image Could Speak

While Eusebius may not have been the first to bring "John the Presbyter" into the conversation about the authorship of Revelation, he was probably the most impactful through his volumes on Church History, quoting from a previous writer, Papias.

But Eusebius says "it is probably", not it is definite and he also references the apostles as "elders" in his quote from Papias, "If, then, any one came, who had been a follower of the elders, I questioned him in regard to the words of the elders — what Andrew or what Peter said, or what was said by Philip, or by Thomas, or by James, or by John, or by Matthew."

So, while there probably was a follower of Christ known as "John the Presbyter", we can also surmise that John, as well as the other apostles, were known as elders.

Eusebius' work did not go uncontested. In the early 1900s, the Catholic encyclopedia stated that the distinction between John the Presbyter and John the Apostle "has no historical basis" and gives a very convincing argument for the writer of Revelation, as well as the other books by John accepted into the canon, to be written by one man – John the Apostle.

John Mark

John Mark, also known simply as Mark, was who, it is traditionally believed, wrote the Gospel of Mark and was the son of Mary as we see in Acts, *"^{12}So, when he had considered this, he came to the house of Mary, the mother of John whose surname was Mark, where many were gathered together praying."* (Acts 12:12)

He accompanied Paul on his first missionary journey to Cyprus, but for an unknown reason, left Paul and Barnabus in Pamphylia. Paul saw this as abandonment of the ministry, but later forgave Mark and actually called for him on his deathbed, *"^{9}Be diligent to come to me quickly; ^{10}for Demas has forsaken me, having loved this present world, and has departed for Thessalonica—Crescens for Galatia, Titus for Dalmatia. ^{11}Only Luke is with me. Get Mark and bring him with you, for he is useful to me for ministry."* (2 Timothy 4:9-11)

Appendix I – Who wrote Revelation?

It is interesting that I could not find any attribution to John Mark as the writer of Revelation in any of the early church historians' work. It may exist, but I couldn't find it so I'm not sure how John Mark's name came to be included as a possible author of the book of Revelation.

One of the theories is that those who challenged the authorship of John the Apostle tossed out these names, along with various other Johns of the period, as potential authors. However, even those who challenged the authorship as apostolic, could not agree on which John it was, so there was no concise argument that it was not John the Apostle.

One of the arguments is that John Mark, the author of the Gospel of Mark, must have written it because it was written in the mid first century AD. Of course, that time frame has also been challenged and it seems to be circular logic to imply it was written by someone simply because of the time frame (often contested and with which most of the early church historians disagree) and that, therefore, the book (Revelation) must have been written in the mid first century. We'll delve more into that timing further down, but for now, I think we can put aside that John Mark, the author of the Gospel of Mark, wrote the Book of Revelation. As we'll see further on, many of the early church historians agree that John the Apostle was the author of Revelation.

Unknown John

This is another instance where those who opposed the apostolic source of the book of Revelation tossed a name into the mix for consideration. But there is no, at least none that I could find, evidence supporting there was an unknown man, named John, who authored the book of Revelation. In fact, the book itself would seem to refute this. As we've seen in the scriptures listed above in the first verses in Revelation, John identifies himself as, simply, "John". That would seem to imply this John was sufficiently well known among the early church that there was no need to further identify himself – his credibility was already well-established. As we'll see further on, many of those early church historians attributed the book of Revelation to John the Apostle.

John the Apostle

So the Image Could Speak

John, the author of the Book of Revelation, identifies himself within the text of that book only four times:

"¹The Revelation of Jesus Christ, which God gave Him to show His servants—things which must shortly take place. And He sent and signified it by His angel to His servant John, ²who bore witness to the word of God, and to the testimony of Jesus Christ, to all things that he saw." (Revelation 1:1-2)

"⁴John, to the seven churches which are in Asia: Grace to you and peace from Him who is and who was and who is to come, and from the seven Spirits who are before His throne, ⁵and from Jesus Christ, the faithful witness, the firstborn from the dead, and the ruler over the kings of the earth." (Revelation 1:4-5)

"⁹I, John, both your brother and companion in the tribulation and kingdom and patience of Jesus Christ, was on the island that is called Patmos for the word of God and for the testimony of Jesus Christ." (Revelation 1:9)

"⁸Now I, John, saw and heard these things. And when I heard and saw, I fell down to worship before the feet of the angel who showed me these things." (Revelation 22:8)

While that seems precious little to go on, there are a few things we can deduce from these four verses. In the very first verse of Revelation, John identifies himself as the Lord's servant, *"²who bore witness to the word of God."* While that "bore witness" could be translated as one who personally witnessed and was present with Jesus during his time on earth, we must go to the original Greek to see what was actually written. The word used here is martureó (Strong's 3140), which is translated as testify. John is simply stating that he is a believer in Jesus Christ and willingly testifies to His saving grace.

In the next verse where John is identified, Revelation 1:4-5, the phrase *"⁴John, to the seven churches which are in Asia:"* would imply that John had a relationship to those churches. We know from historians that John the Apostle returned to Ephesus – one of those seven churches - after his release from Patmos and is buried there.

Appendix I – Who wrote Revelation?

The most revealing of these four verses where John is identified is Revelation 1:9, *"⁹I, John, both your brother and companion in the tribulation and kingdom and patience of Jesus Christ, was on the island that is called Patmos for the word of God and for the testimony of Jesus Christ."* So we know that the John who wrote the book of Revelation was on the island of Patmos while he was writing it. In the time of this writing, Patmos was a small island in the Aegean Sea and was used as an exile for criminals and political prisoners. The Apostle John was sent there by the Roman government for his testimony of Jesus Christ.

What else do we know about John the Apostle? Well, not much actually. We know he was the son of Zebedee, and he was one of the fishermen called by Jesus on His way through Galilee.

"¹⁸And Jesus, walking by the Sea of Galilee, saw two brothers, Simon called Peter, and Andrew his brother, casting a net into the sea; for they were fishermen. ¹⁹Then He said to them, "Follow Me, and I will make you fishers of men." ²⁰They immediately left their nets and followed Him. ²¹Going on from there, He saw two other brothers, James the son of Zebedee, and John his brother, in the boat with Zebedee their father, mending their nets. He called them, ²²and immediately they left the boat and their father, and followed Him." (Matthew 4:18-22)

John, and his brother James, were called "Sons of Thunder" for their, shall we say, rash and impulsive ways.

"¹³And He went up on the mountain and called to Him those He Himself wanted. And they came to Him. ¹⁴Then He appointed twelve, that they might be with Him and that He might send them out to preach, ¹⁵and to have power to heal sicknesses and to cast out demons: ¹⁶Simon, to whom He gave the name Peter; **¹⁷James the son of Zebedee and John the brother of James, to whom He gave the name Boanerges, that is, "Sons of Thunder";** *¹⁸Andrew, Philip, Bartholomew, Matthew, Thomas, James the son of Alphaeus, Thaddaeus, Simon the Canaanite; ¹⁹and Judas Iscariot, who also betrayed Him. And they went into a house."* (Mark 3:13-19) (emphasis added)

So the Image Could Speak

One example of the boldness of the two brothers is given in Mark 10, where they ask Jesus to place them on either side of Him: *"³⁵Then James and John, the sons of Zebedee, came to Him, saying, " 'Teacher, we want You to do for us whatever we ask.' ³⁶And He said to them, 'What do you want Me to do for you?' ³⁷They said to Him, 'Grant us that we may sit, one on Your right hand and the other on Your left, in Your glory.' "* (Mark 10:35-37)

Of course, they were humbled by Jesus' response to their request, but we get an idea of their zeal and lack of humility, at least at this point, in their request. It didn't win them friends among the other apostles, either, though that rift was short-lived.

We can read other accounts of the two brothers' zeal and rashness in Mark, chapter 9 and in Luke, chapter 9, but we know that, at some point, the two brothers grew in wisdom and became part of Jesus' inner circle, along with Peter. It was those three – John, Peter, and James – that Jesus called to go with Him to what we now call the Mount of Transfiguration.

"¹Now after six days Jesus took Peter, James, and John his brother, led them up on a high mountain by themselves; ²and He was transfigured before them. His face shone like the sun, and His clothes became as white as the light. ³And behold, Moses and Elijah appeared to them, talking with Him." (Matthew 17:1-3)

John matured and grew in wisdom and patience. It was he that Jesus, on the cross, asked to look after His mother.

"²⁵Now there stood by the cross of Jesus His mother, and His mother's sister, Mary the wife of Clopas, and Mary Magdalene. ²⁶When Jesus therefore saw His mother, and the disciple whom He loved standing by, He said to His mother, "Woman, behold your son!" ²⁷Then He said to the disciple, "Behold your mother!" And from that hour that disciple took her to his own home." (John 19:25-27)

John is not named specifically in this passage, but called "the disciple whom He loved", but history records that this was John, the son of Zebedee and brother of James.

Appendix I – Who wrote Revelation?

John's zeal for truth was unmatched in the Gospels, except by Jesus Himself, yet, that zeal was balanced by love of his brothers and sisters in Christ, as reflected in his letters. *"¹The Elder, To the elect lady and her children, whom I love in truth, and not only I, but also all those who have known the truth, ²because of the truth which abides in us and will be with us forever: ³Grace, mercy, and peace will be with you from God the Father and from the Lord Jesus Christ, the Son of the Father, in truth and love."* (2 John 1:1-3)

Scripture doesn't record much of John's ministry after the crucifixion, but we know he rejoined some of the Apostles for a fishing trip and Jesus appeared to them, *"¹After these things Jesus showed Himself again to the disciples at the Sea of Tiberias, and in this way He showed Himself: ²Simon Peter, Thomas called the Twin, Nathanael of Cana in Galilee, the sons of Zebedee, and two others of His disciples were together. ³Simon Peter said to them, "I am going fishing." They said to him, "We are going with you also." They went out and immediately got into the boat, and that night they caught nothing. ⁴But when the morning had now come, Jesus stood on the shore; yet the disciples did not know that it was Jesus. ⁵Then Jesus said to them, "Children, have you any food?" They answered Him, "No." ⁶And He said to them, "Cast the net on the right side of the boat, and you will find some." So they cast, and now they were not able to draw it in because of the multitude of fish."* (John 21:1-6)

Paul acknowledged John as a "pillar" in his letter to the Galatians after hearing about the false teaching they were receiving, *"⁶But from those who seemed to be something—whatever they were, it makes no difference to me; God shows personal favoritism to no man—for those who seemed to be something added nothing to me. ⁷But on the contrary, when they saw that the gospel for the uncircumcised had been committed to me, as the gospel for the circumcised was to Peter ⁸(for He who worked effectively in Peter for the apostleship to the circumcised also worked effectively in me toward the Gentiles), ⁹and when James, Cephas, and **John, who seemed to be pillars**, perceived the grace that had been given to me, they gave me and Barnabas the right hand of fellowship, that we should go to the Gentiles and they to the circumcised."* (Galatians 2:6-9) (emphasis added)

However rash and judgmental John, and his brother James, may have been in the early years, it is evident he grew in wisdom, patience, love and forbearance and is an early leader of the church.

We can learn, from early church leaders and historians, that it was widely believed to have been John the Apostle who penned the book of Revelation. Historians such as Justin Martyr (c. 100-165 AD), Melito of Sardis (mid – late second century), and Irenaeus of Smyrna (c. 130-202 AD) seemed to point to the writer of Revelation as John the Apostle. It is interesting to note that Ireneaus knew Polycarp as a child. Polycarp was one of John the Apostle's disciples.

Even into the third century, church historians are referencing John the Apostle as the author of the book of Revelation, including Tertullian (c. 155-220 AD), Hippolytus (c. 170-235 AD), and Origen of Alexandria (c. 185-253 AD).

However compelling the words of these historians may be, the most convincing argument of John the Apostle's authorship of the book of Revelation is the Bible itself. While some argue the style of writing may be different between the Gospel of John and the book of Revelation, there can be no argument in the similarities between the Gospel and the book of Revelation. For example:

1. Jesus is the Word, or Logos. John is the only one of the four Gospels, or any of the writers of the New Testament, that references Jesus as The Word.
2. Jesus is the True Witness. Again, John is the only one to use this reference.
3. The Two Witnesses. John is the only one who fully references the Mosaic requirement for Two Witnesses.

Appendix I – Who wrote Revelation?

	Gospel of John	Revelation
1.	"*¹In the beginning was the Word, and the Word was with God, and the Word was God.*" (John 1:1) "*¹⁴And the Word became flesh and dwelt among us, and we beheld His glory, the glory as of the only begotten of the Father, full of grace and truth.*" (John 1:14)	"*¹²His eyes were like a flame of fire, and on His head were many crowns. He had a name written that no one knew except Himself. ¹³He was clothed with a robe dipped in blood, and His name is called The Word of God.*" (Revelation 19:13)
2.	"*³¹'If I bear witness of Myself, My witness is not true. ³²There is another who bears witness of Me, and I know that the witness which He witnesses of Me is true.'* " (John 5:31-32) "*¹⁴Jesus answered and said to them, "Even if I bear witness of Myself, My witness is true, for I know where I came from and where I am going; but you do not know where I come from and where I am going*" (John 8:14)	"*¹⁴'And to the angel of the church of the Laodiceans write, 'These things says the Amen, the Faithful and True Witness, the Beginning of the creation of God:'* " (Revelation 3:14)
3.	"*¹⁷'It is also written in your law that the testimony of two men is true. ¹⁸I am One who bears witness of Myself, and the Father who sent Me bears witness of Me.'* " (John 8:17)	"*³And I will give power to my Two Witnesses, and they will prophesy one thousand two hundred and sixty days, clothed in sackcloth.*" (Revelation 11:3)

So the Image Could Speak

It would take multiple volumes to fully explore the possibilities of who penned the book of Revelation, but why do we need to know that? The first verses in the first chapter of the book of Revelation tell us who the source of the writing that follows is: *"¹The **Revelation of Jesus Christ**, which God gave Him to show His servants—things which must shortly take place. And He sent and signified it by His angel to His servant John, ²who bore witness to the word of God, and to the testimony of Jesus Christ, to all things that he saw."* (Revelation 1:1-2) (emphasis added)

Whose Revelation? The Revelation of Jesus Christ.

Whoever penned the words on the scroll that became the Book of Revelation was doing so by the inspiration of Jesus Christ Himself. But knowing who picked up the reed pen and placed the words on the scroll does help narrow down the time of writing the Book of Revelation. Understanding and accepting when it was written will help determine the time frame for those events depicted.

Of the original twelve disciples, all were martyred except for John and Judas. We know what happened to Judas, the apostle who betrayed Jesus for thirty pieces of silver. Judas was then replaced by Matthias, chosen by lots drawn. James, the brother of John, was the first to be martyred for his faith and testimony. *"¹Now about that time Herod the king stretched out his hand to harass some from the church. ²Then he killed James the brother of John with the sword."* (Acts 12:1-2)

Legends of the deaths and martyrdom of the other apostles abound but are not recorded in Scripture. We do know that only John lived to an old age, and we know John was exiled to Patmos by Domitian. Eusebius, in his History of the Church, writes about Domitian, "Domitian, having shown great cruelty toward many, and having unjustly put to death no small number of well-born and notable men at Rome, and having without cause exiled and confiscated the property of a great many other illustrious men, finally became a successor of Nero in his hatred and enmity toward God. He was in fact the second that stirred up a persecution against us, although his father Vespasian had undertaken nothing prejudicial to us."[92]

---

[92] Eusebius of Caesarea, "Church History, Book III, Chapter 17", https://www.newadvent.org/fathers/250103.htm

Appendix I – Who wrote Revelation?

Eusebius adds, "1. It is said that in this persecution the apostle and evangelist John, who was still alive, was condemned to dwell on the island of Patmos in consequence of his testimony to the divine word."[93]

So church historians, such as Eusebius and Ireneaus, record that it was John the Apostle who was exiled to Patmos, and he was exiled by Emperor Domitian. Domitian did not come to power until 81 AD and it was on his death in 96 AD that John's exile ended and he returned to Ephesus. Ireneaus, in his writing Against Heresies, says he received information from those who had met with John, the author of Revelation[94] and that he, John, recorded his revelation "almost in our day, toward the end of Domitian's reign."[95]

We don't know exactly when John was exiled to Patmos; some believe he was only there for about 18 months before being released. But we know he could not have been exiled by Emperor Domitian prior to 81AD because Domitian was not yet the emperor.

To summarize, it was John the Apostle who put pen to scroll and wrote the divinely inspired Book of Revelation during his exile to the island of Patmos by Emperor Domitian. According to Ireneaus, the Book of Revelation was written "toward the end of Domitian's reign."[96] Most Bible scholars today agree John wrote the book of Revelation in the 95-96 AD timeframe.

Could it be that John the Apostle, the only one of the Apostles who lived to die a natural death, was protected because of the plans God had for him to record the images given to him?

---

[93] Eusebius of Caesarea, "Church History, Book III, Chapter 18.1", https://www.newadvent.org/fathers/250103.htm
[94] Ireneaus, Against Heresies, 5.30.1
[95] Ireneaus, Against Heresies, 5.30.3
[96] Ibid

So the Image Could Speak

Appendix II – The Letters to the Churches

	Meaning of Name	Commendation	Concern	Promise to the Overcomer
Ephesus	Desired, Lovely	Hate deeds of Nicolaitans	Lost first love	Tree of Life
Smyrna	Sweet, fragrant Myrrh	Rich in good works	None	Crown of Life
Pergamos	Mixed Marriage	Held fast in faith	Idol worship	Hidden Manna and White stone
Thyatira	Sacrifice	Good works, love, and patience	Jezebel, idolatry	Power over nations
Sardis	Remnant	None	Dead	White raiment, Book of Life
Philadelphia	Brotherly love	Kept Christ's Word	None	Kept from the hour of trial
Laodicea	A Just people	None	Lukewarm, spiritually poor	Sit with Christ on His Throne

Appendix III – 70 Weeks Timeline

Appendix III – 70 Weeks Timeline

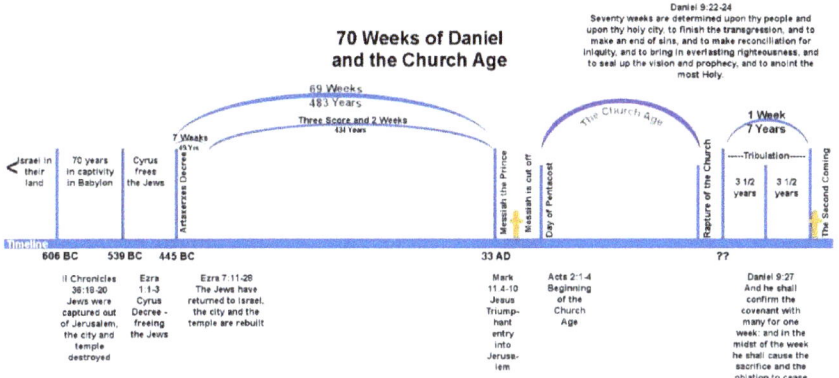

So the Image Could Speak

Appendix IV – Revelation Order of Events

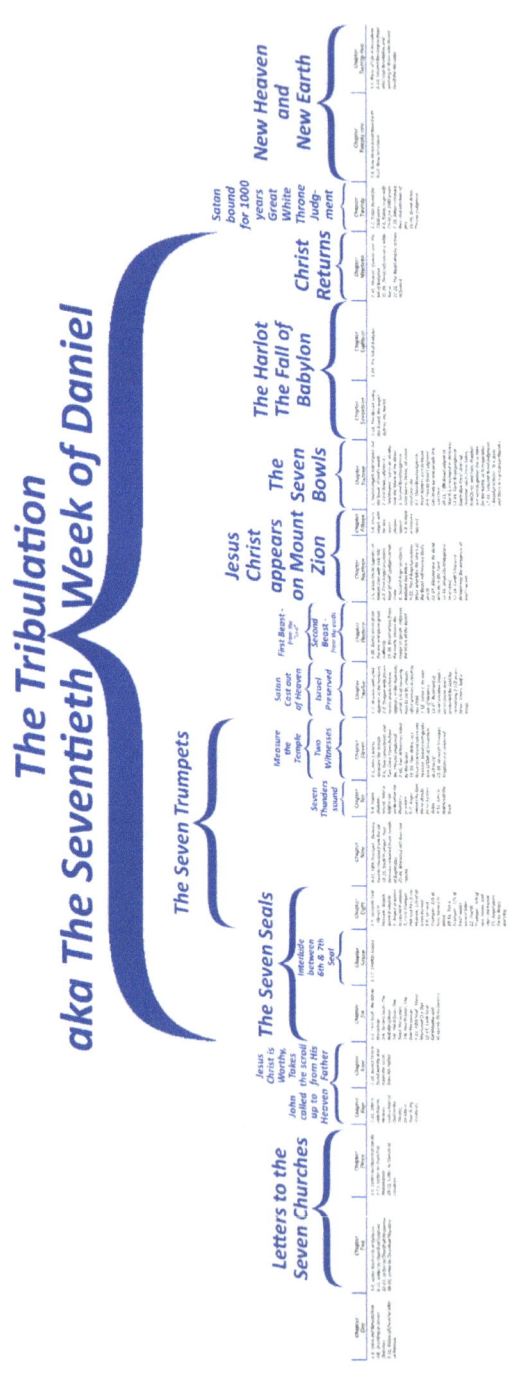

Appendix V – Specific Times in Revelation

Appendix V – Specific Times in Revelation

1. Letter to the church of Smyrna
   "*¹⁰Do not fear any of those things which you are about to suffer. Indeed, the devil is about to throw some of you into prison, that you may be tested, and you will have tribulation ten days. Be faithful until death, and I will give you the crown of life.*" (Revelation 2:10)

2. Silence in Heaven
   "*¹When He opened the seventh seal, there was silence in heaven for about half an hour.*" (Revelation 8:1)

3. Fourth Trumpet
   "*¹²Then the fourth angel sounded: And a third of the sun was struck, a third of the moon, and a third of the stars, so that a third of them were darkened. A third of the day did not shine, and likewise the night.*" (Revelation 8:12)

4. Fifth Trumpet
   "*⁴They were commanded not to harm the grass of the earth, or any green thing, or any tree, but only those men who do not have the seal of God on their foreheads. ⁵And they were not given authority to kill them, but to torment them for five months. Their torment was like the torment of a scorpion when it strikes a man.*" (Revelation 9:4-5)

5. John is told to measure the temple.
   "*²But leave out the court which is outside the temple, and do not measure it, for it has been given to the Gentiles. And they will tread the holy city underfoot for forty-two months.*" (Revelation 11:2)

6. The Two Witnesses
   "*³And I will give power to my two witnesses, and they will prophesy one thousand two hundred and sixty days, clothed in sackcloth.*" (Revelation 11:3)

7. Death of the Two Witnesses
   "*⁸And their dead bodies will lie in the street of the great city which

spiritually is called Sodom and Egypt, where also our Lord was crucified. ⁹Then those from the peoples, tribes, tongues, and nations will see their dead bodies three-and-a-half days, and not allow their dead bodies to be put into graves." (Revelation 11:8-9)

8. Remnant of Israel flees.
   "⁶Then the woman fled into the wilderness, where she has a place prepared by God, that they should feed her there one thousand two hundred and sixty days." (Revelation 12:6)

9. Remnant of Israel protected.
   "¹⁴But the woman was given two wings of a great eagle, that she might fly into the wilderness to her place, where she is nourished for a time and times and half a time, from the presence of the serpent." (Revelation 12:14)

10. Satan gives AntiChrist authority.
    "⁵And he was given a mouth speaking great things and blasphemies, and he was given authority to continue for forty-two months." (Revelation 13:5)

11. The ten kings receive authority.
    "¹²The ten horns which you saw are ten kings who have received no kingdom as yet, but they receive authority for one hour as kings with the beast." (Revelation 17:12)

12. Judgment of Babylon
    "⁹The kings of the earth who committed fornication and lived luxuriously with her will weep and lament for her, when they see the smoke of her burning, ¹⁰standing at a distance for fear of her torment, saying, 'Alas, alas, that great city Babylon, that mighty city! For in one hour your judgment has come.' " (Revelation 18:9-10)

13. Satan is bound.
    "¹Then I saw an angel coming down from heaven, having the key to the bottomless pit and a great chain in his hand. ²He laid hold of the dragon, that serpent of old, who is the Devil and Satan, and bound him for a thousand years; ³and he cast him into the

Appendix V – Specific Times in Revelation

bottomless pit, and shut him up, and set a seal on him, so that he should deceive the nations no more till the thousand years were finished. But after these things he must be released for a little while." (Revelation 20:1-3)

14. *"⁴And I saw thrones, and they sat on them, and judgment was committed to them. Then I saw the souls of those who had been beheaded for their witness to Jesus and for the word of God, who had not worshiped the beast or his image, and had not received his mark on their foreheads or on their hands. And they lived and reigned with Christ for a thousand years."* (Revelation 20:4)

15. *"⁵But the rest of the dead did not live again until the thousand years were finished. This is the first resurrection."* (Revelation 20:5)

16. *"⁶Blessed and holy is he who has part in the first resurrection. Over such the second death has no power, but they shall be priests of God and of Christ, and shall reign with Him a thousand years."* (Revelation 20:6)

So the Image Could Speak

Appendix VI – First Song of Moses

[1] "I will sing to the Lord,
For He has triumphed gloriously!
The horse and its rider
He has thrown into the sea!
[2] The Lord is my strength and song,
And He has become my salvation;
He is my God, and I will praise Him;
My father's God, and I will exalt Him.
[3] The Lord is a man of war;
The Lord is His name.
[4] Pharaoh's chariots and his army He has cast into the sea;
His chosen captains also are drowned in the Red Sea.
[5] The depths have covered them;
They sank to the bottom like a stone.

[6] "Your right hand, O Lord, has become glorious in power;
Your right hand, O Lord, has dashed the enemy in pieces.
[7] And in the greatness of Your excellence
You have overthrown those who rose against You;
You sent forth Your wrath;
It consumed them like stubble.
[8] And with the blast of Your nostrils
The waters were gathered together;
The floods stood upright like a heap;
The depths congealed in the heart of the sea.
[9] The enemy said, 'I will pursue,
I will overtake,
I will divide the spoil;
My desire shall be satisfied on them.
I will draw my sword,
My hand shall destroy them.'
[10] You blew with Your wind,
The sea covered them;
They sank like lead in the mighty waters.

[11] "Who is like You, O Lord, among the gods?
Who is like You, glorious in holiness,
Fearful in praises, doing wonders?

Appendix VI – First Song of Moses

¹²*You stretched out Your right hand;*
The earth swallowed them.
¹³*You in Your mercy have led forth*
The people whom You have redeemed;
You have guided them in Your strength
To Your holy habitation.

¹⁴*"The people will hear and be afraid;*
Sorrow will take hold of the inhabitants of Philistia.
¹⁵*Then the chiefs of Edom will be dismayed;*
The mighty men of Moab,
Trembling will take hold of them;
All the inhabitants of Canaan will melt away.
¹⁶*Fear and dread will fall on them;*
By the greatness of Your arm
They will be as still as a stone,
Till Your people pass over, O Lord,
Till the people pass over
Whom You have purchased.
¹⁷*You will bring them in and plant them*
In the mountain of Your inheritance,
In the place, O Lord, which You have made
For Your own dwelling,
The sanctuary, O Lord, which Your hands have established.

¹⁸*"The Lord shall reign forever and ever."*
(Exodus 15:1-18)

So the Image Could Speak

Appendix VII – Second Song of Moses

[1] "Give ear, O heavens, and I will speak;
And hear, O earth, the words of my mouth.
[2] Let my teaching drop as the rain,
My speech distill as the dew,
As raindrops on the tender herb,
And as showers on the grass.
[3] For I proclaim the name of the Lord:
Ascribe greatness to our God.
[4] He is the Rock, His work is perfect;
For all His ways are justice,
A God of truth and without injustice;
Righteous and upright is He.

[5] "They have corrupted themselves;
They are not His children,
Because of their blemish:
A perverse and crooked generation.
[6] Do you thus deal with the Lord,
O foolish and unwise people?
Is He not your Father, who bought you?
Has He not made you and established you?

"Remember the days of old,
Consider the years of many generations.
Ask your father, and he will show you;
Your elders, and they will tell you:
[8] When the Most High divided their inheritance to the nations,
When He separated the sons of Adam,
He set the boundaries of the peoples
According to the number of the children of Israel.
[9] For the Lord's portion is His people;
Jacob is the place of His inheritance.

[10] "He found him in a desert land
And in the wasteland, a howling wilderness;
He encircled him, He instructed him,
He kept him as the apple of His eye.
[11] As an eagle stirs up its nest,

Appendix VII – Second Song of Moses

Hovers over its young,
Spreading out its wings, taking them up,
Carrying them on its wings,
¹²*So the Lord alone led him,*
And there was no foreign god with him.

¹³*"He made him ride in the heights of the earth,*
That he might eat the produce of the fields;
He made him draw honey from the rock,
And oil from the flinty rock;
¹⁴*Curds from the cattle, and milk of the flock,*
With fat of lambs;
And rams of the breed of Bashan, and goats,
With the choicest wheat;
And you drank wine, the blood of the grapes.

¹⁵*"But Jeshurun grew fat and kicked;*
You grew fat, you grew thick,
You are obese!
Then he forsook God who made him,
And scornfully esteemed the Rock of his salvation.
¹⁶*They provoked Him to jealousy with foreign gods;*
With abominations they provoked Him to anger.
¹⁷*They sacrificed to demons, not to God,*
To gods they did not know,
To new gods, new arrivals
That your fathers did not fear.
¹⁸*Of the Rock who begot you, you are unmindful,*
And have forgotten the God who fathered you.

¹⁹*"And when the Lord saw it, He spurned them,*
Because of the provocation of His sons and His daughters.
²⁰*And He said: 'I will hide My face from them,*
I will see what their end will be,
For they are a perverse generation,
Children in whom is no faith.
²¹*They have provoked Me to jealousy by what is not God;*
They have moved Me to anger by their foolish idols.
But I will provoke them to jealousy by those who are not a nation;
I will move them to anger by a foolish nation.

So the Image Could Speak

²²For a fire is kindled in My anger,
And shall burn to the lowest hell;
It shall consume the earth with her increase,
And set on fire the foundations of the mountains.

²³'I will heap disasters on them;
I will spend My arrows on them.
²⁴They shall be wasted with hunger,
Devoured by pestilence and bitter destruction;
I will also send against them the teeth of beasts,
With the poison of serpents of the dust.
²⁵The sword shall destroy outside;
There shall be terror within
For the young man and virgin,
The nursing child with the man of gray hairs.
²⁶I would have said, "I will dash them in pieces,
I will make the memory of them to cease from among men,"
²⁷Had I not feared the wrath of the enemy,
Lest their adversaries should misunderstand,
Lest they should say, "Our hand is high;
And it is not the Lord who has done all this." '

²⁸"For they are a nation void of counsel,
Nor is there any understanding in them.
²⁹Oh, that they were wise, that they understood this,
That they would consider their latter end!
³⁰How could one chase a thousand,
And two put ten thousand to flight,
Unless their Rock had sold them,
And the Lord had surrendered them?
³¹For their rock is not like our Rock,
Even our enemies themselves being judges.
³²For their vine is of the vine of Sodom
And of the fields of Gomorrah;
Their grapes are grapes of gall,
Their clusters are bitter.
³³Their wine is the poison of serpents,
And the cruel venom of cobras.

³⁴'Is this not laid up in store with Me,

Appendix VII – Second Song of Moses

Sealed up among My treasures?
³⁵Vengeance is Mine, and recompense;
Their foot shall slip in due time;
For the day of their calamity is at hand,
And the things to come hasten upon them.'

³⁶"For the Lord will judge His people
And have compassion on His servants,
When He sees that their power is gone,
And there is no one remaining, bond or free.
³⁷He will say: 'Where are their gods,
The rock in which they sought refuge?
³⁸Who ate the fat of their sacrifices,
And drank the wine of their drink offering?
Let them rise and help you,
And be your refuge.

³⁹'Now see that I, even I, am He,
And there is no God besides Me;
I kill and I make alive;
I wound and I heal;
Nor is there any who can deliver from My hand.
⁴⁰For I raise My hand to heaven,
And say, "As I live forever,
⁴¹If I whet My glittering sword,
And My hand takes hold on judgment,
I will render vengeance to My enemies,
And repay those who hate Me.
⁴²I will make My arrows drunk with blood,
And My sword shall devour flesh,
With the blood of the slain and the captives,
From the heads of the leaders of the enemy." '

⁴³"Rejoice, O Gentiles, with His people;
For He will avenge the blood of His servants,
And render vengeance to His adversaries;
He will provide atonement for His land and His people."
(Deuteronomy 32:1-43)

So the Image Could Speak

Appendix VIII – Two Battles of Gog and Magog

	Ezekiel 38 & 39	Revelation 20
When?	Unknown, though many believe pre-Tribulation - Eze 38:8	End of Millennium - Rev 20:7
Who?	Armies from specific lands, led by Gog, the Prince of Magog - Eze 38:3-5 and 15	Armies from the four points of the globe led by Satan, all over the world - Rev 20:7-8
Who is Attacked?	Israel, at a time of peace - Eze 38:11-12	Camp of the saints - Rev 20:9
Purpose of attack?	For plunder and to carry off spoils - Eze 38:12	Unstated, but most likely rebellion - Rev 20:9-10
How is the battle ended?	Earthquake, internal fighting, plagues, rain, hailstones, fire, and sulphur - Eze 38:19-22	Fire from Heaven - Rev 20:9
Aftermath	They will fall in the mountains of Israel and will be consumed by wild beasts and birds - Eze 38:4-5 and 39:17-20	Fire from Heaven consumes them and the devil is thrown into the Lake of Fire - Rev 20:9
Burial ground of the enemy	The Lord will create a burial place for the enemy, called Hamon-Gog, Eze 39:11-12	None - not needed as armies are all consumed by fire, See above.
Clean-up time	Seven months to bury the dead and Israel will use the weapons for energy for 7 years - Eze 39:12 and Eze 39:9-10	None - not needed as armies are all consumed by fire, See above.

Appendix IX – The Temples of Jerusalem

Appendix IX – The Temples of Jerusalem

1. Solomon's Temple

   David, once he conquered Jerusalem, longed to build a Temple, but the ongoing battles in and around Jerusalem prevented him from achieving it.

   When his son, Solomon, came into power and there was less unrest, the decision to build the temple was made.

   "³You know how my father David could not build a house for the name of the Lord his God because of the wars which were fought against him on every side, until the Lord put his foes under the soles of his feet. ⁴But now the Lord my God has given me rest on every side; there is neither adversary nor evil occurrence. ⁵And behold, I propose to build a house for the name of the Lord my God, as the Lord spoke to my father David, saying, 'Your son, whom I will set on your throne in your place, he shall build the house for My name.' " (1 Kings 5:3-5)

   Solomon was determined to build a Temple to God that was worthy of God.

   "⁵And the temple which I build will be great, for our God is greater than all gods. ⁶But who is able to build Him a temple, since heaven and the heaven of heavens cannot contain Him? Who am I then, that I should build Him a temple, except to burn sacrifice before Him?" (2 Chronicles 2:5-6)

   The Temple Solomon built was impressive; overlaid with gold and precious stones, and it awed all who entered within the gates.

   "³This is the foundation which Solomon laid for building the house of God: The length was sixty cubits (by cubits according to the former measure) and the width twenty cubits. ⁴And the vestibule that was in front of the sanctuary was twenty cubits long across the width of the house, and the height was one hundred and twenty. He overlaid the inside with pure gold. ⁵The larger room he paneled with cypress which he overlaid with fine gold, and he

So the Image Could Speak

carved palm trees and chainwork on it. ⁶And he decorated the house with precious stones for beauty, and the gold was gold from Parvaim. ⁷He also overlaid the house—the beams and doorposts, its walls and doors—with gold; and he carved cherubim on the walls.

⁸And he made the Most Holy Place. Its length was according to the width of the house, twenty cubits, and its width twenty cubits. He overlaid it with six hundred talents of fine gold. ⁹The weight of the nails was fifty shekels of gold; and he overlaid the upper area with gold. ¹⁰In the Most Holy Place he made two cherubim, fashioned by carving, and overlaid them with gold. ¹¹The wings of the cherubim were twenty cubits in overall length: one wing of the one cherub was five cubits, touching the wall of the room, and the other wing was five cubits, touching the wing of the other cherub; ¹²one wing of the other cherub was five cubits, touching the wall of the room, and the other wing also was five cubits, touching the wing of the other cherub. ¹³The wings of these cherubim spanned twenty cubits overall. They stood on their feet, and they faced inward. ¹⁴And he made the veil of blue, purple, crimson, and fine linen, and wove cherubim into it." (2 Chronicles 3:3-14)

When the Temple was complete, Solomon called the Priests together to bring up the Ark of the Covenant and place it in the Holy of Holies within the new Temple.

"⁷Then the priests brought in the ark of the covenant of the Lord to its place, into the inner sanctuary of the temple, to the Most Holy Place, under the wings of the cherubim. ⁸For the cherubim spread their wings over the place of the ark, and the cherubim overshadowed the ark and its poles. ⁹The poles extended so that the ends of the poles of the ark could be seen from the holy place, in front of the inner sanctuary; but they could not be seen from outside. And they are there to this day. ¹⁰Nothing was in the ark except the two tablets which Moses put there at Horeb, when the Lord made a covenant with the children of Israel, when they had come out of Egypt." (2 Chronicles 5:7-10)

Then a miracle took place, *"¹³indeed it came to pass, when the*

Appendix IX – The Temples of Jerusalem

trumpeters and singers were as one, to make one sound to be heard in praising and thanking the Lord, and when they lifted up their voice with the trumpets and cymbals and instruments of music, and praised the Lord, saying: 'For He is good, for His mercy endures forever,' that the house, the house of the Lord, was filled with a cloud, ^{14}so that the priests could not continue ministering because of the cloud; for the glory of the Lord filled the house of God." (2 Chronicles 5:13-14)

"For the glory of the Lord filled the house of God." The Shekinah glory of the Lord filled the house of God. Wow

Solomon's Temple, the first Temple, was completed circa 966 BC and was used for worship, oblations, and sacrifices by such as Isaiah, Jeremiah, and Ezekiel until it was destroyed by Nebuchadnezzar's army circa 586 BC.

2. Zerubbabel's Temple

Once the Israelites were freed from Babylon, many returned to Jerusalem and decided to rebuild the Temple, as they had been commanded by Cyrus the Great. They did not have the resources available to them that Solomon had, so the Temple that was built by Zerubbabel was not as glorious as Solomon's Temple. In fact, many of those who had been to Solomon's Temple were dismayed at the sight of the new Temple.

"^{12}But many of the priests and Levites and heads of the fathers' houses, old men who had seen the first temple, wept with a loud voice when the foundation of this temple was laid before their eyes." (Ezra 3:12a)

The dimensions of this Temple are not recorded in Scripture, but it is assumed the dimensions of the actual Temple structure would have been the same as Solomon's Temple. The difference was in the size of the inner and outer courts and the level of furnishings – gold and precious jewels – in this second Temple.

This Temple was dedicated circa 515 BC and stood until about 20 BC, most of that time in relative peace. However, in 198 BC, there was an upset in the realm. The Ptolemies were defeated by the Seleucids and their king, Antiochus Epiphanes (reigned 175-164 BC) hated the Jews. He desecrated the Temple, though he did not destroy it.

The Seleucids retained control for about thirty years until a family known as the Maccabees came along and revolted circa 168 BC. Amazingly, they were able to wrest control away from the Seleucids and, after much cleansing and sacrifices, rededicate the Temple.

3. Herod's Temple

Herod (reigned circa 40 BC – 4 BC), was king of the Jews, being half-Jewish. It is believed he rebuilt the Temple for two main reasons, 1) to glorify his own name and 2) to convince the Jews in his realm – who didn't altogether trust him – that he was their friend.

The Temple Herod build is also referred to as the Second Temple, as it was a rebuilding and extension of Zerubbabel's Temple, not a replacement.

The size of the Temple itself would have remained the same as the First Temple, aka Solomon's Temple, but the outer and inner courts were greatly enlarged. Herod determined that this Temple would match or exceed Solomon's Temple and, according to Josephus, he succeeded.

"Accordingly, in the fifteenth year of his reign, Herod rebuilt the temple, and encompassed a piece of land about it with a wall, which land was twice as large as that before enclosed. The expenses he laid out upon it were vastly large also, and the riches about it were unspeakable." [97]

"Now the outward face of the temple in its front wanted nothing that was likely to surprise either men's minds or their eyes; for it was covered all over with plates of gold of great weight, and, at

---

[97] The Wars of the Jews, Josephus, ca 75AD, Book 1, chapter 21.1

Appendix IX – The Temples of Jerusalem

the first rising of the sun, reflected back a very fiery splendor, and made those who forced themselves to look upon it to turn their eyes away, just as they would have done at the sun's own rays. But this temple appeared to strangers, when they were coming to it at a distance, like a mountain covered with snow; for as to those parts of it that were not gilt, they were exceeding white."[98]

It was in this Temple that Joseph and Mary found twelve year old Jesus conversing with the Elders, after he had wandered away from them in Jerusalem after the Passover feast. (Luke 2:41-52) It was also in this Temple where Jesus toppled the tables of the moneychangers.

"[12]Then Jesus went into the temple of God and drove out all those who bought and sold in the temple, and overturned the tables of the money changers and the seats of those who sold doves. [13]And He said to them, "It is written, 'My house shall be called a house of prayer,' but you have made it a 'den of thieves.' " (Matthew 21:12-13)

This Temple was the religious, political, and social center of the Jews until 70 AD, when General Titus, later to become Emperor Titus, destroyed Jerusalem and the Temple.

There has not been another Temple in Jerusalem, or anywhere else, since Herod's Temple was destroyed.

4. Tribulation Temple

We don't know much about the dimensions, or scale, or how lavish the Temple built during the Tribulation will be, but we do know there has to be a Temple for it to be desecrated by the AntiChrist.

*"[27]'Then he shall confirm a covenant with many for one week; but in the middle of the week **he shall bring an end to sacrifice and offering**. And on the wing of abominations shall be one who makes desolate, even until the consummation, which is*

---

[98] The Wars of the Jews, Josephus, ca 75AD, Book 5, chapter 5.6

determined, Is poured out on the desolate.' " (Daniel 9:27) (emphasis added)

This Temple will, most likely, be built in the style and dimensions of the Second Temple, Herod's Temple, but I don't know that for sure. Unfortunately, I don't have an "in" with either the Temple Mount Faithful or the Temple Institute to see their plans for this next Temple.

But there is one other Temple described in Scripture, in the book of Ezekiel. The dimensions of this Temple do not match either Solomon's Temple or Herod's Temple. We do know it will be built, but not when.

It could be Ezekiel's plan that will be used for the Temple built during the Tribulation, or…it could be the Temple that is built during the Millennium. I suspect the latter, but I am no prophet.

There is an excellent video posted by Israel MyChannel on Youtube that addresses several questions about the Ezekiel Temple, including why there are still sacrifices in the Millennium, the size of the Temple described in Ezekiel, and much more. I would invite you to watch it at **https://www.youtube.com/watch?v=7xnDh5YsadQ**.

www.ingramcontent.com/pod-product-compliance
Lightning Source LLC
Chambersburg PA
CBHW070633160426
43194CB00009B/1452